Tony Benn

Tony Benn

A Political Life

DAVID POWELL

ORCA BOOK SERVICES

CONTINUUM
London and New York

Continuum
The Tower Building, 11 York Road, London SE1 7NX
370 Lexington Avenue, New York, NY 10017–6503

First published 2001

British Library Cataloguing-in-Publication Data
A catalogue record for this book is available from the British Library.

ISBN 0–8264–5699–5 (hardback)

Library of Congress Cataloging-in-Publication Data
Powell, David 1930–
    Tony Benn : a political life / David Powell.
        p. cm.
    Includes bibliographical references and index.
    ISBN 0-8264-5699-5
    1. Benn, Tony, 1925–   . 2. Politicians—Great Britain–Biography.
    3. Great Britain–Politics and government—1945–
    I. Title

DA591.B36 P69 2001
941.085'092-dc21

                                                            2001037097

Typeset by YHT Ltd, London
Printed and bound in Great Britain by CPD, Ebbw Vale.

Contents

Foreword *by Tony Benn*   vi

Acknowledgements   ix

Introduction   1

1   Common Sense   11

2   In Place of Strife   40

3   The Great Schism   62

4   New Labour: 'A Little Bit of Leninism'   78

5   The Enemy Within   109

6   A Special Relationship: The Last Colony   139

7   Interview   173

A Note on Sources   193

Bibliography   194

Index   197

Foreword

One of the most powerful weapons in the hands of the establishment, in its mission to control the people it governs, is to keep us in ignorance. Indeed, if information can be withheld, presented selectively or adjusted to suit the interests of those at the top, a consensus can be artificially constructed which appears to suggest widespread support for what is being done or proposed.

Knowledge is power, which is why the maintenance of official secrecy has always been so important to successive governments; and 'Truth is the first casualty' in war, since the mobilization of a nation for a conflict has to be sustained by identifying and vilifying the enemy to the point where victory becomes a moral necessity.

Again, while the case for selective education is supposed to be based on ability, it is best understood as an artificial barrier set up to limit real education to a small, future elite, and to provide an excuse to shunt everybody else onto the labour market, trained to obey, but not to question or challenge orders.

Perhaps the most successful example of opinion manipulation, however, is the one provided by the treatment of history and the way in which progressive ideas, and the story of those who campaigned for them, are quietly forgotten, so that a sanitized account of the past is presented to give a sense of continuity to the tradition of subservience to our betters.

The most obvious instance of this is the way in which nations occupied by other nations find that their culture and history is obliterated, and has to be rediscovered when a national liberation movement wins back their independence. On a day-to-day basis, the mass media assist this process by selecting which stories to place at the top of their agenda, and which to omit, on the grounds that they either are not newsworthy or might arouse unwelcome controversy. And the world's religions have also played their part over the years in promoting those ideas which strengthen the faithful in their allegiance to their spiritual leaders, while identifying all others as potentially heretical.

This practice of information control has played, and continues to play, a major role in the shaping of our politics. In fact, limiting the freedom of action that democracy should have given us when it was won by electing governments committed to radical change has, in practice, produced all-powerful party machines that also want to control the thought processes of their members and the public.

Therefore, to establish what is really going on, what has actually happened in the past and what policies should be followed in the future, it is essential that knowledge, now held back, is relevant and intelligible to the people. In short, a historical perspective is the key to democratic politics, which if denied can bury the real issues and confine the news coverage to high-level gossip about the rich and the powerful, reducing us to the role of spectators of our fate, rather than active participants in building our own future.

Looking back over my own experiences after fifty years in the House of Commons – and far longer as a student and political activist – I have been struck by the way in which these factors have influenced the history of the period, and have led to so many avoidable mistakes being made.

For example, if the hard-right sympathies of successive governments had been better understood, we might have responded more positively to the proposals put by the Soviet Union for an alliance to prevent Hitler from launching the Second World War; we might also have avoided the subsequent Cold War, which cost so many lives and required the diversion of so much money from economic progress and development, which could have made peace more secure.

Again, if a better understanding of the colonial liberation movements, and what they represented, had been encouraged, could we have prevented the Algerian and Vietnamese wars from taking place, and helped to create a real 'new world order'?

Or yet again, if the trade union movement had not been

demonized and, more recently, nearly destroyed, could we not have saved our manufacturing industry and built up an effective counterweight to the overwhelming power of the multinationals for whom profit and power are the dominant considerations, regardless of the cost to those whose lives are ruined or made insecure?

But most important of all, could we not have realized the full potential we have for change if our contemporary political debates had been illuminated by an understanding of the frequent occasions in the past when many of the same issues were addressed and fought over by our predecessors?

At present, media headlines reflecting the prejudices of the establishment deliberately encourage us to live from day to day, while our long-term perspectives are conditioned by those professors who entrench their own prejudices in the official histories which they write.

The obliteration of the past strengthens the short-term calculations that pass for political thought, and for me the real heroes are those few who try to explain the world in order to help us to understand what we can best do to improve our lot. The most passionate critics of these free thinkers come from the ranks of the establishment, who are clever enough to see that such writing can be very influential unless it is so effectively distorted and denounced that people can be persuaded not to listen.

This book presents contemporary politics in its proper historical context in a way which gives us greater confidence to think for ourselves, and for that reason deserves to be widely read.

Tony Benn
April 2001

Acknowledgements

This book has taken more than two years to write, and I owe a debt of gratitude to many people, most notably Nick Bagnall, Arthur Butler, Greg Elliott, Chris Freeman, Joe McCarney, Liz Mandeville and Brian Morris. To them all, my thanks.

My thanks also to Sarah and George Mallen and their team at SSL for having invested their confidence in the project, for establishing the website that 'trailed' the work's publication and for providing Tony Benn with a chat room where he can engage with what he termed his 'new constituency'.

Above all, my thanks to Tony Benn. From the outset he insisted that while I was free to interpret his career in whichever way I chose ('warts and all' were the exact words that he used), he would, nonetheless, be happy to assist me in every way possible with my research. And it is precisely this that has made the work possible.

Finally, my thanks once again to Rachel, who for the past couple of years has lived, uncomplainingly, 'A Political Life'. As always, this book is dedicated to her.

Introduction

*Britain is the traditional land of dissent, of dissent not only in
its original religious connotation, but of dissent itself; of, if
you will, dissent for dissent's sake.*

John Strachey, *The Strangled Cry* (1962)

Ten days after announcing his intention to 'retire from Westminster and go into politics' Tony Benn was approached by a Labour peer on the terrace of the Commons and invited to 'join us in the Lords'. Possibly the irony of the situation escaped his Lordship, that Benn had spent three years of his political life renouncing what was now on offer. Or possibly he failed to appreciate what the offer revealed about the mind-set of the Labour establishment. Where Benn had once been damned as a maverick, beyond political redemption, not least for his outspoken critique of the constitution, he was now being invited to join the very institution he had anathematized.

Ingenuous as it may have been, there was nothing new about the practice. On the contrary, the labour movement has long made heroes of its rebels, provided, of course, that they no longer pose a threat to the party establishment. Like resurrection men, the Labour leadership has regularly called up the ghosts of dissent – Winstanley and the Levellers, Tom Paine and the Revolution Society, Feargus O'Connor and the Chartists, William Morris and the Social Democratic Federation, Jimmy Maxton and the Independent Labour Party – to legitimize its own lineage.

Of course, the creation of political mythology has always been a potent force. It is only in the past half-century, however, that the engineering of political consent in Britain has become an art form, though Orwell provided a disturbing foretaste of things to come in *Nineteen Eighty-four*, depicting a world in which Newspeak had been devised to eradicate all heretical thoughts specifically in order to meet 'the ideological needs of Eng. Soc. [English Socialism]':

> All words grouping themselves round the concepts of liberty and equality, for instance, were contained in the single word 'Crimethink', while all words grouping themselves round the concept of objectivity and rationalism were contained in the single word 'Oldthink'.[1]

More was required in Orwell's scenario of Oceania than the acquisition of a new language, however. For the nomenklatura to achieve their ends, they required a new philosophy, hence doublethink, which enabled its practitioners to believe in a proposition at one level and in its antithesis at another. Oldthink! Newthink! Doublethink: the emasculation of reason by linguistic means. Imperceptibly, but nonetheless inexorably, Orwell's warning has gained in substance in the past half-century.

Indeed, it was Ralf Dahrendorf who, in a turn-of-the-millennium analysis of the New Labour project, echoed many of Orwell's fears:

> The Third Way is not about either open societies or liberty. There is indeed a curious authoritarian streak in it, and not just in practice. ... the Singapore model is not very far from present trends, even public preferences; let those up there deal and leave us in peace! Thus the political class becomes a kind of nomenklatura, which remains unchallenged because of the apathy of the many; *and when those who do not fit are silenced, nobody raises his or her voice.* (author's italics)

Or possibly because Newthink has already been substituted for Oldthink. Thirty years have passed since Andy Warhol and the avant-garde made a radical statement about the nature of contemporary culture by creating false objects and images, as if truth was becoming outmoded. It was left to Rupert Murdoch to exclaim when it was revealed that the Hitler diaries were forgeries:

1. George Orwell, *Nineteen Eighty-four* (Secker and Warburg, 1949).

'We are just in the entertainment business'; and doubtless he was entertained by an article in the *Sun* purporting to be based on an analysis of Benn's character: 'Benn on the couch. Is he crazy?' Apparently Bernard Shaw was wrong: 'My way of joking is to tell the truth.'

In Benn's case this is the problem, how to distinguish fact from fiction in order to establish where the truth lies as far as the man and his politics are concerned. For half a century a Member of the Commons, he was once widely tipped to become leader of the Labour Party, only to be anathematized for his burgeoning radicalism. But what was it that led him to challenge a system of which he, himself, was a part? Why was it that he sacrificed a promising future, to be demonized for his political views?

It appeared at times as if he was willing his own destruction, like a man possessed. Or was it that, like his puritan forebears – 'The more we understand individual things, the more we understand God' – he was on a voyage of self-discovery; that in pursuit of 'individual things' he shared common cause with the Levellers, holding that 'Not one word was spoken in the beginning that one branch should rule over another.'

Democracy is the cat's-paw of politics. For Burke (Benn's predecessor as an MP for Bristol) it was 'the tyranny of the multitude'; for Oscar Wilde 'the bludgeoning of the people by the people for the people'; and for Plato the Noble Lie, which helps to disguise the reality that democracy is little more than a device to secure the authority of the Guardians, a sham of which Bertrand Russell was to write:

> Continuity [in government] represents no real need of national safety, but merely a closing up of the ranks of the governing classes against their common enemy: the people. Ever since 1832 [the year in which Russell's grandfather was party to the passing of the Great Reform Bill], the upper classes of England have been faced with retaining as much as possible of the substance of power whilst abandoning their forms to the clamour of democrats.[2]

2. Bertrand Russell, *The Practice and Theory of Bolshevism* (George Allen and Unwin, 1920).

The clamour of democrats, the substance of power – for a century the Labour Party represented the former, yet the substance of power has remained largely unchanged. Indeed, it is arguable that by enabling Russell's 'governing classes' to abandon the forms while retaining the substance of power, the party has, at times, served as an agent for exactly the class it was intended to replace.

And it was this, the democratic deficit that he found at the heart of governments, that was to shape the character of Benn's political career. His father, Viscount Stansgate, who for more than half a century had been a member first of the Commons and then of the Lords, laid the foundations for Benn's scepticism about the 'illusions of democracy'. During his early years in the House, however, Benn did not share Stansgate's disillusion. Proud to call himself 'a Commons man', he believed intensely if not unreservedly in the merits of parliamentary democracy. Indeed, there was something naive about the 25-year-old who first took his seat in the House in November 1950, to write shortly afterwards:

> I am a very new Member of Parliament and it is still exciting
> to bump into Winston Churchill in the Members' lavatory ...
> It is still pleasant to be called by my Christian name by
> Aneurin Bevan and to call him Nye.

His campaign to renounce his peerage was to change all that. Viscount Stansgate died in November 1960, and for the next three years Benn was to devote all his energies to retaining his seat in the Commons. It was a salutary experience which, in providing him with an insight into the arcana of Britain's unwritten constitution, revealed the democratic deficit at the heart of government. And if it was this that laid the foundations for his radicalization, his subsequent experience in the Wilson government was to convince him of the need for root-and-branch reform of the constitution of the Labour Party itself, an experience which prompted him to write in 1970:

> Parliamentary democracy and the party system have in recent
> years been criticised not only for their inability to solve some
> of our problems but also to reflect others adequately ... It is
> not only some members of the public who are disenchanted.
> There are people inside active politics, of whom I am one,

who have long begun to feel uneasy that the alienation of Parliament from the people constituted a genuine cause for concern.[3]

A foretaste of things to come, this was not something that the Labour establishment wished to hear. Since its foundation, the cat's-cradle of interests that make up the party – the constituencies, the unions, the National Executive Committee (NEC), the Parliamentary Labour Party (PLP) – has inevitably meant that it has been an agency of compromise. Walking a tightrope, the leadership has spent the last century edging its way across a political Niagara, Labour's survival depending on its ability to mediate between the disparate factions that comprise the movement.

Compromise does not come easily to Benn, and the more he saw of the inner workings of the party – the deals being struck, the agendas being rigged – the more he questioned whether the huzzahs for unity were not being employed to disguise the authoritarian nature of the Labour establishment, particularly when it appeared that key elements in the establishment were bent on jettisoning the party's socialist principles. Since Anthony Crosland had published *The Future of Socialism* in 1956, to assert that Britain was no longer a capitalist society, revisionists had been sapping at the essence of socialism. Throughout the 1970s Benn led the counterattack against what he believed to be a betrayal of Labour's founding principles, developing in the process a strategy aimed at, on the one hand, breaking the stranglehold of the Labour hierarchs in order to democratize the party and, on the other, strengthening rather than diminishing the role that any future Labour government would play in the economy.

Radical as it may have appeared, Benn's prescription was firmly rooted in history. In 1647, Cromwell and Ireton had rejected the republican Thomas Rainborough's call for manhood suffrage on the grounds that 'it may happen that the majority' would introduce economic changes 'by law, not in a confusion'. Alarmed at the prospect, the Commonwealth grandees would have no truck with democracy, maintaining that it would lead to a levelling economic

3. Sources for the frequent quotations from Tony Benn's own writings, speeches and interviews have not been given in footnotes (*see* 'A Note on Sources', p. 193, and the Bibliography).

policy carried out by due process of law. Like Rainborough, Benn recognized that each element in the programme was dependent on the other, that without the former there would be no prospect of achieving the latter.

If a radical economic strategy ran counter to the revisionists' inclinations, then the democratization of the party threatened to undermine the roots of their power. It was all very well for Benn to protest, 'You can't go on for ever and ever pretending you're a socialist party when you are not, pretending to do something when you won't', but this, in essence, was precisely what the revisionists were intent on doing. Convinced that Labour had little hope of recovering power without repositioning itself, they intensified their efforts to write socialism out of the party's script.

Before achieving their goal, however, it was essential to neutralize the challenge of the left and to marginalize Benn, whom Peter Shore was to describe as 'the man who was more superbly equipped than anyone else to fulfil the functions of a really dynamic and successful Labour leader'. This was exactly what the revisionists feared, and abetted by the right-wing media, who saw in Benn the spectre of an unreconstructed socialist, they set about demonizing him and all that he represented. The bitterly fought contest for the deputy leadership of the party in 1981, leading to Healey's victory, was to prompt Giles Radice's subsequent assertion that the result had 'saved the Labour Party'. Pragmatic as always, the party, or at least the party establishment, wanted no part of Benn's revolution, preferring, rather, the placebos of New Labour and neo-liberal appeal of Thatcherism.

While sharing nothing in common but their contempt for the existing order, Benn and Thatcher revealed something of their nonconformist upbringing in their prescriptions for change, though from diametrically opposed directions. Almost five centuries have passed since Calvin formulated his doctrine of predestination: 'By the decree of God ... some men and angels are predestinated unto everlasting life, and others foreordained for everlasting death.' Grounded on the belief that the world existed only for the glorification of God, the best that humankind could do was 'to labour to promote His greater glory'. The economic rationalism of the Calvinist doctrine, which was to provide the ethical foundation for the economic revolution to come, left only one question unanswered: For whose benefit should such labour be employed, that of the individual or of society?

The issue has polarized opinion since Calvin first preached the gospel in Geneva, and led the economic historian R. H. Tawney to conclude: 'Both an intense individualism and a rigorous Christian Socialism could be deduced from Calvin's doctrine.'[4] Each was to animate its own disciples, and Thatcher's declaration that 'there is no such thing as society' served only to prompt an equal and opposite response from Benn. Indeed, Ian Gilmour, who served for two years in Thatcher's first administration, was later to note the near-messianic fervour which affected the government at the time, and 'the monetarist frenzy that swept through much of the Conservative Party with the force of revelation'. It was a 'frenzy' generated by possessive individualism that was to shift the political centre of gravity sharply to the right.

The Thatcherite revolution, and Labour's response, was to realign British politics and compound Benn's isolation. Within two years of taking office in 1983, Kinnock was to renounce what remained of his radical past to dismiss 'the stale vanguardism of the ultra left' and to assert 'that the market is potentially a powerful force for good'. And possibly Kinnock was right. Possibly, a new generation of voters wanted nothing of redistribution and arguments in favour of equality, opting, rather, for the vagaries of the free market and the obscurantist mysteries of the Third Way peddled by New Labour and the apparatchiks of Millbank.

Only one maxim was absent from the authoritarian credo of Oceania – UNITY IS POWER. It was an omission that New Labour was quick to rectify. Indeed, there was a certain irony in the fact that where Benn had once been demonized for talking up the need to democratize the party, the party modernizers subsequently appropriated the principle as their own in order to parody its meaning, with New Labour's marketing guru, Philip Gould, confessing to a certain fondness for the authoritarian practices of Leninism: 'I think that in periods of change a little bit of Leninism goes a long way.' Seemingly, there are no limits to irony in the Doublethink of the party's nomenklatura.

Cynical as it was, however, the 'spin' of New Labour did much

4. R. H. Tawney, *Religion and the Rise of Capitalism* (John Murray, 1926).

to account for the party's victory in the election of May 1997, a seismic shift in the political landscape which prompted the Tory philosopher Roger Scruton to write: 'Labour have accepted that Mrs Thatcher was right', and encouraged *The Times* and *The Economist* to recommend a vote for New Labour in June 2001 in order that Blair could complete the Thatcher project. Or could it be that the old prestidigitator, history, was simply repeating itself? Whatever the case, it was Benn's sense of history that gave substance to his widening critique of the democratic deficit.

Once begun, in fact, there could be no turning back from what was to become the moving force of his career, and if his half-century in the House provided him with the material for a critique both of the British constitution and the constitution of the Labour Party, then his eleven years in government provided the evidence for his critique of the 'imperial bureaucrats' of the European Union, and what he came to regard as the hegemonic ambitions of the USA. With Britain's retreat from empire, he was to write in the early 1960s: 'The question now is whether Britain will become a satellite of the Common Market or a colony of the US?' In the four decades that followed he found both wanting, maintaining that each was an adherent of the Noble Lie that belied his own definition of what constitutes democracy.

But Benn has been more, much more, than a critic of the existing order. Since publishing his proposals for a reform of the House of Lords in the mid-1950s – a pre-emptive strike against his own ennoblement – he has drafted a range of bills directed at eliminating the deficit which, he believes, disguises the true nature of power. And while, to his critics, he may be many things – self-righteous, stubborn, contumacious – even they are unable to gainsay the fact that he has remained consistent in his champion-ship of 'the password primeval: democracy'. In paying lip service to the ideal, however, they have shown little inclination to implement it in practice, which may account in some way for Benn's decision to quit Westminster and 'go into politics', allowing him the freedom to continue with his examination of the 'options for democracy' in the twenty-first century.

The groundwork for such a project has already been laid, based on the myriad issues which have engaged Benn's attention during his half-century in the Commons. And this, in essence, is what the present work is about: tracing the evolution of Benn's ideas in areas as diverse as globalization and post-colonial power; post-war capitalism and the welfare state; law and order and human rights; open government and freedom of information; British sovereignty and the European Union; and always, the cohering factor, the prospects for democracy in the century that lies ahead.

In short, *Tony Benn* is a biography of the evolution of ideas that have shaped Benn's fifty-year career in Westminster, and more especially of what he regards as 'the democratic deficit' that is a feature of contemporary politics. As such, Chapter One develops his critique of the deficit within the constitution, and the consequent dangers of the emergence of an 'elective dictatorship'; Chapters Two to Four chart his campaign to democratize the Labour Party, leading to the fratricidal disputes of the 1980s and the subsequent emergence of New Labour; Chapter Five examines his critique of the authoritarian nature of the trade unions; while Chapter Six turns to his long-standing reservations about the EU project, and his critique of not only what he regards as Britain's political subordination to US interests but also the reach of US economic imperialism. The final chapter is devoted to an interview with Benn, in which he reflects on the future prospects for the issues that have engaged his attention for the past half-century.

This is not to say that the man or his ideas make for a bloodless recital. How could they, when his whole career has been grounded as much in an historical consciousness of dissent as in the memories of his own radical upbringing: memories of the time when, as a six-year-old, he was introduced to Mahatma Gandhi; when, as a ten-year-old, he distributed Labour pamphlets for the election of 1935; when, as a thirteen-year-old, he saw Oswald Mosley and his Blackshirts strutting their stuff in London's East End; when, as a nineteen-year-old, he heard of the death of his elder brother, Michael, on active service, and learned he was heir to a title, with all that that implied for his own future.

But if it is the past that has conditioned Benn, it is the future that has been his overriding concern, which does something to explain why, since entering the lists against the revisionists, he has been at the storm centre of national and party politics: a provocateur who, at times, brought the party he professed to love close to breaking-point in the belief that he, and he alone, had read the seeds of time. To ask whether he was right or wrong, whether the electorate's preference for gradualism was well founded and whether Benn's radical prescriptions would have resolved the problems that he identified is to play the game of alternative histories at the expense of *realpolitik*.

But if the future is out there, waiting, it nonetheless demands an appreciation of the past – a past which in the case of the Labour Party has been animated by the century-long debate about the nature of the New Jerusalem, and how it can best be achieved. While Labour may be 'a tale of two parties', it is precisely this capacity to enter into such a debate, and to allow its members to contend for their own vision of the future – 'the one country', as Oscar Wilde remarked, 'at which humanity was always landing' – that has provided the party with its vitality and life force.

Yet now it seems as if New Labour has made its landfall, which fuels Benn's suspicions not only of Blair's 'Napoleonic traits', and the implications of this for the emergence of what Lord Hailsham once termed 'an elective dictatorship', but also of the Orwellian mind-set of a party that shows ever-diminishing tolerance for any ideas but its own. Contrary to Orwell, however, the traditional language of Eng. Soc. was not about eliminating dissent. While critics left and right might not like what they heard, nonetheless they listened. There were always exceptions to the rule, of course, the ghosts of those radicals which the movement once dismissed as extremists – Gerarrd Winstanley, Tom Paine, William Morris, Jimmy Maxton, Harold Laski, Nye Bevan – but even they were posthumously rehabilitated, to be raised as the icons of socialism.

As for Benn, the iconoclast, he politely declined the invitation to 'join us in the Lords', and poured himself a fresh cup of tea.

CHAPTER ONE

Common Sense

My Nation was subjected to your Lords.
It was the force of Conquest; force with force
Is well ejected when the Conquer'd can.
John Milton, Samson Agonistes (1671)

We are light years away from being a true democracy.
Tony Blair (July 1995)

The coincidence went unremarked, but for all that, it was noteworthy. On Tuesday, 26 October 1999, as the Lords were voting away the rights of all but ninety-two hereditary peers to sit and vote in the upper chamber, Tony Benn was warning the Commons that unless the House asserted its authority over government 'it will virtually disappear'. The issue at stake was the independence of the Speaker, Betty Boothroyd, amid rumours that New Labour apparatchiks were attempting to remove her, in the hope of placing a more emollient MP in the chair. A small coincidence, perhaps, but for Benn it revealed a disquieting symmetry; a suspicion, no more, that the government's talk of constitutional reform concealed an altogether more insidious design aimed at reinforcing the executive power of No. 10.

During his half-century in the Commons, Benn had become adept at reading the minds of the nomenklatura, not that he had any quarrel with Labour's plans for reforming the Upper House. After 800 years of asserting their inherited privileges, there could be no question but that their Lordships had outlived their time, a case which he had been arguing even before the death of his father,

Viscount Stansgate, forty years earlier. In a pre-emptive strike against his own ennoblement, the 32-year-old backbencher had published the Fabian tract *The Privy Council as a Second Chamber* in 1957, in which he detailed plans for a root-and-branch reform of the Lords:

> The fact that the House of Lords has remained unchanged for so long cannot be attributed to any lack of effort on the part of the peers. In the last hundred years there have been dozens of attempts by individual peers ... to bring their House into conformity with the spirit of the age.

All of these attempts were stillborn, as were Benn's own proposals, which partly accounted for his amusement when, in the autumn of 1999, he read the seventy-five words each inherited peer had been allowed to write in order to justify the retention of their political rights, some typed, some handwritten, some illegibly scrawled: 'It is hardly for me to proselytise my candidature. It is a matter for my peers.' (Lord Morris) ... 'Writes Lords Diary. Brings flowers.' (Baroness Strange) ... 'All cats to be muzzled to stop the agonising torture of mice and small birds.' (Viscount Monckton of Brenchley).

Albeit unwittingly, the petitions mocked the intentions of their authors, and confirmed Benn's belief that a radical shake-up not only of the Lords but also of the entire constitution was long overdue – a cry for reform that long predated his own three-year campaign to renounce his peerage. After the death of the first Viscount Stansgate on the afternoon of 17 November 1960, the Speaker issued orders on the following day that, as his successor to the title, Benn should be kept out of the chamber of the Commons, and that the free copies of Hansard to which he had been entitled as an MP should be withdrawn.

While the constitutional niceties had to be observed, the brutality of the decision compounded Benn's sense of loss. It was not so much that he had been deprived of his seat in the Commons, more that he had lost his political mentor. Since childhood, the second son of William Wedgwood and Margaret Benn had been raised in a highly charged, political environment, both his paternal and maternal grandfathers having served as Liberal MPs; yet during that evening of 17 November, his sense of loneliness was hardly to be borne, for 'the one man who could advise me wasn't there to do so'.

A bestriding figure, 'Wedgie' Benn, as he was known to his colleagues, first entered the Commons as a Liberal MP in 1906, to serve as a junior Lord of the Treasury under Lloyd George. At the outbreak of the First World War, however, he quit Parliament to join, first, the Middlesex Yeomanry, and later the fledgling RFC, where he received both the Distinguished Service Order and the Distinguished Flying Cross.

Two years after the end of 'the war to end wars', and having returned to the Commons, Wedgwood Benn married Margaret Holmes, the daughter of Daniel Holmes, a Scottish classics master and one-time Liberal MP for Govan. Independently minded and intellectually gifted, Margaret Benn had long been a committed feminist, who on meeting the Archbishop of Canterbury, Randall Davidson, had been quick to assert that she wanted her sons 'to grow up in a world in which the Churches will give women equal spiritual status'.

As a Congregationalist, one of the first denominations to accept women into the ministry, her husband agreed. But while the issue of feminism provided table-talk for the Benn household at 40, Millbank – a site that was later to become the headquarters of New Labour – there were altogether more pressing issues to hand. Wedgwood Benn had refused to join Lloyd George's Liberal–Tory coalition following the election of 1919, preferring to align himself with the Liberal rump under Asquith, derisively known as the Wee Frees. With the break-up of the coalition in 1923, an attempt was made to reunite the Liberals under Lloyd George. When a *rapprochement* was finally achieved in 1927, Benn quit the party in disgust, to join Labour and later to win North Aberdeen under the militant slogan: 'The Labour Party is a socialist party and I am a socialist.'

With the return of Ramsay MacDonald's minority government in 1929, Benn was appointed Secretary of State for India, but his time in office was short-lived. Following the economic debacle of 1931, and the subsequent election in which the National Government was returned to power, Benn lost his seat in the House. He remained in the political wilderness until 1937, when he was returned as MP for Gorton, Manchester. His absence from the Commons, however, did little to diminish his standing with the Party, and in 1938 he came fifth in the ballot for membership of the Parliamentary Committee of Labour MPs.

The long weekend of peace was already coming to an end, and with the outbreak of the Second World War, Benn re-enlisted in the RAF at the age of sixty-three, rising to the rank of Air Commodore; at much the same time, he was invited by Churchill to enter the Lords. Since the fall of the Chamberlain government in May 1940, Churchill had been leading a broad-based coalition, and his aim was to reinforce the small group of Labour peers in the Upper House. Contemptuous of the honours system, Benn only accepted on the understanding that Churchill would make it clear that he was accepting a peerage as a duty, not as an honour, and it was on these terms that he entered the Lords in December 1941. He could never have imagined the far-reaching consequences of his decision.

Little more than two years later his eldest son, Michael, a night fighter pilot, was killed in an air crash near Chichester, and Tony Benn became heir to the title. While he was quick to grasp the implications of his brother's death, it was not until he was barred from the House in 1960 that the full reality of his situation came home. Since 1950, he had been the sitting MP for Bristol South-East, but now it seemed as if he were trapped by the arcane procedures of an unwritten constitution which his own, nonconforming, forebears had defied.

Religion and politics, politics and religion: for Benn they are the agents of dissent, the bedrock of beliefs, of which he once wrote: 'I was brought up on the Old Testament, on the conflict between the kings who exercised power and the prophets who preached righteousness. Faith must be a challenge to power.' Although Benn was later to declare that he had only come lately to a detailed knowledge of the English Civil War and the Commonwealth, the entire history of the Benn family was rooted in dissent, reaching back to a time when the republican Rainborough had declared that 'the poorest He in England hath a life to lead as the greatest He' and the grandees feared that they 'raised those spirits them could not lay'. While couched in theological terms, the debate that racked England in the mid-seventeenth century turned, ultimately, on the secular issue of the constitution. The king was down, but who ruled, and on what terms?

In fighting the Civil War, the radicals had begun by appealing to the sovereignty of Parliament. All too soon, however, they discovered that Parliament was as unrepresentative and repressive as the rule of kings which it had replaced. The Lords may have been abolished in 1649 (to be re-established eight years later), but in proclaiming that the people were superior to both Parliament and the laws, the radicals demanded more, much more. They had not fought to replace one tyranny with another, or to become the bondsmen to a new generation of grandees such as Cromwell and Ireton, who were quick to dismiss any talk of extending the franchise on the grounds 'that it takes away that which is the most original, the most fundamental civil constitution of this kingdom and, which is above that, that constitution by which I have any property'.

Gerrard Winstanley, the Leveller, was right. The 'Army of England's Commonwealth' may have won the war, but it lost the peace which followed. Even before the Restoration of 1660 the radicals' God-given vision of a New Jerusalem had been subordinated to the rights of property, but it was to be another quarter of a century before John Locke would provide the grandees with the text which they were to employ as their rationale throughout the eighteenth century: 'The great and chief end of men uniting into Commonwealths, and putting themselves under government, is the preservation of their property.'[1] The fact that the majority were property-less made no difference. Indeed, their continuing disenfranchisement was central to maintaining the authority of the magnates who made the Glorious Revolution of 1688 – a revolution that was glorious only in name. The folk memory of a time when 'the poor and the mean things of this earth had confounded the mighty and the strong' nonetheless remained powerful enough for John Wilkes to declare, when being tried in 1763 as the author of 'a seditious and treasonable paper':

> My Lord, the Liberty of all peers and gentlemen, and what touches me more sensibly, that of all the middling and inferior set of people who stand in most need of protection, is in my case this day finally to be decided upon, a question of such importance as to determine at once whether English Liberty shall be reality or a shadow.

1. John Locke, *Two Treatises of Government* (1690).

That it was more shadow than substance was of no consequence; on his acquittal, the huzzah of 'Wilkes and Liberty' was heard on the streets of London for the first time. However, it was the French Revolution that was to revive 'the restless spirit' which the upper classes had feared for so long, and which they had long been so successful in suppressing. Two centuries on, Benn was to nominate Tom Paine as his Man of the Millennium. The son of a Quaker staymaker, and a 'Godfather of American independence' (Thomas Edison), Paine's *Rights of Man* exploded in the public's consciousness on its first appearance in 1792, terrifying the Pitt government with the possibility that 'the French disease' might well be infectious.

In a devastating critique of the monarchy ('Hereditary succession is a burlesque on monarchy ... It requires some talents to be a common mechanic, but to be a King requires only the animal figure of man – a sort of breathing automaton'), of the Lords ('The idea of hereditary legislators is as inconsistent as that of hereditary judges or hereditary juries; and as absurd as an hereditary mathematician or an hereditary wise man') and of the constitution itself ('All hereditary government is in its nature tyranny ... To inherit a Government is to inherit the people, as if they were flocks and herds'), Paine argued that as 'the Nation is essentially the source of all sovereignty', and that as every man was a 'proprietor in society', it followed that the constitution of a country was not the act of its government but of 'the people constituting a Government'.[2]

The tone and the style are different, but the content of Benn's writing on constitutional issues echoes much of the flavour of the *Rights of Man* – a work which, shortly after its first appearance, was to be proscribed by government for the next three decades. Not that Paine was alone in protesting the need for reform. In fact, it was the growing clamour for a radical extension of a franchise that restricted the vote to all but 4 per cent of the population which placed the issue forcibly on the political agenda of the mid-nineteenth century.

While the Reform Act of 1832 satisfied the political ambitions of the new industrial bourgeoisie by supplying them with the vote, it

2. Thomas Paine, *Rights of Man, Part One* (1791).

did nothing to improve the representation of the mass of the population. Like the 'Army of God's Commonwealth', they had provided the foot soldiers in the campaign for reform, yet when reform came they were quick to learn that their trust had been betrayed – a betrayal that was to provide the impetus for the Chartist movement, with its far-reaching demands for constitutional reform, and the later emergence of the short-lived, but nevertheless influential, Christian Socialist movement, whose leader, Denison Maurice, was to write in 1849: 'I feel that they [the Chartists] should be made to feel that communism, in whatever sense it is a principle of the New World, is a most important principle of the Old World ... The idea of Christian communism has been a most vigorous, generative one in all ages.'

Christianity and socialism. Socialism and Christianity. In a symbiotic relationship, it seemed at times as if the two were inseparable and that given time a Christian Commonwealth would be achieved. The Act of 1832 had gone so far in reforming the franchise, but not far enough, and in 1867 the boundaries of manhood suffrage were again extended, convincing the advocates of gradualism of the inevitability of their prescriptions – depending, that is, on the definition of inevitability. Indeed, it was to be another half-century before women – or more precisely, women over the age of thirty – were to receive the vote, while the question of reforming the Lords became the cockshy of political debate. In 1891, as part of their election package, the Liberals had pledged to 'mend or end' the House of Lords, a foretaste of the party's clash with the Upper House when Benn's father was serving as a junior Lord of the Treasury.

Challenged from the left by the embryonic Labour Party, Liberal policies had become radically more progressive in an attempt to retain the working-class vote, and in the Budget of 1909 the Chancellor, Lloyd George, did nothing to disguise the bill's redistributive intentions: 'This is a War Budget. It is to raise money to wage implacable war against poverty and squalidness.' The Tories were incensed, and the greater their ire, the more radical Lloyd George became, mocking the vanities of the great and the good – 'a fully equipped Duke costs as much to keep up as two Dreadnoughts' – with the cant of their principles.

While Ramsay MacDonald was quick to endorse Lloyd George's

tax-raising proposals ('an epoch-making measure'), he was equally quick to assure the Commons that this was because 'Socialism was not in it.' The Lords disagreed. The House of Commons' exclusive control of finance bills was a central tenet of Britain's unwritten constitution, but after a six-day debate in November the Upper House threw out Lloyd George's budget, and precipitated a constitutional crisis. In February 1910, the Liberals went to the country under the slogan 'People versus Peers', to be returned with a reduced majority. The party subsequently introduced a package of constitutional reforms reinforced by a pledge that if the Lords continued to block legislation the government would create five hundred new peers to swamp their resistance.

The threat was enough. After a second election later in the year, Lloyd George's 'People's Budget' was approved. Their Lordships were reprieved, but with reduced powers to delay legislation, and the majority returned to their somnolent ways for the next half-century. Twice during the interim there had been talk of reform, but it signified little, and on 17 November 1960, Viscount Stansgate died:

> At the moment of his death, the only thing on my mind was all the arrangements that would have to be made. One had to begin the job of fighting the peerage at the very moment when one was least inclined to think of anything else at all ... The funny thing was that I never had the chance to discuss the tactics with him as I'd always imagined I would ... But it didn't work like that. As soon as Father died the escalator was beginning to move. The gates had clanged in the Commons and I was moved, against my will, up to the other end of the building.

The other end of the building. For Benn it might just as well have been the other end of the world. What had long been an abstraction had now become a reality. It had been all very well to theorize about the absurdities of an unwritten constitution, but now he was caught up in its cat's-cradle of protocol and conventions, in its semi-feudal mysteries and surreal rituals, and, above all else, in the catch-all ruling of 1626 which declared that a peerage 'is an incorporeal hereditament affixed in the blood and annexed to posterity'. If anything was to concentrate Benn's mind on the need for reform it was what he was to learn of the arcane practices of the Palace of Westminster during the three-year campaign to renounce his peerage.

Even Benn could never have envisaged the difficulties that lay ahead after the death of his father, though the reaction of the leader of the Labour Party, Hugh Gaitskell, to the news that he intended to contest the case provided a foretaste of what was to come. Where once, and comparatively recently, Gaitskell had regarded Benn as an invaluable aide (in 1959 he had won election to the NEC for the first time, and later was appointed shadow spokesman on transport), three differences were to sour the relationship between the two men – Clause IV, defence policy and the collective responsibility of shadow cabinet members. All were subsequently to play a defining role in Benn's career, yet he can hardly have read the seeds of time when he opposed Gaitskell's line on each of the above issues. An autocrat, who was as little inclined to forgive as to forget, Gaitskell's response to Benn's approach for support in contesting his elevation to the Upper House was as dismissive as it was mean-minded: 'You can't expect the party to make a fuss over you.'

Although accepting that Gaitskell's irritation at the independent line he had taken was appreciable, the full extent of Benn's bitterness at the brusque treatment he had received was revealed in an interview in 1962:

> When it [the renunciation campaign] has been in the news and leading articles have been coming out, then he joins in and makes a wonderful speech attacking the primitive tribal customs which hold a member back ... But as soon as the thing goes out of the headlines and becomes submerged, he forgets it. He thinks that the public forgets it and he thinks that there is nothing much worth doing about it.

But Gaitskell was wrong. A significant element of the Labour Party, and not least his constituency party, rallied behind Benn. Since the foundation of the party in 1900, reform of the Lords had been one of those issues on which the leadership had blown the trumpet to advance, to cover a retreat from their principles. Now there could be no escaping the issue. Not that support for his case split on party lines. Backing for Benn's campaign came from, among others, a cross-party group of MPs which included the maverick Tory Gerald Nabarro and the Liberal leader, Jeremy Thorpe, while the media would have a field day championing what the *Daily Sketch* hailed as 'this contest between David and Goliath'. Ironically, in the light of what was to come later, Benn wrote at the time that he regarded the press 'all along as my friend'.

And he would need all the friends he could muster in the knock-down, drag-out political campaign that was to follow his father's death. Twelve days later, the Leader of the Commons, R. A. Butler, announced that he intended to summon the Committee of Privileges to review a petition that would have allowed Benn to renounce his peerage. With a built-in Tory majority, the outcome was a foregone conclusion, and when the committee reported in March 1961 it found that Benn's petition was invalid, and that the ruling of 1626 still held good. And the Commons agreed. In a three-hour debate in April, it voted that Benn should not be heard in his own defence, that there was no further need to review his case and that the committee's report should be accepted *in toto*.

Seemingly, it was the beginning of the end. In fact, however, it was only the end of the beginning. In a pre-emptive strike against the Commons' decision, Benn's constituency party had voted unanimously that it would back him in the event of a by-election being fought following his disqualification as an MP. Benn's case no longer turned on constitutional niceties, but offered a direct challenge to the political establishment. Even if the Commons rejected him, his constituents wanted Benn to remain, a decision that was to receive the backing of Labour's NEC. When the writ for the Bristol South-East election was issued on 18 April 1961, only two candidates were listed: for the Tories, Malcolm St Clair, and for Labour, Anthony Wedgwood Benn.

Two centuries before, John Wilkes had stood three times for the Middlesex seat, to be returned three times by the electorate, only to be rejected on each occasion by the Commons. Now Benn was to test the nerve of the political establishment again, to determine where the rights of freeborn Englishmen really lay, whether 'English liberty be reality or shadow'. The decision, when it came, was clear-cut, Benn being returned with a 13,044 majority. Not that it did anything to resolve the case. At Westminster the old order still applied. On 8 May, at much the same time as Conservative

Central Office were lodging a petition in St Clair's name to unseat Benn, Benn was closeted with the Speaker, Hylton Foster, in an attempt to discover whether, if he was unable to resume his seat as an MP, he would be allowed to address the Commons from the bar of the House.

Hylton Foster was adamant: 'You can't come beyond the door', and Benn equally assertive: 'If you intend to stop me you must give orders that force is to be used to keep me out. That's the only condition under which I am prepared to bow to your authority.' The deadlock was complete. It was only to be broken when Benn presented himself at the door of the Commons early that afternoon with the election certificate from the returning officer for Bristol South-East in his hand. The occasion was unprecedented, and upwards of fifty MPs, and almost as many journalists, had gathered to watch the saga being played out. As he reached the door, Benn offered the certificate to Mr Stockley, the doorkeeper, who held up his hand and said: 'You can't enter, sir.' Only one question remained to be asked: had the Speaker ruled that, if necessary, he should be prevented from entering the Commons by force? The answer was perfunctory: Yes.

The ritual had been played out, and for a second time Benn had lost. That evening he issued a press release of the speech that he had been intending to make if allowed to speak at the bar of the House: 'I come now not as a supplicant for special favours but as the servant of those who must be sovereign ... Are the people of Bristol South-East to have the right to choose their own Member, or is this right to be usurped by the government of the day?' On 8 May he had the answer, recalling the words of a former Member for the Bristol constituency, Edmund Burke: 'Those who are not for governing with an attention to the circumstances of times, opinions, situations and manners, they will not govern wisely, they cannot govern long, because [of] the powers they impiously attempt.'[3]

The times may have changed since Burke had reflected on the British constitution, but all too often the old circumstances, the old opinions, still prevailed. And in Benn's case, it appeared that the prospect of changing them was rapidly diminishing. Only one

3. Edmund Burke, *Thoughts on the Cause of the present Discontents* (1770).

hope remained, albeit a slim one: the Election Court. With memories still fresh in his mind of his treatment at the hands of the Committee of Privileges, Benn initially had doubts about contesting St Clair's petition, but not for long. Although in the immediate aftermath of his confrontation at the door of the Commons, he had suffered from a bout of 'suicidal depression', it proved short-lived, and by early June he was deeply engaged in preparing his case for the court. It proved to be a *tour de force*. In his 22-hour address, during which he answered 537 questions, Benn reviewed the centuries-long history of the rights of peers to their inherited privileges, to conclude that in law the Commons were not entitled to disqualify him.

The judges were impressed, describing Benn's performance as 'magnificent', but it made little difference. Their judgment took two hours to read, but long before its conclusion, Benn realized that he had lost. It became clear that while the hereditary system was retained there was no way in which it could be modified. This was the constitutional impasse at which he had arrived, and on which he was later to reflect:

> The idea that the hereditary system was necessary took precedence over the democratic element in our constitution. This is a view of our constitution that simply does not fit in with the facts, because in no respect ... does the hereditary system have anything but a very minor role to play in the government of this country.

Thirty years were to pass before the facts were finally corrected to fit the case.

Meanwhile, even before the judges had announced their verdict, Gaitskell had performed yet another about-turn, demanding that Benn should not stand again in the event of a Bristol South-East by-election, or at least not until his constitutional position had been legitimized. If this was not enough, the blow was compounded when he learned that the party leadership had rejected his nomination for membership of the NEC on the grounds that he was no longer an MP.

Like some latter-day Prometheus it seemed that he was being crushed by his own exertions, that there was, indeed, no place to go but the Upper House. In the previous eight months he had explored, and exhausted, every avenue of escape, and now it was not only the door of the Commons and the obscurantism of the constitution that barred his way but also the machinations of the party leadership. Where once he had been regarded as an asset by the party, it appeared that he had now become a political liability, to be marginalized with unseemly haste.

A historic condition, based as much on a conflict between the personalities involved as on the policies they pursued, the internal disputes of the Labour Party have always been venomous. It was not altogether surprising that, having helped to deny Benn a platform at the 1961 party conference, Richard Crossman, the conference Chairman, later confessed: 'At the conference for the first time I really did something dirty to Anthony Benn. I really damaged him.' And not for the last time, either. A man whose talents were matched only by his envy of the talents of others, Crossman was already averse to Benn. On one issue, however, the two shared common cause: a belief that the British electorate were the victims of what Plato had termed 'the Noble Lie'; that while being encouraged to believe they were part of a self-governing democracy, they were, in effect, the dupes of government by oligarchy. As Anthony Howard was to write in his Introduction to *The Crossman Diaries*, this was 'the guilty secret at the heart of the British governmental system'.[4]

In 1961 it must have seemed that, in having no truck with government by oligarchy, Benn himself had become the victim of the Noble Lie. However, such philosophical considerations were no consolation for what amounted to his political disenfranchisement. Only recently he had lived with the prospect of a promising political career. Now all that remained was the consideration of what might have been.

Benn has never been a man to live his life retrospectively, and within a year of Crossman's conference snub he had won back his seat on the NEC, while in December 1962 came the breakthrough for which he had long been hoping but feared would never occur. In 1961, Ian Macleod had succeeded R. A. Butler as the Tory Leader

4. Anthony Howard, Introduction to Richard Crossman, *The Crossman Diaries*, Vols 1–3, edited by Anthony Howard (Hamish Hamilton and Jonathan Cape, 1975, 1976, 1977).

in the Commons, and embarrassed by the seemingly interminable wrangle over the peerage issue, he established a select committee to examine the whole tortured affair. When the committee reported in December 1962, their conclusion was straightforward: heirs to a peerage should have the retrospective right to renounce their titles. Another five months were to pass before the Peerage Bill came before the Commons, five months during which Benn lobbied hard in its support, with the full backing of the new leader of the Labour Party, Harold Wilson.

After a brief illness, Hugh Gaitskell died on 18 January 1963. Benn's reactions were mixed, his regrets ('I have worked closely with him for twelve years and when he was at his nicest he could be very kind indeed') being tempered by memories of Gaitskell's less-than-sympathetic attitude on the peerage issue. But if Benn was ambivalent about Gaitskell, he had few reservations about his successor. In a shift to the left, Harold Wilson was elected leader of the party on 14 February 1963, and Benn made a note in his diary:

> It is a great shot in the arm and opens up all sorts of possibilities for the party. I have known him well personally, have always agreed with his general line and voted for him [in the party leadership contest] against Gaitskell in November 1960. He is an excellent chairman, gets on well with people and has some radical instincts where Hugh had none.

While it was clear that Wilson respected Benn, the latter's future remained in abeyance until the Commons debated the select committee report. For a further three months Benn remained in political limbo, and it was not until late May that the House debated the Peerage Bill and accepted the committee's recommendations. For a brief moment it seemed as if the case had been won, on the sole condition that no peer should be allowed to renounce his or her title until after the next general election. But history is rich in ironies, and never more so than when the Lords rejected the Commons' proviso. After more than three years contesting his right to remain an MP, it was the Lords who finally allowed Benn to renounce his title on the day that the Peerage Bill received the royal assent.

Benn's diary for the period catches something of his sense of elation ('I shall be back in the Commons before Christmas and maybe even before'), and something more besides: 'this was the beginning of a much bigger fight which I was sure we would win too.' In the first instance he was right, as St Clair resigned his seat when the bill became law, allowing Benn to be returned for Bristol South-East in August 1963, with a 15,569 majority; but it was the second issue that was to engage his attention in the years ahead, namely the need 'to put pomp and pageantry back in the museum'. Indeed, his subsequent thirty-year campaign for reform of the constitution, culminating in the tabling of his Commonwealth of Britain Bill in 1992, could well be regarded as a posthumous tribute to his father.

There was little indication of what was to come, however, when Benn submitted his innocuously titled paper *The Honours System* to the Home Policy Committee of Labour's NEC in January 1964. Only five months had passed since his re-election, and it may have been that in raising a comparatively incidental issue, he was simply testing the nerve of the party on the broader, and altogether more contentious, question of root-and-branch constitutional reform. But even then there were traces of the radicalism that was to become a feature of Benn's later campaigns:

> Hereditary honours are wrong in themselves since they confer status and privilege on those who succeed to them ... Where this also carries a seat in Parliament it represents a political threat to the supremacy of the Commons.

And again:

> Even where [those honours carrying a personal title] are not hereditary they undoubtedly buttress the class structure in Britain, dividing people into social categories built on the idea of superior and inferior human beings. Every society includes people who think they are better than others. What characterises Britain is that those who are supposed to be inferior have been persuaded that they actually are and accept their predetermined lot. There is no more depressing social phenomenon than this.

Restrained as it is by contrast, the echo was of Tom Paine: 'Titles ... mark a sort of foppery in the human character which degrades it.' Possibly the radical tone of *The Honours System* proved too alarming, and it remained unpublished until 1974.

In the autumn of 1964, the Conservative government under Alec Douglas-Home went to the country, only to see Labour returned with a four-seat overall majority, and for Benn to be appointed Postmaster-General, a job that was to provide him with his first experience of the workings of power, not least when it touched, however peripherally, on the role of the monarchy. One of his first acts on taking office was to call for a redesign of Britain's postage stamps. What followed had all the makings of a Whitehall or, rather, a Buck House farce.

The issue at stake was whether or not the Queen's head should remain on certain stamps, and at an audience with the Queen, Benn gained the impression that she approved of a new set of designs:

> I then knelt on the floor and one after the other passed up to the Queen the Battle of Britain stamps bearing the words 'Great Britain' and no royal head on them. It was a most hilarious scene ... At the end I packed up and said I would take them away but I was delighted to hear she approved of a scheme under which we could submit things to her for her consideration.

He had underestimated the Machiavellian mind-set of the establishment, even if he did suspect that the entire conversation had been monitored by the Queen's Private Secretary, Sir Michael Adeane. It was the beginning of a ritualized contest during which Benn issued instructions to his own department relating to the redesigned stamps, only to have them ignored; during which the Garter King of Arms insisted that if the Queen's head continued to appear she should be wearing either a coronet or a crown; during which Sir Kenneth Clark, of the Stamp Advisory Committee, reminded Benn of George V's charge 'Never to let the sovereign's head come off the stamps'; during which the Prime Minister, Harold Wilson, had a 75-minute audience with the Queen, ten minutes of which were devoted to reviewing the Rhodesian crisis, and the remainder to discussing Benn's redesigned stamps; and during which, always and everywhere, Adeane played the *éminence grise*: 'The real enemies, of course, are those forces of re-action – the Tory Party, the Civil Service, the Palace flunkies and courtiers – who use the Queen as a way of freezing out new ideas.'

A shadowy presence, insidious yet powerful, the establishment ensured that Benn's proposals were rejected, an experience that would reinforce his conviction of the need to revitalize Britain's institutional structures if the country was to have any hope of competing successfully for a place in the future. The evidence was conclusive. The pace of change was accelerating at an exponential rate, and Benn never tired of quoting the examples of the technological revolution that presaged a post-industrial age. All too often, however, it seemed that the hierarchs of power were trapped in a never-never land on which the sun never set, and in which Britannia continued to rule the waves. As the old blues number had it: 'Ain't got a future, but O Lord, what a past.'

And it was precisely this, the past, that Benn hoped to exorcize on being appointed Minister of Technology. When he moved into his new offices in the Millbank Tower on 4 July 1966, however, he may well have wondered whether he could, indeed, harness the potential of what Harold Wilson termed 'the white heat' of technology to revive the British economy. Almost two years later, at a conference of the Welsh Council of Labour, Benn was in an uncharacteristically bleak mood. After conducting an exhaustive examination of the state of British industry, he concluded that its problems reflected a malaise that affected the entire fabric of society:

> Our educational system, our system of local government, the civil service and the legal system are all now under critical examination because technology has made them obsolescent. And what of Parliament itself? Can we assume that it will go on in exactly the same form as we have it now, for ever and ever? I very much doubt it.

Only days had passed since the student uprisings of May 1968, and Benn's reflections caught something of the troubled mood of the times: 'Much of the present wave of ... discontent is actually directed at the present parliamentary structure ... The pressure for the redistribution of political power will have to be faced ... People want a much greater say.' As a first step towards achieving such a 'participating democracy', Benn listed six requirements, among them the devolution of power to Scotland, Wales and the regions; the need to enforce the public's 'right to know' about the workings of government and, conversely, the government's need to know more about the public's frame of mind, possibly through the development of electronic referenda. And the alternative?

> The pressures for changes are as inevitable as was the incoming tide that engulfed King Canute ... However unwelcome this pressure may be to those who now believe that the parliamentary system of government is the finest expression of man's constitutional genius, adjustments will have to be made. If they are not, discontent, expressing itself in despairing apathy or violent protest, could engulf us all ... It is no good saying it could never happen here. It could.

The delegates remained silent. They suspected that Benn was right. In the previous six months more than three million working days had been lost due to strikes, as workers sought to shore up their incomes against inflation. Aware of the damage that burgeoning industrial unrest was inflicting on the government, Wilson asked Barbara Castle, the Minister of Labour, to tackle the problem. When published, her solutions exacerbated rather than resolved the situation. While she insisted that *In Place of Strife* was a charter of union rights – among them the right to belong to a union and safeguards against unfair dismissal – nothing could disguise the fact that in return the charter imposed certain conditions, not least that the government should be given the power to order a ballot among strikers and that fines could be imposed on employers, unions or individual strikers in the case of certain disputes.

In militant mood, the unions would have nothing of it, and in the years ahead it seemed at times as if Benn's apocalyptic forecast could well be realized. In June 1970, a Conservative government under Edward Heath was returned to power, pledged to curb union militancy. Four years later, with the pledge unfulfilled, Heath went to the country to catechize the electorate with the question 'Who Rules?', concluding: 'Only one thing can threaten our future. This is our continued record of industrial strife. We can't afford the luxury of tearing ourselves apart any more.' It made little difference. Although Labour won the February 1974 election with a wafer-thin majority, it, too, was later to be locked into growing disputes with the unions, culminating in the Winter of Discontent, of which the Prime Minister, Jim Callaghan, was later to write:

> The serious and widespread industrial dislocation caused by the strikes of January, 1979 ... set the government's fortunes cascading downhill, our loss of authority in one field leading to misfortunes in others just as an avalanche, gathering speed, sweeps all before it.[5]

Albeit faintly, Callaghan's epilogue catches something of Benn's warning of 1968 that 'discontent, expressing itself in despairing apathy or violent protest, could engulf us all'. Not that Benn was despairing. His critique of the constitution was a challenge as much to himself as to his audience: a challenge to which he was to devote an increasing amount of attention. A decade had passed since his father's death, when the Fabian Society published Benn's pamphlet *The New Politics, a Socialist Reconnaissance*:

> It is arguable that what has really happened has amounted to such a breakdown in the social contract, upon which parliamentary democracy by universal suffrage was based, that the contract now needs to be re-negotiated on a basis that shares power much more widely, before it can win general assent again.

Benn had chaired the society in the mid-1960s, but six years in government, particularly his time as Minister of Technology, had fostered his latent radicalism. Indeed, it was arguable that the inevitability of gradualism favoured by the Fabians was itself becoming obsolescent, a victim of the technological revolution that was transforming the entire socio-economy. It was a theme which, in messianic mode, Benn was to adopt as his own and which, in pursuit of extending the frontiers of democratic participation, was to lead to his championship of referenda as touchstones of public opinion.

Based on his own experience, Benn was slowly yet consistently developing his critique of government in order to formulate a new model of the constitution. And as the industrial situation deteriorated during the 1970s, his critique became ever more

---

5. James Callaghan, *Time and Chance* (Collins, 1987).

radical. A parliamentarian fiercely jealous of the rights of the Commons, he already had suspicions about the burgeoning power of the executive at the expense of the legislature when the Tories were returned to government in 1979, and Mrs Thatcher delivered her homily at the door of No. 10: 'Where there is discord may we bring harmony. Where there is error may we bring truth. Where there is doubt may we bring faith. Where there is despair may we bring hope.' On her own terms, of course. Nominally contemptuous of ideology, Thatcher was nonetheless quick to set the cabinet dancing to her own, free-market dogma, reinforcing Benn's fears that 'the centralisation of power in the hands of one person has gone too far and amounts to a system of personal rule in the very heart of our parliamentary democracy ... The premiership, today, is, in effect, an elective monarchy.' The jigsaw of power might be complex, but the pieces fitted together for all that.

First, there was the power of patronage, and the fact that during his four terms in office over an eight-year period, Harold Wilson had appointed or reshuffled 100 cabinet ministers and 403 ministers of state and junior ministers, had created 243 peers, had appointed 24 chairmen of nationalized industries and 16 chairmen of Royal Commissions, not to mention his control of all senior appointments within the civil service and, yet again, the composition of the honours list:

> For not one of these appointments is a prime minister constitutionally required to consult cabinet, Parliament, public or party ... No medieval monarch in the whole of British history ever had such power as every modern British prime minister has in his or her hands.

Second, there was the power over ministerial conduct, and the fact that on their appointment all ministers were issued with a personal minute of procedure which detailed precisely their powers and functions, and their collective responsibility to the cabinet:

> The prime minister's power to secure compliance with these rules rests on his or her power to dismiss those who breach them. However, as James Callaghan once made clear ... he regarded the application, or non-application, of the rules of

collective cabinet responsibility as being entirely within his own personal discretion.

Third was the power of determining the government's business agenda and the fact that, in the five years from 1974 to 1979, there were 23 standing committees of the cabinet, together with some 150 *ad hoc* committees, all of whose business was subject to the approval first of Wilson and then of Callaghan:

> From this it will be clear that the prime minister is able to use the government to bring forward the policies which he or she favours, and to stop those to which he or she is opposed ... To this extent the conduct of government business can be said to reflect a personal or autocratic rather than a collective and democratic spirit.

Fourth came the power of determining the 'right to know', and the fact that, alone among ministers, prime ministers had the power to inform or withhold from Parliament and the public any matter relating to the government's business:

> He or she has the power to classify documents to any level, and to establish a leak enquiry ... into any suspected disclosure by a minister, or any official, of which he or she ... believes should not have been disclosed, and he or she may withhold the results of that enquiry from the cabinet even when cabinet ministers have been questioned.

And buttressing all the rest was the power of the security services into whose ranks Benn had once been invited to enlist. In the late 1940s, he had been introduced to 'a certain colonel who was in plain clothes' and asked whether he would like a job. Explaining that he one day hoped to stand as an MP, he was told: 'Oh, that is no problem. You could do both jobs.' When his father heard of the encounter, he was adamant: 'Whatever you do, don't get mixed up in that sort of business.' Benn heeded his advice, though years later he did come across the name of 'a certain colonel' in an article about the security services.

Theoretically, only the prime minister is entitled to know the full extent of the operation of the security services, yet Harold Wilson, who was widely rumoured to have been a victim of the machinations of MI5, was to confess that 'The prime minister is occasionally questioned on matters arising out of his responsibilities. His answers may be regarded as uniformly uninformative' – largely because prime ministers, too, remained uninformed.

Secret agents of the state, responsible solely to themselves, the security services were the ill-omened piece in the jigsaw of power that fortified Benn's conviction that open government ultimately depended on the passage of a comprehensive Freedom of Information Bill. As he was apt to point out, three centuries and more had passed since the Levellers had declared 'common people have been kept under blindness and ignorance, and have remained servants and slaves to the nobility and the gentry', yet the public's right to know still remained in abeyance. Twice during the 1970s attempts were made to introduce a Freedom of Information Bill, and twice they were aborted, prompting Benn to write in 1981:

> There was more hostility to the idea of a Freedom of Information Act than to almost any other measure, because it really touched the centre of power. Knowledge is power, and weak ministers and strong civil servants – we have had plenty of both in British government in recent years – live on the maintenance of secrecy: they can't be challenged.

But if these were the powers of an elective monarchy, what of the monarchy itself? If successive premiers had derived their ultimate authority from the prerogative powers vested in the crown (among others, the power to declare war, enter into treaties and implement EEC legislation without obtaining the approval of Parliament), what of the role of the crown? Benn's answer was clear:

> Our parliamentary democracy now finds itself with an elective monarch – the prime minister – who uses powers notionally vested in the crown to bypass the legislature, which in its turn has agreed to abandon key legislative powers. This constitutes a major reversal of the advances we had made towards democracy, even allowing for the fact that we hadn't in any case completed the democratic process begun in the seventeenth century.

As Benn saw it, this was the unfinished business of the Glorious Revolution of 1688. Half a century on, Voltaire had written an encomium to the beauties of the English constitution, of the checks and balances of the three estates – executive, legislature, judiciary – that regulated government, while in 1867 Bagehot had reflected on the 'dignified capacity' of the monarchy. The pomp remained, but the circumstance had changed, and it was this shift in power from the crown-in-Parliament to the purlieus of No. 10 that Benn feared was leading to the progressive erosion of democracy:

> The trend to centralisation of power is there for all to observe ... Strong leadership there must be, but it must be open, collective, accountable, and must learn to exercise its necessary powers by persuasion and, above all, through the development of a constitutional premiership.

And in an altogether darker mood, as if anticipating his own demonization, he made the following appeal:

> Dissenters must be protected. They must be protected from the witch-hunters, from the heretic burners, from the Thought Police ... from MI5 and Special Branch who in this country as in any country in the world are always looking for difficult men who may be saying something that in some way undermines the authority of society.

Benn was that difficult man. It may be, of course, that the chimera of an elective dictatorship was a product of Benn's own imaginings, or it may be that Tom Paine had been right when he wrote in 1776: 'A long habit of not thinking a thing *wrong* gives it a superficial appearance of being *right.*' Whatever the case, Benn was to employ Paine's words, together with the title of Paine's first, great tract, when he published *Common Sense* in 1993.

An extension of Benn's existing critique, the 123-page work (written in collaboration with Andrew Hood) filled in the background to two bills he had tabled in 1992, the Commonwealth of Europe Bill and the Commonwealth of Britain Bill:

> The two constitutional Bills advanced in this book offer specific and detailed alternatives both for the British and European arrangements. The Commonwealth of Britain Bill offers a new constitution for this country and the Commonwealth of Europe Bill suggests a looser and wider form of co-operation across the continent as a whole.

While the two could not be divorced, the one from the other, the fifty-four clauses in the Commonwealth of Britain Bill, together with its Charter of Rights, revealed the primacy that Benn attached to the measure. It was not so much his belief that the Treaty of Rome now substituted for Britain's unwritten constitution, or even his long-standing suspicion regarding the European project, as his conviction that the ragbag of measures that passed for a constitution perpetuated the power of the privileged at the expense of the general public and democracy itself:

> Despite the suffrage gains, the British political system is so steeped in hierarchy that real progress is hindered at every point ... as Britain draws close to the twenty-first century its people still enjoy no entrenched rights, not even the right to vote; only obligations.

> The culture of subservience inculcated by this peculiar and hierarchical history [has] ... certainly led people to accept their situation in the belief that it could be changed peacefully by parliamentary means.

If this was an illusion, then it was equally illusory to pretend 'that we live in a real democracy'. Like an inverted pyramid, the entire constitutional edifice continued to rest, if only notionally, on the crown. The real power might lie elsewhere, but the myth remained, to provide legitimacy for all the rest, each part of the constitutional architecture being necessary to secure the authority of the whole. The danger, as Benn saw it, was that where power had once resided in the court, a lost world in which state business had been conducted 'backstairs', it was now being replaced by a new court and new courtiers: the estate of an elected monarchy.

Power, it seemed, was in the process of recycling itself, especially under the Thatcherite regime, whose court philosopher, Roger Scruton, warned in 1980 of the 'contagion of democracy'. A miasma, it had haunted the establishment's thinking since Burke conjured up the vision of a 'swinish multitude', and Bagehot had declared that the *vox populi* was, in reality, the *vox diaboli*. Based on the principle that the 'mere people' were incapable of governing themselves, the prescription had provided a historic justification for government by the great and the good.

It was a notion that Benn rejected in its entirety. For him, the damage resulting from the perpetuation of elitism, as much in economic as in constitutional terms, was incalculable, and as long as the constitution remained unwritten, the condition would prevail. Thus, the need 'to refound our public institutions upon the principles of the common weal, democracy and internationalism more in tune with the needs of the twenty-first century', and thus the Commonwealth of Britain Bill. The key to all the rest lay in the Foreword to *Common Sense*, in which Benn declared that Britain should become a republic and

> that every Briton would become a citizen of a democratic, federal and secular commonwealth dedicated to the welfare of all and with fundamental human rights enshrined in a charter dealing with political, legal, social and economic dimensions.

A utopian conceit? Possibly, and to thwart the sceptics, Benn listed seven measures which he regarded as essential to realizing his goal: that the monarchy should be replaced by a presidency; that power should be devolved to Scotland, Wales and the English regions; that the Lords should be abolished and replaced by a House of the People; that the voting age should be reduced to sixteen, and that there should be equal representation of the sexes in Parliament; that church and state should be separated, and the resultant disestablished Church of England allowed to decide its own structure and to choose its own leaders; that there should be comprehensive reform of the legal system; and finally that the security services should be subject to parliamentary supervision, and that a Freedom of Information Act should be enacted.

Benn's proposals for what the *Guardian* described as 'the first Parliamentary attempt to abolish the monarchy since Cromwell's time' fell victim not so much to the pressures of parliamentary business as to *realpolitik*, and not only among the Tories. In private, significant elements of the Labour Party might subscribe to republicanism. In public, the subject was taboo, not least among the party leadership, which was quick to recognize that, if accepted, Benn's programme could well undermine the edifice of power on which the premiership relied – notably the delegated power vested in the royal prerogative to enact business without reference to Parliament.

For all the short shrift that Benn's proposals received in 1992, significant elements of his programme – among them, devolution, reform of the Lords and the publication of a Freedom of Information Bill – were to feature prominently during New Labour's first term of office, albeit in radically curtailed forms. Equally significantly, however, the party made clear that it had no truck with Benn's republican proposals, with Blair declaring that he was 'an ardent monarchist' and the Leader of the Lords, Baroness Jay, pledging that the monarchy was safe with Labour.

Much else might be sacrificed, but never this, the capstone of executive power. Not that Blair had any reason to feel threatened during New Labour's first term in office. Although commanding an unassailable majority, the Labour intake of 1997 remained supine, while the cabinet became little more than a token assembly, with ministers having to submit their papers for scrutiny before they were tabled at the weekly cabinet meetings, many of which lasted for no more than twenty minutes. And with power came contempt, with Blair voting in only 14 of 325 divisions in 1998, a record which prompted Patrick Dunleavy, Professor of Government at the London School of Economics, to describe him as 'the least active premier for 120 years in terms of prime ministerial accountability'.

But even this was not enough. Indeed, there was a hint of paranoia evident when Labour spin doctors began circulating rumours that it was time for the Speaker, Betty Boothroyd, to be replaced. Within two months of New Labour taking power in May 1997, she was warning the government that the Commons was 'rightly jealous of its role of holding ministers to account', an assertion that she was to repeat in July 1998 – 'I cannot deprecate strongly enough the leaks and briefings that go on behind our backs' – and would reiterate in December of the same year:

> What is happening is that this House and the status of this House is being devalued and I deprecate it most strongly. I hope that those on the front bench, senior Members, will note what I have said and see that there is no recurrence of this.

It was not something the Labour hierarchy wished to hear, and in the gossip-shop of Westminster the rumours began to circulate –

Boothroyd must go. This led the veteran Labour backbencher, Tam Dalyell, to reflect that there was 'something to be said for the House of Commons having a Speaker that the prime minister of the day doesn't want'. Benn agreed: 'I feel very strongly that if this House doesn't assert itself it will virtually disappear as a factor in our political society.'

And it was in defence of the legislature that Benn tabled an early-day motion in November 1999, noting 'the emergence of a semi-presidential style of government, bypassing the cabinet and taking this House for granted, with few checks and balances on the power of the executive', and 'inviting' MPs to reassert their role as elected representatives with the concomitant responsibility 'for maintaining the role of this House as a democratic legislature holding governments to account, having been elected by the people for that purpose'.

The appeal was to the historic consciousness of the Commons, and in a subsequent adjournment debate Benn was to trace, briefly, the centuries-long contest that had been waged to secure parliamentary government, and the altogether more recent erosion of what had been so hard-won:

> I think that without any announcement of change being made, this country is moving from a parliamentary to a presidential system. It appears to me that, increasingly, all effective power comes from No. 10, Downing Street ... The issue raised is enormous – the future of democracy itself.

Eight months later, on 12 July 2000, Betty Boothroyd announced her intention to retire as Speaker before the next election, warning the House once again that it was 'the function of Parliament to hold the executive to account ... It is in Parliament in the first instance that ministers must explain and justify their policies.' In the contest for succession, a number of backbenchers, both Labour and Tory, urged Benn to stand for the vacant position. The irony was inescapable, that at this late stage in his career he appeared to be in the process of being rehabilitated – 'It was quite extraordinary, the number of faces hovering in the tea room smiling at me for the first time' – though, as the *Observer* was to reflect, 'the news of his candidature will send a shudder through Downing Street'.

Honoured as he was by the proposal, Benn declined to pursue

his candidature, preferring rather to press for a reform of the whole arcane procedure that precedes the election of a new Speaker:

> Today we need a strong and independent Commons comprising people who genuinely represent those who elected them, are faithful to their convictions and who have the courage to vote according to their deeply held beliefs. That means that we also need as Speaker an independent person who will stand up for us against the executive.

For Benn, the quintessential House of Commons man, it was his last campaign in defence of the system of parliamentary democracy he had championed since the day he had been shut out of the Commons following his father's death. In the days before the election a growing number of senior ministers, and ex-ministers – including John Major and Kenneth Clarke – joined the lobby pressing for a new voting system. It made little difference. The old order prevailed. Benn, however, remained undeterred, and in early November 2000, he canvassed members to support his call for an early-day motion 'to strengthen the powers of the House of Commons over the executive'.

The draft motion included eight proposals, among them the need for a ballot when electing the Speaker; the right of the Speaker to recall Parliament; the use of a ballot to elect select committees; the right of the Commons to approve European laws before such laws are made; and the right of the Commons to exercise control over prime ministerial patronage. The provisional date set for the debate was 29 November. It never took place. On 22 November Caroline Benn died. It was the end of a partnership that had begun in 1948, when he proposed to her after a lightning, eight-day courtship. An American, Caroline Benn had played a leading role in the campaign for comprehensive education in Britain. Indeed, the *Times Educational Supplement* was to write of her: 'Caroline Benn, who has died at the age of 74, may have influenced British society more than the members of the political dynasty into which she married.' As for Benn, his diaries are punctuated with references to 'my Caroline', who had shared his faith in Tom Paine's dictum that 'We have it in our power to begin the world all over again', and had provided him with her unfailing love and support during the nightmare years when he was anathematized.

On the day of Caroline's death, her son Hilary, himself an MP, collected the *Spectator* magazine's Parliamentarian of the Year award on behalf of his father, in recognition of the fifty years Benn had served in the Commons; whilst it was during a debate in which Benn made his valedictory speech that he was to win his final parliamentary battle. Following the farrago that surrounded the election of the Speaker, and in part as a result of Benn's previous efforts, the Procedure Committee of the Commons decided to examine the whole fraught issue. On 22 March 2001, their recommendations were debated by the House.

For a final time, Benn rose from his seat on the back benches to invoke the Speaker to protect the Commons from 'the triple powers of Buckingham Palace, Millbank and Central Office'; to warn that 'the real danger to democracy is not that someone will burn Buckingham Palace and run up the Red Flag ... but that if people don't vote they destroy by neglect the legitimacy of the government that has been elected'; and to reiterate his own long-held fears for the future of democracy: 'I'm referring not to demonstrations, but to the power of the media, the multinationals, Brussels, the World Trade Organization. They are wholly unelected.'

At the close, the House voted that future Speakers should be elected by secret ballot, but rejected Benn's call that such elections should be open rather than closed, but not before one Tory backbencher, John Bercow, had commended Benn to his fellow MPs as Britain's 'greatest living parliamentarian'. Such again are the ironies of history.

CHAPTER TWO
In Place of Strife

The Labour Party, that sad failure of Socialism.
G. D. H. Cole, *The World of Labour* (1913)

On the evening of 18 November 1999, following the news that Ken Livingstone had made it onto Labour's shortlist to run for the Mayor of London, the Prime Minister, Tony Blair, launched an uncompromising attack on the three men he claimed 'had almost knocked the Labour Party over the edge of the cliff into extinction' – Livingstone, Scargill and Benn. And possibly he was right. Possibly, the radical policies adopted by the party in the early 1980s had made it unelectable. It was not so much this, however, as Blair's subsequent assertion that he would have to 'go out and fight for the Labour Party I believe in' which, in Benn's case, raised the question of what, precisely, did Blair believe?

There was a time when he thought he knew. During the internecine disputes that racked the party following the fall of the Callaghan government, Benn had delivered a speech setting out his own position. In 1994 he received a fulsome note from Tony Blair congratulating him on his statement asserting Labour's socialist principles, and reminding him that the speech in question had been delivered during the by-election when Blair first stood for Parliament in 1982. Apparently, Benn had not so much captivated Blair's imagination as inspired him with a prospect for the future. Sixteen years on, however, it seemed all that had changed: Benn had now become one of those 'extremists' whom Blair wished to distance himself from, if not to hound out of the party.

In this, of course, Benn was keeping good company. The charge of extremism has been employed to stigmatize dissidents since the Labour Party was first established. Indeed, there has always been something slightly paradoxical about a party which, while laying claim to political nonconformity, has nonetheless had little truck with nonconformists who do not subscribe to its own, prescribed version of socialism – a word which, in pursuit of Blair's agenda, has been written out of New Labour's political lexicon.

Like so much else in the party, the past is another country, to be visited only occasionally – yet for Benn the history of the labour movement is a palpable thing, redolent with meaning, and he reaches back to a time when Christ was damned as a dissenter and condemned for his extremism. In fact, it is not accidental that he devotes much of the opening chapter of *Arguments for Socialism* to the impact that Christianity has had on the movement, for Benn's religious commitment is pivotal to all he believes in: a militant rather than a quietist faith. As he sees it, the foundations of socialism are grounded in the radical traditions of the church militant, in the denunciation issued by the fourteenth-century cleric John Wycliffe:

> It is in such ways that the great devour poor men's goods, and so in a manner the rich eat men's flesh and blood and become manquellers such as God hath condemned;

in the proclamation of the seventeenth-century Leveller Gerarrd Winstanley, for whom Christ was the Head Leveller:

> The poorest man in England hath as true a title and as just a right to the land as the richest man ... True freedom lies in the free enjoyment of the earth;

and in the assertion of the twentieth-century Archbishop of York, William Temple:

> The existing system is challenged on moral grounds. It is not merely that some who 'have not' are jealous of some who 'have'. The charge against our social system is one of injustice.

For Benn this is the bedrock of his socialism, the seamless tradition of Christian militancy which, transmuted, has shaped the thinking of secular radicalism. The problem is to translate what the mid-nineteenth-century Chartists termed The Great Political Truths into reality:

> Labour must no longer be the common prey of masters and
> rulers ... God and Reason have condemned this inequality,
> and in the thunder of the people's voice it must perish for
> ever.[1]

Whether it was rational or metaphysical, there could be no
question but that the New Jerusalem was out there, somewhere,
although no one could agree as to exactly where. In laying claim to
the future, Christian Socialists and Chartists, trade unionists and
co-operators, anarchists and Marxists disagreed, vehemently, as
much about the ends to be achieved as about the means to achieve
them – differences that were to be brought into sharp focus in the
acrimonious dispute between G. B. Shaw and William Morris in the
years immediately preceding the foundation of the Labour Party.

Where Shaw vested his hopes in the Fabian's gradualist vision of
socialism, 'which could be adopted either as a whole or by
instalments by any ordinary, respectable citizen', Morris wanted
nothing of socialism on the instalment plan, preferring militancy
instead:

> If by any chance any good is to be got out of the legislation of
> the ruling classes, the necessary concessions are most likely to
> be wrung out of them by fear of such a body [of socialists]
> than they are to be wheedled and coaxed out of them by the
> continual life of compromise.

The difference went deep, and was subsequently to divide the
Labour Party against itself throughout the twentieth century. As if
to disavow his own militant sympathies, Benn wrote in 1981 that to
characterize the party as a contest between moderates and left-
wingers was misleading: 'The Labour Party, being avowedly
socialist in its aims, is itself left wing, and so are all its members ...
Moreover, the term moderate is equally confusing. By any
standard of socialism, the Labour Party is exceptionally moderate'
– a purely semantic defence. Benn must have known that the
history of the party contradicted him.

From the first day of the party's existence in 1900, when Keir
Hardie had cobbled together a compromise to secure at least the

---

1. *The People's Charter* (1838).

appearance of unity, Labour has been an uneasy alliance between right and left, with the right generally in the ascendancy. Ben Tillett, Tom Mann and the syndicalists may have called for extra-parliamentary action, holding that 'Labour MPs are revolutionary neither in their attitude towards existing society nor in respect of present-day institutions', but Ramsay MacDonald was quick to see off such 'impossibilists' in the years before the First World War. Jimmy Maxton and the Independent Labour Party may have rejoiced in the fall of MacDonald's first ministry in 1924, maintaining that 'every day they were in they led us further from socialism', but it was MacDonald who was returned to office in 1929.

Harold Laski, Stafford Cripps and the Socialist League (named in honour of William Morris) may have attacked the party's gradualist agenda of 'sensible socialism' during the 1930s, but it was 'the irreproachable and colourless Attlee' who became leader of the party in 1935, reflecting:

> There is today as much criticism of the Labour Party as ever, especially from those whose enthusiastic desires make official policy and action appear too slow. I am glad that this should be so. Self-criticism is a healthy thing so long as it does not lead to a paralysis of the will.[2]

This may do something to account for the success of Attlee's government in the post-war years. Irreproachable and colourless as he may have seemed to Beatrice Webb, Attlee had the capacity to canalize the fissile talents of one of the most talented ministries of the century, a capacity of which Nye Bevan declared: 'Clem's never put forward a single constructive idea, but by God, he's the only man who could have kept us together.' Benn entered the Commons in the last days of Attlee's government, and while 'feeling like a very new boy', he was nonetheless quick to note evidence of differences emerging on Labour's front bench.

In the autumn of 1950, Gaitskell had been appointed Chancellor, much to Bevan's chagrin, who believed that he deserved the post. There was more to it than pique, however. Simplistic as it may be, the two men represented, exactly, the innate divisions within the

2. C. R. Attlee, *The Labour Party in Perspective* (Victor Gollancz, 1937).

party. While Gaitskell, the autocrat, a product of Winchester and New College, Oxford, was contemptuous of populism, Bevan, a one-time miner who had served his apprenticeship in the hothouse of South Wales politics, was equally contemptuous of the grandee he had once described as a 'desiccated calculating machine'.

It was a difference, personal as much as ideological, that even Attlee could not reconcile, and as if anticipating the dilemma that was to rack him throughout his career in the House, Benn wrote in January 1951 of a problem which all Labour MPs had to face: 'whether to stay as loyal members accepting what is done and try to shape policy or whether to rebel and become lone voices in the wilderness'. A newcomer to the House, and more of a loyalist than a loner, he had little difficulty in deciding where his allegiance lay, though his principles were soon to be put to the test when Gaitskell announced in his first and only Budget that he intended to impose a charge on teeth and spectacles to finance an increase in defence expenditure. If Benn was troubled, Bevan was incensed. This was sapping at the very foundations of his creation – the National Health Service – and in April 1951 Bevan resigned.

For six years Attlee had succeeded in holding together his coalition of talents. Now it was disintegrating, and following the fall of the Labour government in the autumn of 1951 all the old differences re-emerged, provoking Crossman to write that the division within the parliamentary party 'was quite grotesquely obvious to anyone looking down from the gallery [of the Commons]. It really does look like two parties.' An inveterate gossip with a waspish tongue, even Crossman was unable to capture the full extent of the poisonous mood engendered by the dispute, Gaitskell at one point going so far as to consider that it would be better if Bevan quit the party altogether: 'Indeed there would be some advantage, for it would have left us much freer to attack him.'

No more than a hint of expulsion, the remark nonetheless smacked of the witch-hunts and purges that had been a feature of the party since left and right had first contested for the adoption of their own vision of socialism, and Morris had mocked Shaw and the Fabians for carrying their moderation to extremes. Indeed, there may have been a touch of unconscious irony in the title of Bevan's work *In Place of Fear*, published in 1952. Not for the first time, and certainly not for the last, it appeared that the party was on the verge of civil war, and with experience of the blood-lettings of the 1930s Bevan knew full well what that could entail, having been expelled in 1938 for supporting the Popular Front against fascism.

Dismissed by Bevan's biographer, John Campbell, as 'the wordy last gasp of a dying political tradition, not the herald of its rebirth', *In Place of Fear* lacked what the left required: a constructive agenda for the future. It was a failing that was to have damaging consequences in the years immediately ahead, for it was precisely this – a reappraisal of the Labour project – that Tony Crosland was to provide for Gaitskell and the revisionists in 1956. A seminal work, *The Future of Socialism* rejected the Marxist assumption that the inner contradictions of capitalism would lead to its collapse, to conclude 'that the much-thumbed guide books of the past must be thrown away'. Indeed, did socialism continue to have any relevance? Apparently only in qualified form:

> Today traditional capitalism has been transformed and modified almost out of existence – revisionism draws attention to this new reality. A people enjoying full employment and social security has lost its dreams, and lost the need for struggle.[3]

But if the party was to reject its history, what should be put in its place? While 'the indolent-minded people on the left' were unable to adapt their socialism to the contemporary scene, Crosland was confident in his prescription for Labour's future:

> The ideal (or at least my ideal) is a society in which ownership is thoroughly mixed up – a society with a diverse, diffused, pluralist and heterogeneous pattern of ownership, with the State, the national-industries, the Co-operatives, the Unions, Government financial institutions, pension funds, foundations, and millions of private families all participating.[4]

Persuasive as it was, Crosland's optimism for the prospects of a mixed economy was flawed by two assumptions: that unfettered

3. C. A. R. Crosland, *The Future of Socialism* (Jonathan Cape, 1956).
4. *Ibid.*

capitalism would never recover its *élan vital*; and, given that economic expansion was infinitely sustainable, all would share in the consequent bonanza without having to tackle the fundamental problem of wealth redistribution and the inequities which that entailed. An alluring prospect, not least for Gaitskell, it was to be another thirty years before Thatcher and the free-marketeers exposed the flaws in Crosland's scenario.

Beyond asserting that he was wrong, the left failed to develop an effective response to Crosland's revisionism, preferring to retreat into a bunker of ideological purism, and Benn found himself caught up in the resulting crossfire. It was a situation he loathed. He had not entered politics to become involved in internecine party feuding, yet during his first six years in the Commons the party was 'absolutely polarized'. And in the mid-1950s, a time when it seemed that Britain had, indeed, never had it so good, Crosland's thesis may well have had a certain attraction for Benn, who was to note in his diary in June 1955 that the Conservative election victory resulted from them having 'good luck with the economic climate' and people being 'generally better off'.

If the cumulative evidence of embourgeoisement was accepted, then Labour needed to realign its policies, which Gaitskell set about doing when he was elected leader of the party in December 1955. While Benn found Bevan mesmeric, he nonetheless cast his vote for Gaitskell. In his turn, Gaitskell was quick to appreciate Benn's talents, particularly during the Suez crisis when he played a major role in shaping Gaitskell's broadcast opposing Eden's military venture and received, in return, a note saying that if the talk was effective it was due, largely, to Benn's efforts.

Even then, however, there were traces of latent dissent. Today, it is difficult to recall the psychosis of the Cold War period, of a time when the world lived in the shadow of Mutually Assured Destruction (MAD) and Slim Pickens rode an H-bomb to eternity to the backing of Vera Lynn's 'We'll Meet Again' in Stanley Kubrick's mordant satire *Dr Strangelove*. All else, apparently, was subordinate to survival, the question being how could survival best be assured? It was an issue that came to symbolize the fundamental differences that divided the Labour Party.

Bevan had once remarked that 'the language of priorities is the religion of socialism', but since the late 1940s it seemed to the left that the party's priorities were being subordinated to ever more insistent US demands for an increase in UK defence expenditure. Overstretched as the country's post-war economy was, Britain entered the nuclear arms race in 1947, and in the following year spent 10 per cent of its national income on defence – a higher proportion than the USA – yet it appeared that Washington was never satisfied. Seemingly, one priority overrode all the rest, and it was to lead to Bevan's resignation from the government in 1951, and later played a role in the formation of the H-bomb National Committee.

In 1952, the Tory government had taken a decision in secret to go ahead with the manufacture of a hydrogen bomb. By 1954, however, it was the worst-kept secret in Westminster and in April a small group of MPs, among them Tony Benn, formed a committee to organize a national petition in support of Attlee's call for a summit meeting of nuclear powers to explore the possibilities for arms reduction. The call came to nothing. The world continued to arm for the Armageddon it feared, but when the secret of Britain's H-bomb was finally revealed in a Defence White Paper of 1955, only sixty-four MPs, including Benn, abstained from voting in the subsequent debate.

Ironically in light of his record, little more than two years were to pass before Benn was invited by Gaitskell to become one of the opposition's spokesmen on the RAF. At thirty-two years of age, it was a recognition both of his growing standing as an MP and of the role that he was playing in helping to reshape the party's broadcasting strategy. If Benn was flattered by the appointment, however, it was quick to test his conscience. How, in practice, could he represent Labour's defence policy, dependent as it was on nuclear weaponry, when in private he was unable to endorse it?

On the evening of 8 March 1958, he told Geoffrey de Freitas, Labour's front-bench spokesman on the RAF, that after giving a great deal of thought to the matter he had come to the conclusion that 'under no circumstances would it be right or sensible for Britain to use the hydrogen bomb' and thus that he could not, conscientiously, remain a spokesman for a policy with which he disagreed. Only one option remained open, and Benn resigned. Even then, however, he was quickly forgiven, being appointed shadow transport minister in November 1959. Nonetheless, the doubts remained, doubts as much about the quality of Gaitskell's leadership as about the direction in which his leadership was taking the party.

In microcosm, Benn's dilemma reflected the crisis of conscience that was racking the party itself. Always sensitive to the charge of militarism, the left was intensifying its campaign for the party to adopt a policy of nuclear unilateralism, a campaign that was to be powerfully reinforced at grassroots level with the formation of CND in 1958. Gaitskell, however, was dismissive. Committed as he was to the US policy of 'massive deterrence', he regarded the left's scruples as little better than a form of moral flagellation.

But more was at stake than whether or not Labour should quit the nuclear arms race. Important as it was, the issue tended to disguise the recrudescence of the debate about the essence of socialism, as the right were quick to exploit the left's failure to develop an effective response to revisionism. In a Fabian pamphlet of 1956 Gaitskell questioned the continuing validity of Labour's commitment to nationalization, and two years later he was to recommend that the party should seriously consider redrafting Clause IV of its Constitution.[5]

As far as the left was concerned, this was not so much revisionism as downright heresy. Since Sidney Webb and Arthur Henderson had drafted the clause in 1918, it had been the keystone of the Labour edifice, yet it now seemed that the revisionists were hell-bent on dismembering the party's founding principles piecemeal, a threat which led Harold Wilson to protest: 'We are being asked to take Genesis out of the Bible. You don't have to be a fundamentalist to say that Genesis is part of the Bible.'

In 1959, Gaitskell was forced to abandon his attempts to revise Clause IV, but remained obdurate in his defence of multilateralism. Always a fissile issue, it was to explode at the party's conference in 1960. As a member of the party's NEC, Benn tried to broker a compromise agreement between the rival factions, but the party was in an uncompromising mood. At a meeting of the NEC on the

---

5. 'To secure for the producers by hand or by brain the full fruits of their industry, and the most equitable distribution thereof that may be possible, upon the basis of the common ownership of the means of production, and the best possible system of popular administration and control of each industry and service' (Clause IV of the Labour Party Constitution until 1995).

afternoon of 2 October, as CND demonstrators marched past the conference hotel chanting 'Ban the bomb. Gaitskell must go', Gaitskell rejected Benn's peace initiative. For a moment it seemed that there was no more to be said. After the vote had been taken, however, Benn raised a point of order to declare that he had 'tried to bring peace', only to be cut short by the Chairman, George Brinham. For an instant, Benn lost his cool and, announcing that he intended to resign from the executive, walked out of the room. At a crowded press conference early that evening, Benn sought to justify his decision:

> I have resigned because it is the only way in which I can warn the conference of the great danger in which the party stands. What we are facing is a crisis of confidence and leadership … No single statement or policy on defence or anything else can possibly satisfy everybody or do justice to all the different traditions which have come to enrich our movement. But if we are to gain strength from unity there must be leadership that transmits our sense of common purpose in a pulse that can be felt at every level of the party.

Six months had passed since Benn had expressed his private reservations about Gaitskell, remarking to Crossman that 'With him as leader, we can't get anything done.' Now his disillusionment with the leadership was a matter of public record. While critical of unilateralists on the pragmatic ground that even if Britain did establish a moral precedent by abandoning its nuclear arsenal, it was unlikely that others would follow, Benn was equally critical of Gaitskell's intransigent mind-set, and his inability to see any other argument but his own. It was a trait to which Gaitskell would give free rein on 5 October when he tongue-lashed the 'pacifists and fellow travellers' of unilateralism to declare that he would 'fight, fight, and fight again' to reverse the conference decision that Britain should withdraw from the nuclear arms race.

Ten days after the conference ended, Viscount Stansgate died, and Benn found himself in political limbo. For ten years he had been on a political learning curve, to become increasingly radicalized, not least as a result of his dealings with Gaitskell. The experience did more than serve as a catalyst for his radicalization, however. It was all very well for the left to protest

that the revisionists were betraying their socialist principles, when
the left itself was party to the betrayal by failing to provide an
effective reply to the revisionists' critique. Unless such a credible
alternative was on offer all that would remain to the left would be
to read the last rites over socialism. In the autumn of 1960,
however, that was a problem – albeit the overriding one – for the
future.

Although he was no longer in the Commons, the media coverage
generated by Benn's campaign to renounce his peerage made his
name a household word and when he stood for re-election to the
NEC in 1962 he was returned fourth in the constituency section, to
improve on that performance the following year. Significantly,
however, his popularity was not universally endorsed by his fellow
MPs. In August 1963, he was re-elected to the Commons, to poll
only 82 votes in the ballot for the shadow cabinet. Always given to
envy, it may have been that certain members were suspicious of
Benn's popularity with the rank and file of the movement and this
accounted for his poor performance. Or it may have been that he
had still to commit himself in the internecine contest between left
and right and thus had no back-bench following of his own.
Whatever the case, it did little to diminish Harold Wilson's
appreciation of Benn's talents.

After a brief illness, Hugh Gaitskell died in January 1963, to be
replaced as leader of the party by Wilson. Crossman had long
harboured suspicions that Wilson 'was not interested in rethinking
policy', a criticism which was later to be echoed by Denis Healey:
'His short term opportunism, allied with a capacity for self-
delusion which made Walter Mitty appear unimaginative, often
plunged the government into chaos.' In 1963, however, it all
seemed very different. Appointed President of the Board of Trade
by Attlee when he was only thirty-one, Wilson was both a Bevanite
and a member of the Keep Left group, which is what may have
prompted Benn to reflect that his election was 'a great shot in the
arm for the Party ... he has some radical instincts where Hugh had
none.'

While the Mitty factor in Wilson's character was subsequently to
disappoint the left, it was his 'radical instincts' which immediately
concerned the revisionists. Apparently, Gaitskell's attempts to
modernize the party were at risk and the best they could hope for

was that revisionism's time would come again, when the party, or at least its leadership, would recognize that there was no alternative to what Crosland had termed 'new Labour'. Even during Wilson's early days in power, however, the revisionists had less cause for concern than they feared. As always, the prospect of the forthcoming election proved a powerful unifying agent, and on being returned to government with a four-seat majority in the autumn of 1964, the whips were on to ensure conformity with the party line. Ironically, it was after Labour's landslide victory of 1966, when backbenchers felt it safe to rebel without putting the government at risk, that all the old differences began to re-emerge.

Benn himself had worked on one of Wilson's 1964 speeches in which he had pledged to replace 'a system of society where money-making by whatever means is lauded as the highest service' to reassert his belief that 'the fundamental inspiration of our social life should be the age-old principle "from each according to his means, to each according to his needs"'. All too soon Wilson's actions were to belie his words. Within months of being returned to power in 1966, and despite Labour's 86-seat majority, intensifying economic pressures led the government to abandon its policy for the 'planned growth of incomes' in favour of deflation and a statutory wage freeze.

If the right were encouraged that their fears of Wilson had been exaggerated, the left were dismayed by Wilson's *volte-face*. Within twenty months of Labour's return to office, there were six major back-bench revolts, three of them over the government's embryonic prices and incomes policy, and two over defence expenditure related, indirectly, to the government's support for the USA's intervention in Vietnam. For all the signs of dissent, however, Wilson was largely successful in ring-fencing the left, in part as a result of his appointment of Crossman as Leader of the House.

A tactical move, it not only allayed the left's suspicions about the direction of government policy but also their fears that Wilson might conduct a purge of dissenters, for there could be no doubting Crossman's credentials for the post. A critic of social-democratic centralism, he had long maintained that blind acceptance of majority decisions could all too easily be abused 'to concentrate power in few hands and change party democracy into party oligarchy', a danger reinforced by the Standing Orders of the

Parliamentary Labour Party, which Crossman regarded as 'little less ruthless than the Democratic Centralism of Leninist theory'.

This was not to gainsay the need for an element of discipline, for the danger of a rupture along ideological lines had existed since the foundation of the party, which was never more than a loose federation of conflicting interests. The Labour leadership had made a talisman of unity, the overriding question being: on whose terms? For six decades, left and right had contested the issue, leaving Crossman to reflect that the left were never happier than when they believed that they were being betrayed by the leadership and that the leadership harboured a deep-rooted suspicion of the left's intentions, particularly when they were so often bolstered by what appeared to be the ineradicable radicalism of the rank and file of the movement.

For all Crossman's skills as a mediator, even he was unable to keep the peace within the party indefinitely. By the late 1960s, triggered first by a bitter dispute over the government's plans to cut public expenditure, and then, and considerably more ominously, over the trade unions' opposition to the government's proposals detailed in *In Place of Strife*, the party was dividing against itself. Seventeen years had passed since Charles Geddes, leader of the Post Office workers, had summarized the powers and objectives of the union movement: 'The trade unions' influence upon the party is due to two reasons: 1) money, lots of it, and 2) votes, many of them. This money will be spent and these votes will be cast in the direction which will further trade union policy.' In 1969 the same remained true.

Devised to defuse the growing differences between the party and its paymasters, *In Place of Strife* tended, rather, to exacerbate them. In the first half of 1968 more than three million days had been lost due to industrial action, and Barbara Castle's White Paper aimed to bring strikes under legal control, while providing a raft of measures to safeguard trade unionists' rights. Incensed by an attack on what the unions had long regarded as their ultimate sanction – the right for workers to withdraw their labour – the union leadership branded Wilson 'a class traitor', prompting Wilson to retort that 'they're not so much barons as bloody dukes'.

An exaggeration? Possibly, though not so far from the truth. A new generation of union leaders was emerging – Hugh Scanlon of the Amalgamated Engineering Union, Jack Jones of the Transport and General Workers Union (TGWU) and Clive Jenkins of the Association of Scientific, Technical and Managerial Staffs (ASTMS) – that would shift the balance of power to the left in the command centre of Labour strategy, the NEC, with far-reaching, long-term consequences. Not that the government was interested in reading the future in the early months of 1969. It already had troubles enough on its hands. The publication of *In Place of Strife* had divided the cabinet against itself, and Benn mirrored its ambivalence.

Although many union leaders regarded Benn as little more than a political careerist who had been 'born with a silver spoon in his mouth', as Minister of Technology he knew as much about the problems of industrial relations as any member of the cabinet, and a good deal more than most. But there was more to Benn's support for Barbara Castle than his recognition of the need to resolve the union problem. After five years in office he had growing doubts about the quality of Wilson's leadership, as two of his 1969 diary entries revealed:

Thursday, May 8: Harold is a very small-minded man, he always gets to the least important part of the issue ... when events call for a higher degree of statesmanship.

Tuesday, June 17: There was a further cabinet on industrial relations, which went on and on ... Harold threatened to resign several times ... and said they would have to look for a new leader, and so on, people were completely unmoved by it. His bluff was called, and he just looked weak and petty.

Benn's disenchantment did not extend to countenancing the whispering campaign mounted by the Gaitskellites, now led by Roy Jenkins, to have Wilson replaced as leader. Essentially a loner, he remained uncommitted in the venomous contest between revisionists and fundamentalists, preferring to develop his own critique of the government's policies, and to formulate his own political agenda. At times, it seemed that he wanted to be both an outsider and an insider in the political power game, remaining a free agent as far as policy development was concerned, yet continuing to enjoy the influence he could exert on the party leadership.

If this was the case, the need to secure a political power base was paramount, and it may have been this that encouraged Benn to consider standing for the post of General Secretary of the Labour Party in the summer of 1968, and prompted him to reflect that

> the reconstruction of the party is the most important task ...
> The student power movement, the Black Power movement
> and the discontent among trade unions are very powerful and
> important new forces in society, and I believe that the Labour
> Party has got to enter into creative relationship with them.

Benn was not alone in his doubts about the nature of party democracy. Eighteen months before, Richard Crossman had delivered a stinging attack on cabinet elitism:

> Very few members of the cabinet believe in participation ...
> They believe in getting power, making decisions, and getting
> people to agree to the decisions after they have been made ...
> The notion of creating the extra burden of a live and articulate
> public opinion able to criticise actively and make its own
> choices is something which most socialist politicians keenly
> resent.

And it was precisely this sense of exclusion that led to the establishment early in 1968 of the left-wing splinter group, the Socialist Charter. Critical of the fact that in many cases Labour MPs sat for what, in effect, were pocket boroughs, the Chartists' aim was to bring constituency pressure to bear on the PLP. The initiative was short-lived, but it keyed in, precisely, with Benn's growing concern both about the direction that the party was taking and the marginalization of constituency opinion in favour of democratic centralism. If the former was determined by the latter, then it was contrary to the democratic principles on which the party had been founded, as Benn was to assert:

> The power of achieving greater party democracy is now the
> central problem facing the movement. It is not just a question
> of constitutional amendments ... It is not just a question of re-
> opening of old arguments about the relationship of conference
> decisions to the Parliamentary Labour Party ... It is not just
> about the merits or demerits of the [union] block vote. It

involves all these things and it does so by making party democracy a major *political* theme ... which we must come to see as just as important as what policies a future Labour government may one day pursue.

Roy Jenkins was to dismiss Benn's critique as populist rhetoric, 'talking left and acting right', but for Benn the two elements – the nature of party democracy and, consequently, of the policies the party pursued – were inseparable. It was not something that the leadership wished to hear. Democracy was all very well as far as it went, provided that it did not constrain the leadership's freedom of movement. As with the constitutional deficit Benn had identified during the campaign to renounce his peerage, this was the institutional deficit that mocked the notion of democracy in the Labour Party. Both paid lip service to the ideal, only to abuse it in practice. Being the puritan that he was, there could be no compromising with his principles, or those of the party either.

While there could be no disputing that a degree of authority was essential to ensure a measure of unity within the party, the question remained, what limits should be placed on such authority, and how far should its diktat extend? Six years in office had provided Benn with an insight into the workings of power, and with the return of a Tory government in 1970 these were questions that came to dominate his thinking, questions as much about the nature of power as about the policies that such power licensed.

And in this, Benn was not alone. Once again, Labour's defeat had reopened the debate as to whether, during its time in office, the government had been too radical, or not radical enough; as to whether in succumbing to revisionism it had betrayed its socialist principles. The right had no doubts about the matter, revisionism was the only way ahead; but as far as the left was concerned, it was the loss of any progressive vision that had cost the party the election.

In 1951, for all the hardships imposed by a beleaguered, post-war economy, Labour polled more than a million more votes than in 1945, and even after Wilson's first, short-lived administration, Labour's vote rose by 0.8 million in 1966, yet little more than four years later the party's turnout fell by almost a million votes. Why?

What had gone wrong? The impression created, and assiduously fostered by the right, was that socialism had passed its sell-by date. Conversely, the left were convinced that the collapse in the party's support resulted from its failure to engage with socialism, and the consequent disenchantment and demoralization which that had caused.

In keeping with Michael Foot's opinion that what the party needed was a 'strong shift leftwards', the Tribune group of MPs, the posthumous keepers of Nye Bevan's conscience, actively campaigned for extended nationalization and 'the mobilisation of some of the country's enormous financial reserves', a programme that would be endorsed by Jack Jones at the party's annual conference in October 1970. Jones argued that if socialism was to be more than the 'slogan' of Roy Jenkins's contempt, then it was essential to return to social ownership of the means of production, distribution and exchange – in short, to revive the party's basic principle: Clause IV. And this, as far as Jones was concerned, required the building of 'genuine democracy in Britain instead of the sham democracy which exists at the present time'.

Possibly because Jones's philippic touched a chord in the conscience of the party, or more probably because the TGWU commanded a large block of the conference votes, the applause for his sentiments was prolonged, careless of the irony implied. But whatever the reason, the speech itself indicated the extent of the radical shift in union thinking since the controversy over *In Place of Strife*. A foretaste of the bitter encounters to come, Jones's analysis highlighted the fundamental differences that divided the party over the way ahead. For the revisionists, it smacked of imposs-ibilism. For Benn, it served to reinforce his own appraisal of the malaise affecting the party.

And it may well have been this realization that without power there was no prospect of restructuring the party, and thus of radicalizing its agenda, that helped to determine his decision to stand for the deputy leadership. Even then, however, he had doubts about whether the post would compromise his principles: 'If you are going to go simply for high office then you have got to be very cautious, and I am not sure I want to be, I would rather stand up for what I believe.' A personal dilemma that was to continue exercising him, it was to be quickly resolved in 1971.

Since he lacked precisely what he sought, namely an effective power base, the election's outcome provided few surprises, the PLP splitting on right–left lines, with Roy Jenkins polling 133 votes, against 96 for Michael Foot and 46 for Tony Benn. As he was later to say, however, it had been a good thing to 'stand up and be counted', not least for the benchmark the election had provided when it came to future leadership contests. Meanwhile, there was consolation to be gleaned from the fact that, in the autumn of 1971, he became Chairman of the Labour Party.

The office had a twelve-month tenure, and from the outset Benn made his concerns about the nature of democracy clear, highlighting the issue in his first message to the party as Chairman in October 1971: 'If we are to be taken seriously in our desire to revitalise British democracy, we must first prove it by revitalising party democracy.' A month later he fleshed out his critique in a Fabian Society lecture in which he catechized both himself and the Party, demanding answers to what he regarded as three crucial questions:

> *Have we failed because socialism itself is out of date? Have we failed because Labour has been betrayed by its leaders? Have we failed because people are selfish?* (author's italics)

In each case, the answer was no, but with critical provisos. Regarding the obsolescence or otherwise of socialism:

> It is said that if we adopt the policies advocated by the left we shall be kept out of power ... But my impression is that people, when they are confronted by the problems thrown up by modern society, demand more radical collective action, not less, and what we lack is not the means but the will to face the powerful forces in society that would be threatened if that change was carried through.

As to whether Labour had been betrayed by its leaders:

> It is certainly true that political achievement measured against promise is often disappointing. It is also true, almost by definition, that anyone who gets to the top by means of the status quo is bound to see, in the status quo, advantages that are not so apparent to those who do less well out of it.

As to whether socialism had failed because people were selfish,

Benn turned the question on its head, to reiterate his critique of democratic centralism:

> We shall never change society unless we start to do it ourselves by directly challenging the unaccountable power now exercised over us, and prepare to exercise it responsibly ourselves ... Our internal [party] democracy is riddled with the same aristocratic ideas that deface our national democracy ...
>
> The fact is that those who exercise power in the Labour Party are not as accountable as they could or should be. Some people seem to think that this is a very good thing. They almost imply that democratic pressures are by definition improper ... The idea is so deeply rooted in the aristocratic philosophy of politics that it is time we examined it more critically. For if democratic pressures are improper then how do you achieve any accountability of power within the party?

Two centuries had passed since Edmund Burke, Benn's predecessor as a Member for Bristol, had addressed much the same question, though from a radically different perspective:

> Certainly, gentlemen, it ought to be the happiness and glory of a representative to live in the strictest union, the closest correspondence with his constituents ... But his unbiased opinion, his mature judgement, his enlightened conscience, he ought not to sacrifice to you, to any man, or to any set of men living. Your representative owes to you, not his industry only, but his judgement; and he betrays, instead of serving you, if he sacrifices it to your opinion.[6]

Since Burke declared in 1774 that he maintained the interests of the burgesses of Bristol against their opinions, his prescription had become deeply embedded in the British political psyche. Now Benn was to reopen the whole tortured question of the role of the representative, if not in government, then in the Labour Party, convinced that if inclusion rather than exclusion was the basis of democracy: 'the truth is more likely to unite than divide the party, by helping to see its way forward to a new and broader

6. Edmund Burke, *Speech to the Electors of Bristol*, 3 November 1774.

interpretation of modern popular democratic socialism'.

Committed as they had been to rationalism, it was a sentiment to which the Webbs would have subscribed. While Benn's Fabian lecture was to serve as the touchstone for his policies in the decade ahead, his critique of the party's structure alienated much of the Labour establishment, who were quick to note what amounted to little more than a throwaway line in his text:

> Gravest of all, the party, when in power, alienated the most important pressure group of all from it – the British trade union movement. We now need their energy, and they now need our leadership, if we are to succeed.

Politics has always been a game of shifting alliances, and never more so than in the Labour Party, in which the rivalrous factions – left and right, fundamentalist and revisionist, the NEC and the PLP, the unions and the constituencies, and the rivalrous factions within them – all play their expedient power games. Indeed, it is no more than a part of the great game of politics, and for Benn's critics to make a play of the paradox that he talked up democracy while commending the unions merely disguised their own hypocrisy.

Of course, it may have been that Benn was again trying to establish an effective power base, in which case he would have been no different from the leadership or many of his fellow MPs. The unions, however, still harboured suspicions of a minister who had countenanced *In Place of Strife* – even after Benn led the parliamentary campaign against the Heath government's decision to close Upper Clyde Shipbuilders (UCS) and had marched through Glasgow at the head of 30,000 demonstrators in support of a work-in at the yard. More than a year had passed since Barbara Castle had warned the unions that if they did not put their house in order, someone would do it for them, and the Heath government were determined to do just that, promising that there would be no further support for 'lame-duck' industries, and pledging to curb union powers.

Tacitly, it was a policy for which the revisionists had a certain sympathy, but for Benn it represented the abandonment of labour to capital, and in the countdown to the closure announcement he won the support of both Wilson and the PLP for a proposal that the UCS should be nationalized and placed under worker control. It

was a gesture, no more, but one which gave notice of Benn's
growing militancy. When the government's decision to close the
yard was finally announced on 30 July 1971, it was Benn who
mounted a savage attack on the Tories' industrial policies,
provoking the Trade and Industry Minister, John Davies, to dub
him an 'evil genius' – a remark that would be echoed in private by
Reg Prentice. A minister of state in the previous Wilson
administration, Prentice was one of the revisionist coterie who
surrounded the man they fondly hoped was the party's leader-in-
waiting: Roy Jenkins.

An Oxford graduate, who had had a 'good war' serving with the
gunners on the south coast of England, Jenkins's talents were
matched only by his ambitions, and even Crosland had begun to
have doubts about his commitment to the 'agreed ideals' of the
party. And where Crosland had his doubts, Benn had his
suspicions that Jenkins was bent not so much on revising the
nature of socialism as on writing the word out of the party's
agenda altogether – suspicions that would intensify following
Jenkins's support for Dick Taverne when he resigned as Labour
MP for Lincoln in 1971:

> There is a small group of highly dedicated [Common]
> Marketeers led by Roy Jenkins ... [who] see a last opportunity
> to do to the Labour Party what they failed to do over
> disarmament and Clause IV, namely to purge it of its trade
> union element and of its left. The ...   group ... really
> represents a new political party under the surface in Britain.

Ironically, Taverne was a victim of those Labour activists of
whom he was to write that, although they were the chain horses of
the party,

> when they came to exert their democratic right to express
> their views and to formulate policies through resolutions
> submitted to the party's annual conference, the government
> simply pushed them aside. They were cannon fodder and no
> more ... No wonder they felt bolshy.

And it was just this, the growing frustration of the rank and file,
that was to lead to the formation of the Campaign for Labour Party
Democracy (CLPD). Composed largely of left-wingers campaigning

for the mandatory reselection of Labour MPs, the first statement issued by the CLPD mirrored Taverne's concerns:

> We believe that the policy decisions taken by conference should be binding on the Parliamentary Labour Party and undertake to secure implementation of this principle. We call on the National Executive Committee a) to carry out its full responsibility as custodian of conference decisions, b) to be responsive to rank-and-file opinion between conferences and extend the processes of consultation with the constituency Labour parties.

For all their similarities, his sentiments did nothing for Taverne, leading Jenkins to reflect in his memoirs:

> In a most extreme form this contradiction [of Jenkins's invidious position as Deputy Leader of a party that had proscribed Taverne] expressed itself in the Lincoln by-election of 1 March, 1973. Dick Taverne, goaded by the bandelliras of the Lincoln Labour Party, decided to break free, resign, and fight the seat again at a by-election.[7]

Under pressure from the Labour establishment, Jenkins refrained from canvassing for Taverne, who fought the seat on a Democratic Labour ticket, convinced that the time had come to found a new centre-left party. If Taverne was to become the revisionists' first martyr, it would be another eight years before Jenkins nerved himself to follow his protégé's example. Indeed, in 1972 it appeared as if Jenkins was losing his taste for power. Prompted in part by Labour's decision to advocate a referendum on EEC membership, in part by the fact that the forward march of revisionism had been halted, he resigned his posts as shadow Chancellor and Deputy Leader of the party in May, leading one of his closest aides, Roy Hattersley, to write: 'It was at that moment that the great schism began.'

7. Roy Jenkins, *A Life at the Centre* (Macmillan, 1991).

CHAPTER THREE
The Great Schism

Banking establishments are more dangerous than private armies.

Thomas Jefferson (1799)

The empire of human freedom will never be enlarged by a party which fails to apply its principles within its own frontiers.
Michael Foot, *Loyalists and Loners* (1986)

Britain's radical movements have always been victims of their own differences, careless of the damage this has inflicted on their cause. There can be no absolutes when it comes to building a New Jerusalem, and like medieval schoolmen, the precursors of socialism have long danced on the pinheads of their ideological differences. In mid-summer 1973, Benn was 'absorbed by reading about the English Revolution', noting in his diary on 26 June:

All the parallels with the situation today are there. The argument with the king and his court: Heath and the City of London, with the big corporations. Then one can see the right wing of the Parliamentary Labour Party as the Presbyterians, rigid, doctrinaire, right wing but officially on the side of puritanism and socialism. The Socialist Labour League and the International Socialists on the left are the Agitators. The Levellers are broadly the labour movement as a whole. There is an argument about the pulpit and who has access to it, which could be seen as the whole argument about democracy today.

For a time it appeared as if the Agitators in the Labour Party were in the ascendancy, and not only as far as the democratization issue was concerned. With the unions in militant mood, the party was becoming increasingly radicalized. In February 1973, a liaison committee had published a declaration of aims designed to provide a compact between any future Labour administration and the unions. Radical in content, it committed Labour 'to the expansion of investment and control of capital' through the extension of public ownership and state supervision of private investment, together with 'a large-scale redistribution of income and wealth' and an extension of industrial democracy. The left-dominated Industry Subcommittee of the NEC was quick to adopt the initiative and in the party's policy document, *Labour's Programme, 1973*, advanced a plan for the state takeover of twenty-five leading British companies.

As shadow spokesman for industry and, thus, one of the authors of the *Programme*, Benn was to be taxed by Wilson in private for what the latter regarded as the document's woolly-mindedness: 'Who's going to tell me that we should nationalise Marks and Spencer in the hope that it will be as efficient as the Co-op?'[1] In public, however, he had to go with the flow, and by the time of the party's annual conference, Wilson had reversed his position to advance a programme of nationalization involving, among other industries, shipbuilding, ports and docks, aircraft production and parts of the drugs, machine-tool and construction sectors.

Seemingly, the counterattack on revisionism which had alienated Jenkins was gaining momentum. Percipient as Hattersley was in anticipating Labour's times of trouble to come, he seriously underestimated Wilson's manipulative skills. Alternating threats to have him removed as leader of the party with counter-threats of resignation, Wilson played off right against left in a zero-sum game of which Machiavelli would have been proud. And what he lacked in guile was more than compensated for by the growing crisis in government.

Nothing concentrates the mind of the Labour Party more than the prospect of a forthcoming election, and by the close of 1973 the Heath government was looking increasingly vulnerable. For three

1. Philip Ziegler, *Wilson* (Weidenfeld and Nicolson, 1993).

years it had been involved in a relentless contest with the unions. Initially, its imposition of a compulsory wage standstill, followed by phased wage increases, was partially successful in containing inflation, but on 8 October 1973, only two days before Phase Three of the scheme was due to be announced, war broke out in the Middle East, slashing Britain's oil supplies and almost quadrupling oil prices. Encouraged by the improvement in their bargaining position which the crisis had provided, the miners imposed an overtime ban and threatened to strike. Once before, the government had backed down in the face of the miners' demands. Now they determined to tough it out, fuelling speculation that Heath would seek to strengthen his hand against the National Union of Mineworkers (NUM) by going to the country to resolve the question of 'Who rules Britain?'

Or, more appropriately as far as Benn was concerned, who should rule? In December he published an article in *The Times* which, in rebuffing the paper's long-running campaign to promote a third party in the hope that Labour would be defeated if it adhered to its socialist principles, provided the rationale for the party's interventionist strategy. His line of attack was twofold yet complementary: that the historic shortfall of private-sector investment was damaging Britain's industrial base as seriously as the decline in public investment was undermining essential social needs. This was at the core of the crisis which Britain was facing, and he made no attempt to disguise the tough measures, and the consequent hardships, that would be required to resolve it:

> The only basis on which we can appeal to them [the British people] is by adopting policies of social justice and greater equality ... If this is not done we cannot expect and shall not receive their consent for what has to be done. It is against this background that the relevance of Labour's commitment to bring about a fundamental and irreversible shift in the balance of power and wealth in favour of working people and their families by democratic means will be judged.[2]

If these were the ends to be achieved, the means for achieving them had already been spelled out in the party manifesto. Wilson,

2. *The Times*, December 1973.

however, had as little time for Benn's radical sentiments as he had for the party's radical agenda, preferring, rather, to campaign on a platform of 'national unity' in the run-up to the election of February 1974. But while Wilson's appeal for unity proved successful at the polls, with Labour winning a four-seat majority over the Tories, it did nothing to resolve the differences when it came to appointing his post-election cabinet. The old left–right differences remained, but, adroit as always, Wilson temporarily succeeded in neutralizing both by balancing the factions out, one against the other: appointing Roy Jenkins to the Home Office, Jim Callaghan to the Foreign Office, Denis Healey to the Treasury, Michael Foot to Employment and Barbara Castle to Social Services.

Only one wild card remained to be played, Tony Benn, who was guaranteed a place in the cabinet as a result of his previous shadow cabinet position. Ominously, his appointment as Secretary of State for Industry was to presage a rift not between left and right, but between left and left. Already suspicious of his ambitions, Foot's growing hostility to Benn may have been prompted not so much by the fact that he was usurping Foot's role as the champion of the left, more that he appeared to be hell-bent on undermining party unity. Since Nye Bevan's death in 1960, Foot had been the undisputed leader of the left, but after fourteen years he was tiring of the role. One of the great parliamentarians of the post-war years, he had little taste for high office, preferring to play the tribune of socialism from the back benches, though never at the expense of Labour's electoral fortunes. Independent-minded as he was, Foot was above all else a party man, and with his first appointment to office in the mid-1970s he was to make a shibboleth of party unity, frequently at the expense of his own long-held principles. And this, too, is what may have accounted for his growing animosity to Benn: perhaps he saw in Benn the radical he had once been himself.

As for Wilson, he now tolerated Benn only on sufferance. Healey would write later that his hatred for the man who had once been his protégé often 'bordered on the hysterical'. Wilson's dilemma was that his options for marginalizing Benn were limited by the party's shift to the left, since more than half of the newly elected Labour MPs following the February election had joined the Tribune group, of which Foot had previously been the principal spokesman. Although not a member of the group, Benn reflected many of its views. This was to provide him with the political muscle required to fight his own corner in a cabinet that was divided three ways against itself, with Benn representing what came to be termed the 'hard left' as distinct from the 'soft left' stance of Foot and Castle, both of whom were ranged against the right led by Jenkins. And it was Jenkins who, on 25 July 1974, was to warn Wilson of the dangers 'of ignoring middle opinion and telling everyone who does not agree with you to go to hell'.

Five days later, during a two-hour meeting of 'absolute agony and bloodshed', a cabinet committee approved Benn's White Paper *The Regeneration of British Industry*, but not before 'a great struggle'. It recommended the establishment of a National Enterprise Board with powers to acquire not only lame-duck concerns but also profitable companies, most notably in the shipbuilding sector. The right were quick to leak Benn's proposals to the media, providing a cross-section of the national dailies with the material to mount a savage attack on the plan the following day. As a countermeasure, Benn asked his Permanent Secretary at the Department of Industry, Sir Anthony Part, to have a million copies of a popular version of the White Paper printed for circulation to industry, only to be told that this was impossible, as there was the likelihood of a snap election, and such a move would be controversial. When asked why, Part simply retorted: 'I can only tell you that this would not be possible.'

For a moment Benn may have recalled the time when, as Postmaster General, his plan to produce the so-called 'headless stamp' had been frustrated by a conspiracy of mandarins. Apparently, little had changed in the decade between. When challenged, the mandarinate resorts, at best, to obfuscation, at worst to obscurantism, and in the summer of 1974 Part's 'impossibilism' shared common cause with the right in cabinet, where it seemed that a split could well be imminent. Benn noted in his diary on 25 August that if a crisis did occur 'a few people will go; Reg Prentice, Shirley Williams, Roy Jenkins are bound to slip away to the centre ground, and the Labour Party will have to build itself up again'. He underestimated not only how extensive the slippage would be but also how far the apostates would go.

As for Part, he was right in one respect. In October 1974, Wilson went to the country, and in the run-up to the polls, the media campaign against Benn intensified. A media bogey that was to haunt the electorate was in the making, the *Daily Express* running a cartoon of Benn with a touched-in Hitler moustache, the *Daily Mail* reporting that 'Wilson goes cold on Benn', and the normally patrician *Financial Times* going so far as to publish a think piece addressed to Wilson that concluded with the advice: 'AT ALL COSTS keep Tony Benn muzzled.'

With an overall three-seat majority in the new House, there was nothing that Wilson would have liked to do more than follow the *FT*'s advice. This was more easily said than done, however. Benn could be difficult, contumacious, many things, but Wilson could not afford to get rid of him, or at least not precipitately. All that he needed was time, and the assurance that the new political axis between Denis Healey, the Chancellor, and Michael Foot, the Secretary of State for Employment, would hold. While each worked to their own agenda, careless of the fact that their aims were antithetical – Foot's concern being to revive confidence in Labour's pledge to 'create a partnership between the government and the unions'; Healey's being to contain wage inflation regardless of the impact of such a policy on the level of unemployment – it was a combination that Wilson was to exploit to isolate Benn, and to neuter his industrial strategy.

Not that he could say as much in public. Guileful as ever, at the party conference in November 1974, Wilson described Benn's plans to establish a National Enterprise Board as 'the biggest leap forward in economic thinking as well as in economic policy since the war'. In private, however, it was very different. As the Industry Bill progressed through the House in the spring of 1975, Wilson actively plotted to undermine its main thrust, as the MP Ian Mikardo recalled: 'The Prime Minister's intentions were clear in drafting a series of amendments to the Industry Bill in committee. It was clear cut: the bill was being emasculated.' For all his protestations, Wilson wanted no part of Benn's radical measures, and neither did the Foot–Healey axis.

As Benn's relations with Wilson deteriorated, and his isolation in cabinet increased, he resorted to talking off the record to establish the fact that the policy he was pursuing was the one which had been approved by the party itself. If Wilson and the cabinet were bent on reneging on their commitments, then the rank and file of the party deserved to know, the only trouble being that as a member of the cabinet, Benn was supposedly bound by its code of collective responsibility. Although mocking reality, and not least the fact that Wilson, among others, was a past master of off-the-record briefings, it was a long-standing convention that in public the cabinet should appear united.

Yet again, the question for Benn was on whose terms, and at what cost? As to the one, it was at the expense of his long-standing commitment to both open government and party democracy; as to the other, it was at the expense of the policies he had been appointed to pursue. In the first half of 1975, two of the three major issues on which Benn had campaigned (the third being whether or not Britain should enter the Common Market: see Chapter Six) fused, demanding a compromise which he could not accept. Patently, there was a need for the government to secure the loyalty of its MPs, but equally, as far as Benn was concerned, there was the question of whether he should abandon his policies, if not his principles, in pursuit of cabinet unity. And in the 1975 Wilson government, both policies and principles were subordinate to pragmatism, as Michael Foot engaged in a contest to 'keep the cabinet together' in the face of Benn's challenge, which, considering the forces ranged against Benn, posed few difficulties.

A rebel turned loyalist, Foot was subsequently to justify his actions on the grounds that Benn's problems were psychoanalytical rather than political:

> gradually his belief [in collective responsibility] frayed; gradually his other loyalties elbowed out this allegiance; gradually, from the point of view of his cabinet colleagues, or even his smaller group of associates, he became – literally, it is hard to avoid the term – not to be trusted.[3]

Once opened, the rift between the rebel-that-was and the rebel-in-situ was to widen, cavernously, in the years ahead; while as far as Wilson was concerned, he had had enough of what he regarded as Benn's displays of conscience. On 10 June 1975, he sidetracked Benn from the Department of Industry to the Department of Energy in an attempt to pacify the economic hard-liners in the

3. Michael Foot, *Loyalists and Loners* (Collins, 1986).

cabinet, and to curb his burgeoning influence with the party's rank and file.

The following day the *Guardian* carried the story under the headline 'Wilson gives Benn's head to the City', while at a meeting in the Commons Benn accused Wilson that in transferring him to the Department of Energy he was 'capitulating to the CBI [Confederation of British Industry], the Tory press, and to the Tories themselves, all of whom have demanded my sacking'. Whether or not Wilson had sacrificed Benn to the City, it did little to defuse the market's concern about Labour's management of the economy, despite Chancellor Healey's attempt to contain the wage inflation that had been triggered by the hike in oil prices. Initially, he had little success, with wages rising at twice the rate of the cost of living in late 1974, and by early 1975 he was actively considering a monetarist approach 'to make unemployment the automatic reward for excessive pay settlements by keeping monetary creation within predetermined limits'.

Benn was demoted on 10 June, but with price inflation at 26 per cent and the annual wage rate up by 32 per cent, pressure on the pound remained, and at a cabinet meeting at Chequers on 20 June, Healey floated the idea of introducing a statutory incomes policy. Rejected in favour of setting a £10 limit to wage increases, with a fall-back position of imposing a statutory policy if such a voluntary approach failed, it was a compromise which prompted Benn to point meaningfully at a portrait of Ramsay MacDonald as he left the room. The Treasury had lost a battle, but the war had still to be won.

Within five months, and with the markets maintaining their pressure on the pound, Healey opened a second front by asking for a £3.75 million cut in public expenditure – and threatening to resign if he did not have his way. Yet again, a compromise formula was cobbled together, and yet again sterling was kept afloat. Jack Jones issued a reminder to the annual conference of the TGWU: 'The MacDonalds, the Snowdens, the Jimmy Thomases are lurking around, their names do not need to be spelt out', while Barbara Castle reflected bitterly: 'I see no reason for the existence of a Labour government. We have adopted Tory *mores*. The only difference is that we carry out Tory policies more efficiently than they do.'[4]

4. Barbara Castle, *The Castle Diaries* (Weidenfeld and Nicolson, 1980 and 1984).

Her obituary for socialism was premature, though it may have done something to reinforce Wilson's decision to stand down as Prime Minister. Twelve years had passed since he had entered No. 10 with high hopes of transforming the electoral landscape, twelve years during which the realities of power had sapped at his radical credentials. An increasingly isolated figure, he had lost his taste for office and on 16 March he announced his resignation to the cabinet. It was a decision of which Peter Clarke was to write:

> Wilson's departure in fact opened up the era of clarification in the Labour Party. His heritage of manipulative Labourism now faced a double challenge. On the left, the idiom of Marxism acquired a new cachet and a new militancy ... Conversely on the right of the party there was a more self-conscious adoption of the language of social democracy.[5]

The six candidates who stood to succeed Wilson represented the full spectrum of the differences that divided the cabinet: Jenkins, Callaghan, Healey, Crosland, Foot and Benn. Foot, the centre-left candidate, led Callaghan, the right's favourite, in the PLP's first ballot, with Jenkins coming in a poor third with 56 votes, followed by Benn (37), Healey (30) and Crosland (17). Although he was delighted by the result, not least that he had run Jenkins so close and bettered Healey, there were still doubts about Benn's shift to the left, as his aide, Joe Ashton, noted: 'The conversion time hadn't been long enough for some people. Old timers on the left thought he was too much of a careerist.' Significantly, Ashton was to add: 'That was when Tony began to think we'd got to have a better way of picking a leader or it would always be a play-safe, right-wing leader of the PLP.'

In the second ballot, Benn voted for Foot, but in the final ballot it was 'the pike lurking in the shallows', Jim Callaghan, who was returned as leader with 176 votes. Largely self-educated, his first words on hearing the news of his victory were: 'Prime Minister, and I never even went to university.' Callaghan was as politically friendly as his name Sunny Jim implied, commanding a powerful following in the PLP and among trade unionists, who were indebted for the role he had played in sabotaging *In Place of Strife*.

5. Peter Clarke, *A Question of Leadership: From Gladstone to Thatcher* (Penguin, 1992).

Within three years of taking office, Callaghan's *mésalliance* was to return to haunt him, but the makings of the crisis yet to come were already there before he entered No. 10. At his final cabinet meeting, Wilson had declared that 'there were no impending problems or difficulties' which had not already come under discussion – an assertion that belied reality.

Innately hostile to Labour, the City had been talking down the British economy for more than two years. And in this they were not alone. More than half a century had passed since the Treasury had been party to the bankers' demands that the MacDonald government introduce a packet of swingeing cuts in public expenditure in order to secure a balanced budget. More than half a century on, the old orthodoxies still prevailed. Apparently careless of the fact that inflation was falling and unemployment was rising, certain Treasury officials went so far as to mislead the Chancellor, Denis Healey, about the levels of public expenditure in order to reinforce the financial markets' demands that the government introduce further curbs on public expenditure. Keynes might never have been.

A month before Wilson's resignation, the government published a White Paper on public expenditure, freezing all planned increases. Even this was not enough to satisfy the markets, however. In the first week of March, there was a run on sterling, which was to accelerate precipitately in the first weeks of Callaghan's administration, the pound falling by almost 15 per cent against the US dollar in the two months up to June 1976. Apparently, the government had still not got the message that monetarism rather than Keynesianism was now the name of the game. And whatever lingering doubts there may have been about such a *volte-face* were soon to be quashed when it came to raising funds from the IMF to support sterling.

The Republican administration in Washington wanted nothing of Labour's 'profligate' policies and, using the IMF as its stalking-horse, it demanded further massive cuts in public expenditure in return for stand-by credit. The gathering storm had finally broken, and as two leading British economists, Burke and Cairncross, were to write in their study of the financial crisis of 1976:

What seems clear in retrospect is that no matter what the government did, short of repudiating both its history and its supporters, the market would continue to demonstrate its total lack of confidence, unless and until an approach was made to the IMF.[6]

During the first three weeks of July, the cabinet met nine times to discuss what amounted to the markets' ultimatum, which Benn rejected outright. In effect, what the City and its allies were demanding was the government's capitulation to the dictates of *laissez-faire*, and with it the subordination of Britain's economy to forces over which it had no control. And, to achieve their ends, it seemed that the markets were careless about the damage they inflicted on the national economy, for all their protestations that their sole concern was the public good, and that until the government came to recognize that it had no option but to adopt monetarism the country would continue to suffer. As far as Benn was concerned, this, too, was all part of the Noble Lie which secured the authority of the Guardians in Plato's *Republic*: that like 'well-bred dogs', the people had to be saved from themselves.

Constantly recycled to secure the Guardians' hegemony, it was a myth that Benn considered as specious as it was corrupting. The notion that there was, indeed, no alternative – not least, to the dictates of the market and its placebo, monetarism – was no more than a self-fulfilling prophecy which, as is the case with all prophecies, cloaked itself in a mystery of which Benn was to write:

> The argument for it [monetarism] is simple and straight-forward. It is to lift the heavy burden of taxation from industry and commerce by sharp cuts in public investment and public expenditure in the hope that financial incentives will work and market forces will revert to their magical role of reallocating resources to maximise their use. Dr Milton Friedman, the prophet of this school of thought, has succeeded in enthusing a large number of bankers, indus-trialists, and economists with the beautiful simplicity of this approach, which has been embraced by them with all the passion of a religious conversion.

For Benn and the left the problem was to formulate a convincing

6. Kathleen Burke and Alec Cairncross, *'Goodbye Great Britain': The 1976 IMF Crisis* (Yale University Press, 1992).

alternative to the 'frenzy' of monetarism. The National Enterprise Board provided part of the answer, but more was needed if a credible response was to be found to check the charge of the free-marketeers. Since the turn of the Labour government in 1974, Benn and his small team of advisers – led by the economist Francis Cripps – had been working on just such an alternative economic strategy.

Based on a package of measures including the introduction of selective import restrictions and the imposition of controls over banks and other finance houses, the alternative strategy presented a direct challenge to the combined power of the Treasury, the Bank of England and the City, committed as they were to a deflationary policy that was dependent on a fall in real wages and further cuts in public expenditure. And, again, the old orthodoxies prevailed.

While the soft left had a certain sympathy for the alternative strategy championed by Benn, Callaghan was dismissive, declaring that it was 'quite unacceptable . . . I don't see why you wrote it'. On 6 July 1976, the cabinet decided that it had no option but to accept the dictates of the markets. It was not simply Keynesianism, more the entire socialist project that was pawned off to monetarism that day, a reversal which prompted Lord Kaldor, a special adviser to the Chancellor, to accuse Denis Healey of perpetuating the mistakes made by MacDonald and his Chancellor, Philip Snowden, in 1931. It was a ghost that was to haunt the party conference later in the year, where Benn mounted a full-frontal attack on the cabinet's prescription for Britain's economic ills:

> We have played down our criticism of capitalism and our advocacy of socialism . . . The political vacuum we have left has been filled by many voices, by the monetarists, by the nationalists, by the racialists . . . Unless we speak more clearly now we shall be fighting the next election defensively, deep inside our own political territory, instead of being on the offensive on behalf of our own people.

The delegates applauded, but Callaghan was contemptuous:

> For too long, perhaps ever since the war, we have postponed facing up to fundamental choices and fundamental changes in our society . . . We used to think that we could spend our way

out of recession, and increase employment by cutting taxes
and boosting government spending. I tell you in all honesty
that that option no longer exists ... Now we must get back to
the fundamentals.

Milton Friedman, Margaret Thatcher's economic guru, came to
regard Callaghan's speech as a model of fiscal rectitude, and one
that he 'most frequently quoted with approval of any delivered by
any politician anywhere', according to Callaghan's son-in-law,
Peter Jay, who, as economics editor of *The Times* in the mid-1970s,
was a leading proponent of monetarism.

And as if to establish its new-found, fundamentalist credentials,
Callaghan announced in mid-conference that the government was
making an application for a £4 billion IMF loan, while by the close
of the conference Healey (who had taken to referring to the
alternative strategy as the product of 'tiny Chinese minds') had
been persuaded by the Governor of the Bank of England into
making an unqualified commitment to monetarism. For the third
time in the space of a year the government was to capitulate to the
diktat of the markets, to raise interest rates to an unprecedented 15
per cent and inflict further deep cuts in its budget – cuts which for
all her monetarist convictions even Mrs Thatcher never succeeded
in matching.

Although proscribed by government, the alternative economic
strategy nonetheless continued to command widespread support
among the rank and file of the party, and Benn continued to
recommend its merits. Arguably, in fact, it was the extent of the
grassroots support for Benn which did much to account for his
growing demonization. Regarded by the City establishment as an
agent of Satan, the case he advanced for the alternative strategy put
the fear of God into the monetarists, challenging, as it did, the
entire basis of their credo.

Abandoning any claim to logic, and contemptuous of any
arguments but those they wished to hear, the free-marketeers
subscribed to freedom in everything – with the exception of those
opinions they did not share. And the more vigorously Benn
advanced the case that there was an alternative, with all that
implied as far as the closed world of capital was concerned, the
more the markets cast Benn as a bogey figure, a role which the

right-wing media was to promote assiduously in the years immediately ahead. And, albeit covertly, certain elements in the government connived at Benn's demonization, not least Jenkins and his coterie.

In his autobiography, *A Life at the Centre*, Jenkins makes no attempt to disguise his disenchantment with both the Wilson and Callaghan administrations – 'I did not want a future in British politics'; 'I had grown too out of sympathy to be a good or patient member of the government'; 'I had come to believe that Britain was one of the worst governed countries in Western Europe'[7] – a disenchantment fortified by the treatment meted out to one of his closest allies, the 'bravely accident-prone' Reg Prentice.

A former trade unionist, and Wilson's Secretary of State for Education, Prentice's progressive shift to the right had led to a call for his deselection by the Newham Constituency Labour Party. In defence of what he regarded as a serious constitutional principle, Jenkins mobilized a handful of colleagues, including Shirley Williams and Bill Rogers, to campaign for Prentice at a meeting in the East End of London. The event degenerated into farce, and did little to help Prentice's cause. The deselection call was upheld, a decision which may do something to account for Jenkins's remark that in the autumn of 1975 he was 'almost flaking away from the Labour Party to the centre'.

Two years later, he quit the government to become President of the European Commission. Before he left for Brussels, however, a small group of his friends held a farewell dinner in the Commons at which, as Prentice later revealed, Jenkins voiced his growing misgivings about the Labour Party, and hinted at the need for a realignment in British politics. If the Prentice issue helped to crystallize Jenkins's disillusionment with a party which he felt was losing its senses, to the left it appeared that Labour was in the process of recovering them.

Since the formation of the CLPD, with its demand for a comprehensive reform of Labour's constitutional structure, its support among constituency parties had burgeoned, to the growing concern of the party establishment. Although not a member of the Campaign group, Benn supported its aims, which

7. Roy Jenkins, *A Life at the Centre* (Macmillan, 1991).

echoed what he had long been saying, that the party's internal democracy was riddled with the same aristocratic ideas that marred British democracy, and that the problem of democratizing the party was the central issue facing Labour.

In theory, the objective was admirable, but as far as the leadership was concerned it defied the reality of the management of power, more especially when, as in the case of the Callaghan government, it only commanded a one-vote majority in the Commons. Above all else, unity was required, and if that demanded less rather than more democracy, then so be it. But if, unknowingly, Callaghan subscribed to Thomas Hobbes's dictum that 'The power of a man is his present means to obtain some future apparent good', Benn and the CLPD were unwilling to defer the present to the future.

At the party conference in 1976, forty-five constituencies backed the Campaign's call for the mandatory reselection of MPs, together with an instruction to the NEC to appoint a working party to examine alternative ways of appointing the party leader, a warrant then exercised only by Labour MPs. Callaghan was not amused, and in his conference speech he coupled his defence of the new fundamentalism with a carefully qualified attack on constituency activists, maintaining that he had no wish 'to retreat behind the stock defence that "the government must govern" if that becomes a polite way of telling the party to go to hell' while insisting that the NEC investigate 'those elements who misuse the word "socialism" and who seek to infiltrate our party and use it for their own ends ... not because I am on a witch-hunt but because I want the government and the party to work closely together'.

In the Labour canon Callaghan's use of the word 'witch-hunt' was ominous, though it may have been that his conjunction of two themes was accidental, and that he failed to make the connection between the activists' calls to democratize the party and his rejection of the alternative economic strategy. The oversight seems improbable. Callaghan could read the political runes better than most, and at the 1977 conference he toned down his criticism of the left, pleading with rather than browbeating delegates to reject the CLPD's call for the mandatory reselection of MPs. And with reason. In the previous year the campaign had continued to gain momentum, and when it came to the vote the resolution was carried by a million majority. After four years the CLPD had achieved its first objective, a success that reinforced its call for the NEC to complete its study of alternative ways of choosing future party leaders.

The message was as clear as its implications were far-reaching. The whole, carefully crafted edifice of top-down power in the party was being challenged. In a plea that dissenters should be protected from witch-hunters, however, Benn maintained that the call for a new role for political leaders was not 'a charter for anarchism, nor a dream of creating a wholly self-regulating economic or political system', rather an indication that, if power was more widely disseminated, leadership would have to be more widely shared:

> More than five hundred years before the birth of Christ, Lao-Tzu, the Chinese philosopher, had this to say about leadership:
>
> 'As for the best leaders, the people do not notice their existence. The next best the people honour and praise. The next the people fear, and the next the people hate. But when the best leader's work is done the people say, "We did it ourselves." '
>
> To create the condition that will allow people to do it themselves is the central task of leadership today.[8]

8. Tony Benn, *Arguments for Democracy* (Jonathan Cape, 1981).

CHAPTER FOUR

New Labour: 'A Little Bit of Leninism'

We have lived so long at the mercy of uncontrolled economic forces that we have become sceptical about any plan for human emancipation.

Harold Macmillan, *The Middle Way* (1938)

The most convenient world for multinational organisations is one populated by dwarf states or no states at all.

Eric Hobsbawm, *Age of Extremes* (1994)

The Labour government fell in May 1979, an act of political if not of poetic justice. Ten years had passed since Callaghan had helped sabotage *In Place of Strife*, and, careless of their debt to him, the unions wanted no more of the government's fudge and mudge over incomes policies. The Winter of Discontent began with the unions demanding pay increases of between 20 and 30 per cent, the forerunner to a series of wildcat strikes of which Callaghan was to write later:

> The serious and widespread industrial dislocation caused by the strikes of January, 1979 ... set the government's fortunes cascading downhill, our loss of authority in one field leading to misfortunes in others just as an avalanche, gathering speed, sweeps all before it.

On 3 May Britain went to the polls, and the following day the Tories were returned with a 43-seat majority. Benn gleaned only one consolation from the defeat, that after five years in office, during which he had often felt as if he were 'tiptoeing through the corridors of power', he had now recovered 'the freedom to speak my mind, and this is probably the beginning of the most creative period of my life'. He anticipated events, but only by a matter of days. At a meeting of the shadow cabinet on 9 May, Callaghan insisted on the necessity of maintaining collective responsibility, and the following day Benn announced that he had no intention of standing for shadow office on such terms.

At fifty-four years of age, and having served for eleven years in four Labour administrations, he was his own man again, and at a chance meeting with Ted Heath following the state opening of Parliament he expressed some sympathy for Margaret Thatcher 'with her dislike of the wishy-washy centre of British politics'. A conviction politician himself, it was a contempt that Benn shared, though from a radically different perspective. Apparently, the new right were bent on selling the pass, holding that democracy and capitalism were inextricably linked, a notion that Benn rejected in its entirety, maintaining that the primary task of the Labour Party was 'to restore the legitimacy ... of democratic socialism because the press were actively engaged in outlawing any argument to the left of centre of British politics'.

Although now ensconced in Brussels, Roy Jenkins had been following developments in Westminster closely, in particular the intensifying, post-election contest for power in the Labour Party. Seemingly, the party was hell-bent on self-destruction and, unless it could be saved from itself, an alternative had to be found. In the summer of 1979, Jenkins was invited by the BBC to deliver the prestigious Dimbleby lecture, and early in November he test-marketed its contents on Ian Gilmour. Considering his position as Mrs Thatcher's Lord Privy Seal, Gilmour's reaction was significant, as Jenkins recalled in his autobiography:

> He thought much of the end was too right wing. In particular, he objected to the phrase 'the social market economy', saying that he thought it had gone out with Erhard [a committed monetarist, who had served as German Chancellor for three

years in the 1960s] until revived by Keith Joseph [Mrs Thatcher's monetarist guru].[1]

Whatever doubts Jenkins may have had about his text were quickly dispelled by developments at the Labour Party conference. The mood throughout had been poisonous, right and left engaging in charge and countercharge as to who had been responsible for the party's defeat, as to whether the government had been sufficiently radical or not radical enough. At the close, it was the left that carried the day. A resolution calling for the party leader to be elected by an electoral college was only narrowly defeated, while delegates accepted the principle that, in future, control of the manifesto should be vested in the NEC. As for the long-standing issue of mandatory reselection, Ron Hayward, the party's General Secretary, turned on the body of Labour MPs penned in the body of the hall, reminding them:

> I still say that we did not ... select, raise the money, work to send an MP to the House of Commons to forget whence he came and whom he represents. [Applause] ... One [paper] I read the other day said that one MP said 'If I don't get my way at this conference I will resign.' I've got some advice for him. Don't worry about that. I've got a queue a mile long that wants to go to the House of Commons [Laughter] – but it is a very short queue that wants to be a branch secretary. [Laughter and applause]

For Jenkins, the patrician, it can hardly have been the sort of joke he appreciated, or the sort of party of which he wanted to be a part, and in his Dimbleby lecture on 22 November 1979, he provided an insight into his thinking, particularly on the need to develop a new dimension in British politics:

> I believe ... that if [the electorate] saw a new grouping with cohesion and relevant policies it might be more attracted by this new reality than by old labels ... The response to such a situation [of the ideological dogfight racking the Labour Party] in my view should not be to slog through a war of unending attrition, but to break out and mount a battle of movement for new and higher ground.

1. Roy Jenkins, *A Life at the Centre* (Macmillan, 1991).

Significantly, Jenkins concluded by calling for the strengthening of 'the radical centre'. An oxymoron that was later to enter New Labour's vocabulary, it disguised what Benn suspected was a move towards corporatism.

Quite coincidentally, Benn was developing his critique of a school of thought that 'has very powerful friends in high places throughout the Western world' at much the same time as Jenkins was preparing his Dimbleby lecture:

> It is true to describe it [corporatism] as the consensus view of the old British establishment which, for reasons of prudence rather than any personal preference, believe it is their best recipe for survival ... The state and the economy are to be run by a new generation of barons who now occupy their modern castles in the office blocks of London and Brussels.

Benn's critics were quick to dismiss his appraisal as a paranoid fantasy, the work of a conspiracy theorist, careless of the fact that eleven years in government had provided him with a vivid insight into the networking of corporate power and its capacity for corruption, the full extent of which only became apparent following the Scott inquiry into the arms for Iraq affair in 1996 and the Cresson scandal that rocked the EU in 1999. It was not so much the potential for corruption, more the corruption of power that was the by-product of corporatism that Benn suspected, against which he was to pit his faith in democratic socialism, calling up its precursors – the Levellers, Tom Paine, the Chartists, Robert Owen, the Webbs – in defence of a radical agenda:

> We believe that the self-discipline of full democratic control offers our best hope for the future ... Indeed we believe that the nation can earn its living efficiently and profitably only if there is a new balance of wealth and power in favour of working people. And to avoid corporatism creeping in as a by-product of these public initiatives we [the Labour Party] have been working for a wider and deeper accountability of power through greater democratic control by Parliament of government and of finance and industry and of the institutions of the labour movement itself.

Whether the right-wingers in the Wilson and Callaghan

administrations would have agreed with Benn's scenario is doubtful. Indeed, it is altogether more likely that they would have dismissed his remarks as further evidence of his populist tendencies, of which the historian Kenneth Morgan was to write: 'By the end of the 1970s, there seemed hardly a fashionable cause – that of the black activist, feminist, "gay lib" or Greenpeace environmentalist – with which he [Benn] was not passionately identified.' Morgan's remark said more about the prejudices of the party hierarchs than it did about Benn's politics. Contemptuous as the establishment may have been of 'fashionable causes', however, there could be no disguising Benn's growing popularity with the party's rank and file, who continued to snap at the authority of the nomenklatura.

In the aftermath of Labour's election defeat, there was a surge in support for the CLPD – its membership doubling in the twelve months to June 1980 – while by 1981 the Labour Co-ordinating Committee (LCC) had enlisted 800 members, and almost sixty affiliated organizations. Formed in 1977 by a small group of activists who, according to Michael Meacher, 'were disillusioned by the progress of the Wilson–Callaghan government and supported Tony [Benn] as a hope for radicalisation and real progress', the LCC's original aim was to popularize the alternative economic strategy directed, as it was, at 'democratising state services and agencies'. By 1979, however, the committee had become embroiled in the intensifying dispute over 'entryism' into the party.

Since the early 1970s, a range of ultra-left, Trotskyite splinter groups, most notably the Militant Tendency, had succeeded in securing a foothold in a small number of constituency Labour parties. Scornful equally of Benn, whom the Militant leadership referred to as Kerensky, and of the alternative economic strategy, which they regarded as merely reformist, the Militants castigated Labour for the loss of its radical spirit:

> Reliance on the present token and ineffectual parliamentary opposition will advance us nowhere. We must look to new, more militant forms of extra-parliamentary opposition which involve mass popular participation and challenge the government's right to rule.

Benn wanted no part of the entryists' revolutionary posturings, maintaining that 'the debate between extra-parliamentary violence and parliamentarianism' was not only diversionary but was also damaging the reformists' case:

> Their talk of revolution implies, and nobody believes it, that there is a short cut to the transfer of power in this country ... What the socialist groups really do is to analyse, to support struggle, to criticise the Labour Party, to expand consciousness, to preach a better morality. They are all very desirable things to do, but they have very little to do with revolution.

And Benn's actions matched his words. As Chairman of the Home Policy Committee of the NEC, a post he held for ten years up to 1984, he rejected outright a Militant call for the nationalization of 200 companies at the party conference in 1979. Neither his words nor his actions did anything to restrain the increasingly vituperative campaign being mounted against Benn and Bennism, however. While Roy Hattersley was to differentiate between the legitimate left and the Trotskyite entryists ('cuckoos in the Labour Party nest'), others were not so discriminating. Careless of the fact that the Militant Tendency never commanded a significant following in the party, the stigma of militancy was to be exploited, ruthlessly, to demonize the left, Denis Healey going so far as to charge Benn with encouraging 'the sort of People's Democracy the Russians set up in Eastern Europe after the war'.

The charge was not new. In the early 1970s Crossman had said much the same of the democratic centralist tendencies 'of Leninist theory' favoured by the party establishment, a charge which by the early 1980s Healey and the right found it expedient to ignore, preferring, rather, to pursue a campaign of guilt by association against the legitimate left. Damaging as the Trotskyite tactics were, the more so when embellished by horror stories of 'the loony left' in the media, they did nothing to check moves to democratize the party. A decade had passed since Benn had first raised the issue: 'We shall never change society unless we do it ourselves by directly challenging the unaccountable power now exercised over us.' Then it had been little more than a whisper. By 1980 it was the loudest whisper of them all.

If not militant, there was no denying the burgeoning confidence of the left, particularly when the NEC challenged 'the unaccountable power of the capital markets' with the publication of *Peace, Jobs, Freedom* in May 1980. The Thatcher government had been in power for little more than a year, but its messianic commitment to the free market was clear, conscious of the fact that the Callaghan government had already test-marketed the nature of monetarism. A political high roller, it was a trick that Mrs Thatcher could not miss. Benn noted in his diary that during parliamentary Question Time on 6 July 1980, she had made great play of the similarities between her own policies and those of the previous administration: 'quoting what Healey and Callaghan had both said in office'.

The indictment cut deep, and the memory of what many regarded as the betrayal of socialism did much to account for the left's disillusionment and the party's rediscovery of the merits of the alternative economic strategy. A radical, ten-point statement, *Peace, Jobs, Freedom* recommended, among other things, the introduction of statutory planning agreements to 'guide the activities of huge companies that dominate the economy', coupled with the extension of public enterprise to secure a stake in the industrial sector, the introduction of price controls and the imposition of 'strict controls over international capital movements'.

Together with the call for democratization, the NEC's paper was to provide the left with a formidable platform at the Blackpool conference in October 1980 – 'the conference of Tony Benn' according to the political commentator Philip Whitehead: 'He [Benn] seemed to be everywhere, addressing fringe meetings three at a time, if the agenda was to be believed, and mixing a potent brew of instant socialism from the platform.' The word instant gives the lie to the remark. Benn was no pop-up politician, conjuring policies out of the air.

Consistency is not a notable characteristic of power-brokers, and the fact that Benn, particularly since the late 1960s, had been as consistent in his critique of the democratic deficit within the party as of the economic policies that the Wilson and Callaghan governments had pursued did much to fuel the Labour establishment's suspicion of, and animosity towards, him. While his detractors called up memories of Churchill's remark about Benn's predecessor as MP for Bristol South-East, Stafford Cripps – 'There but for the Grace of God goes God' – Benn's consistency was a characteristic that Tom Sawyer, a leading trade unionist, was to applaud, recalling how in 1980 Benn was 'the only man who offered a big change ... it was in our minds absolutely essential to take off in a new and different direction'.

And this is precisely what conference did, endorsing the NEC's economic strategy, reconfirming its support for the reselection of MPs, and approving in principle the establishment of an electoral college to select future leaders of the party. After seven years of campaigning, the CLPD had achieved two of its three goals, the exception being a resolution calling for the NEC's control of the party manifesto. In what Benn came to regard as the best speech of his life, he reversed the right's traditional defence that top-down control was essential to secure party unity: 'The route to unity in this party is not to lecture it to stop quarrelling, but to start listening to the debate, to discuss the policy in advance of the movement, and go on discussing it year after year.'

The constituency delegates applauded ecstatically, heedless of a caution that had previously been issued by Benn's former Parliamentary Private Secretary, Joe Ashton. Disenchanted by Benn's attempts to change the rules of the party, he overrode the slow handclap that punctuated his speech to warn: 'If Roy Jenkins wanted to form a party of twenty-five sacked MPs now in Parliament, they would be in business in six months, and they would be backed by the media.' David Owen was seen to smile. As he was to write, it seemed that the conference was 'in the grip of the far Left', which reinforced the conviction of Jenkins's coterie that the time was fast approaching for them to go it alone. In a full-frontal attack on Callaghan's leadership Owen fomented Labour's troubles: 'We are fed up with this fudging and mudging, with mush and slush ... We must ask our leaders that they stand up for their beliefs with the same conviction and passion and the same skill used by others who have won out on countless issues at this conference.' Coded as it was, the message was clear: unless the party leadership reasserted its authority, an alternative would have to be found.

Callaghan had had enough. Seemingly, the party was running out of control, and twelve days after the conference ended he announced his retirement. Ever the shrewd tactician he realized that to delay the announcement would deprive the PLP of its last chance of taking sole responsibility for the selection of a new leader. At Blackpool it had been agreed to hold a special conference in January 1981 to decide on the composition of the electoral college which, in future, would be responsible for making the choice, a choice that Callaghan pre-empted, preferring to place his trust in the good sense of the PLP rather than to gamble on the outcome of a collegiate election. Although tempted by the prospect, to have stood for the leadership would have compromised Benn's own, long-standing campaign to democratize the party, and in a frank appraisal of his dilemma he wrote a gathering held at his home: 'It was a meeting of the left, and very formidable they are, but they were unanimous I shouldn't stand ... so I bowed to the will of the majority.'

In retrospect, it was a wise decision. Benn's championship of reselection, together with his support for an electoral college, had alienated a significant body of Labour MPs who were as much concerned for their own political futures as they were for their rights to appoint the party leader. And as the contest for power intensified, it became increasingly bitter, Benn writing of the hatred he met in the tea room of the Commons, 'a hatred so strong that I became absolutely persuaded that this was not a party I would ever be invited to lead, and nor could I lead it'.

Five days were to pass between the announcement of Callaghan's resignation and Michael Foot's unwilling entry into the leadership contest. Never happier than when harrying the government in power from the back benches, he had little inclination to take up the post. The party, however, came before his personal preferences, not least the realization that if the right's favoured candidate, and early front-runner, Denis Healey, was elected, it could well split the movement. As the left–right dispute became progressively more acrimonious, the word in the labyrinth of Westminster was that only one man could provide the party with the unity which it required, and on 10 November Foot narrowly defeated Healey for the leadership, appointing Healey as his deputy and recalling the words of his mentor, Nye Bevan: 'Never underestimate the passion for unity in the party.'

Significantly, Foot's victory was secured, in part, by the votes of a handful of MPs who within months were to defect to the SDP. As one of their number, Neville Sandelson, was later to recall, there was a collective move by the cabal

> to wreck the Labour Party by voting for the more extreme
> candidates ... and the number of votes [they cast] in the Foot–
> Healey election were sufficient to tip the balance Foot's way.
> He was the man most likely to lead to the crumbling of the
> Labour Party.

If Benn had stood, doubtless they would have voted for him.

As it was, Benn voted for Foot, though there were some who came to regret the fact that he was not a candidate himself. Peter Shore, a long-time cabinet colleague of Benn's, was later to describe him as 'the man who was more superbly equipped than anyone else to fulfil the functions of a really dynamic and successful Labour leader', a conclusion that Michael Meacher was to endorse, holding that the left had had within their ranks 'someone clearly of leadership potential who was an inspiration, who had a grand vision, who had a sense of purpose, and who was a brilliant communicator'. Dynamism. Inspiration. Vision. These were precisely the qualities which led Shore to describe Benn as 'Labour's lost leader', and which the right and its agents feared, the more so when allied to his commitment to socialist policies with which they had no truck.

Benn did not speak at the Wembley conference held to decide on the composition of the electoral college that would choose the future leaders of the party. He had no need to. His views were already well known:

> It is often argued that MPs are threatened with domination by
> conference, or the NEC, or local parties. In fact the real
> problem is that Labour MPs have fallen under the control of
> the parliamentary leadership through patronage, official
> secrecy and demands for total loyalty to the leader personally.

It was precisely how to redress this distortion of power that the Wembley delegates debated in January 1981, voting in favour of a forty-thirty-thirty weighting between the unions, the parliamentary party and the constituencies when the time next came to elect a party leader. Before the singing of 'The Red Flag', David Owen quit the platform, declaring that 'four trade union barons meeting in smoke-filled rooms is no way to elect a prime minister.' The following day, the Gang of Four (David Owen, Shirley Williams and Bill Rogers flanking Roy Jenkins in the forefront) issued their so-called Limehouse Declaration:

> The calamitous outcome of the Labour Party Wembley conference demands a new start in British politics ... We realise that for those people who have given much of their lives to the Labour Party, the choice that lies ahead will be deeply painful. But we believe that the need for a realignment of British politics must now be faced.

Michael Foot's heartfelt appeal for unity had come to nothing. After little more than two months with him as party leader, the unthinkable had occurred: the Labour Party had divided against itself, and in March 1981 the Social Democratic Party was formed.

Subsequently, Benn and the left were to be made the scapegoats for Labour's times of troubles. In a political sleight of hand, the Gang of Four, who would be followed by twenty-five Labour back-benchers, came to be regarded as, if not the first martyrs, then the first victims of extremism, in a process that was to accelerate as the party began its shift to the right in pursuit of electoral credibility. In the early 1980s, however, there was little evidence to support the view that socialism had passed its sell-by date. Quite the reverse. Even in the 1979 election that followed the Winter of Discontent there had been only a 2 per cent swing to the Tories. Twelve months later, Labour had achieved a 10 per cent lead in the polls, the *Sunday Times* reporting that Mrs Thatcher was 'the most unpopular leader' since polls began, while as Healey was to note: 'The Labour Party's internal troubles did not wipe out its lead in the opinion polls until the autumn of 1981, when the split created the SDP, and the long battle over the Deputy Leadership finally sealed our fate.'[2]

The one front-bench spokesman whom Thatcher really feared, Healey was a born political infighter. Once described by Crossman as 'a very lone mover', he was to compare the post of deputy leader to that of the US vice-president – 'If he is bad he can do much damage, if he is good, he can do nothing'. In the spring of 1981 it

2. Denis Healey, *The Time of My Life* (Michael Joseph, 1989).

was the damage he feared Benn would inflict on the party that persuaded him to contest the deputy leadership, maintaining that if Benn were elected 'there would be a haemorrhage of defections both in Parliament and in the country. I do not believe that the Labour Party would have recovered.'[3] Michael Foot agreed. At a meeting on 24 March, he urged Benn not to stand, arguing that it would 'lacerate' the party. Two days later, the Gang of Four announced the formation of the SDP.

Healey was speaking in Hamburg when he first heard the news that Benn had entered the electoral lists. It was All Fools' Day 1981, an ill-omened date. Fearing that he would be blamed for their defection, Benn had delayed the announcement of his candidature until after the launch of the SDP. Even then there were those who urged him to think again. The General Secretary of ASTMS, Clive Jenkins, invited Benn to an extravagant lunch, at the close of which he presented him with an elegant loving cup, on the front of which were inscribed the words 'Elections can be poisoned chalices, Tony' and on the back, 'Don't do it, Tony'.

Altogether more ominously, elements of the Tribune group, which Benn had only recently joined, had serious reservations about his candidature. Formerly the vanguard of the left, and for a long time the home ground of Michael Foot, Tribunites such as Neil Kinnock had already begun to trim their policies, and wanted nothing of Benn's radicalism. The divide reflected the divisions in the PLP and the unions, though not in the constituencies, which were solid in their support for Benn. As the dispute intensified, it was to become progressively more poisonous, a fratricidal contest between the myriad tribes of socialism that turned as much on the ideologies of the individual candidates as on the characters of those who championed them.

For Healey the next six months were to prove 'the least agreeable of my life'.[4] For Benn, it would be a period of mounting frustration. Early in May he had begun to feel unwell ('I don't have any feeling in my feet, and my hands tingle. I just don't feel well at all'), and on 6 June he was admitted to Charing Cross Hospital where, following a series of neurological tests, doctors diagnosed that he

3. *Ibid.*
4. *Ibid.*

was suffering from Guillain-Barre Syndrome, a disease of the nervous system. When he was discharged in mid-June, the doctor's orders were clear: if he wished to make a full recovery, he would have to rest for the critical three-month period that led up to the deputy leadership election.

Until the campaign to discredit Ken Livingstone two decades later, the campaign mounted against Benn in 1981 ranks among the most venomous in the history of the party, and led Michael Meacher, one of Benn's former aides, to recall:

> There was never less than a half-page of vitriol in the press every day, and the source was the right wing of the Labour Party. They were feeding stuff into the press even though it did cataclysmic damage ... It was more a cause of the defeat in 1983 than the Falklands.

And where innuendo and aspersion failed, the behaviour of the ultra-left always made for good headlines, not least the brawl of entryists led by the Militant Tendency who harassed Healey at rallies in Birmingham and Cardiff. Few of Militant's revolutionary designs were ever stated explicitly, but there can be no question that its tactics did serious damage to the cause it pretended to represent. By generating alarmist coverage, the Militants' menacing conduct not only alienated moderate opinion but also disguised the fact that there was a powerful case to be made for the devolution of power within the party, which was one of the main reasons why Benn had entered the contest, to compel party members to make choices:

> That's what's called polarisation, divisiveness, and all the rest, but it's true. You can't go on for ever and ever pretending you're a socialist party when you're not, pretending to do something when you won't, confining yourself to attacks on the Tories when that's not enough. People want to know what the Labour Party will do and I think that this process is long overdue.

Neil Kinnock provided the curtain-raiser for the Labour Party conference which opened in Brighton in the last week of September. Writing in *Tribune* in the previous week, he had mounted a highly personalized attack on Benn, which set the tone for much that was to come: 'I believe Tony has fostered antagonism in the party, he has undermined the credibility of credible policies, he has not disowned those who insist on support for his candidature as the test of loyalty to Labour policy.'[5]

Regardless of the fact that many of the 'credible policies' had been developed by Benn, and endorsed by Kinnock, it was the man rather than his policies who was the target of Kinnock's antipathy. And in this he wasn't alone. Still in a state of shock following the defection of the Gang of Four, and aware that further defections could follow, the party leadership, together with a significant section of the PLP, and a number of the larger unions, wanted nothing more than to disguise the innate differences that divided the party – differences that had come to be symbolized by Benn.

Condemned by one MP for pursuing 'a personality cult', and by others for what they regarded as his self-righteous championship of socialist verities, Benn's presence haunted the consciousness of the once-and-future revisionists who gathered in Brighton for the party's eightieth annual conference. And on the afternoon of Sunday 27 September, they were to avenge themselves on Benn's presumption, recording the closest vote in the history of the party's deputy leadership contests.

In the first ballot, which eliminated the outsider John Silkin, Healey obtained 45.3 per cent of the votes, against 36.6 per cent for Benn. More than 80 per cent of the constituency votes had gone to Benn, and with the TGWU announcing that it intended to shift its support from Silkin to Benn in the second ballot, it seemed that all would depend on how Silkin's supporters divided their 18 per cent share of the vote, not least the members of the PLP. At the count, 30 per cent of the PLP vote went to Benn, but eighteen Tribune members abstained, prompting Margaret Beckett to denounce Kinnock as a Judas, and for one furious delegate to shout: 'Why don't you stand, Neil [Kinnock], then everyone can abstain.' By then it was too late, Healey had been returned with 50.4 per cent of the vote, against 49.5 per cent for Benn, a 0.9 per cent margin.

Healey's campaign manager, Giles Radice, was to assert that in beating Benn, Healey had 'saved the Labour Party', though that was not immediately apparent. In the spring of 1982, the SDP were a couple of percentage points ahead of Labour in the polls, with the

5. Neil Kinnock, *Tribune*, September 1981.

Tories trailing in third place. The Falklands War was to transform
the political landscape. Shortly after the Argentinian surrender in
June 1982, the Tories had established a 20 per cent lead over
Labour, prompting Benn to write in his diary:

> I feel somehow that we are at a real turning point in politics. I
> can't quite describe it. The military victory in the Falklands
> War, Thatcher's strength, and the counterattack of the right of
> the Labour Party on the left ... make me feel more than ever
> before that I need to pause and think and work out a new
> strategy ... I feel we have just come to the end of an era.

It was to be another year before his forebodings were fully
realized. The jingoistic appeal of the Falkland campaign, and the
mood of triumphalism following the Argentinian defeat, had
revived the Tories' short-term fortunes and provided them with
the launch pad for the election of June 1983.

For Labour, the outcome was disastrous. Although the NEC and
conference had agreed to fight the election on a radical manifesto
based, in part, on the alternative economic strategy, Benn was later
to note: 'In 1983, not only couldn't we persuade the public to
support Labour policy, we couldn't persuade the leadership to
support it.'

The resulting campaign was a shambles. Pressurized by Healey
and the right, yet still teased by memories of his radical past, Foot,
the unifier, was divided against himself – particularly when Healey
threatened to withdraw if Foot campaigned on a manifesto pledge
favouring unilateral nuclear disarmament, an issue which Foot had
long made his own. And this was not all. While both Callaghan
and Wilson openly attacked the manifesto, a right-wing element
within the party was playing an altogether more devious game. As
John Golding, Chairman of the Home Policy Committee, was
subsequently to reveal, the so-called Clause Five group of MPs
deliberately decided to support the manifesto in order to ensure
that, in the event of a Labour defeat, the responsibility for the
defeat would rest solely with Benn and the left. And the outcome
was to justify their machinations.

Careless of the Falkland factor, it was the left's championship of
what Gerald Kaufman subsequently dubbed 'the longest suicide
note in history' that was held to account for the Tories' landslide

victory in which Labour secured only 27.6 per cent of the vote, and in which Benn lost his seat. As a result of boundary changes, his old constituency of Bristol South-East had been eliminated from the political map, and its electors redistributed between Bristol South and Bristol East. Even before being selected to stand for Bristol East, Benn had been warned of the danger of contesting what, currently, was a Tory seat. Benn ignored the advice. He had represented a Bristol constituency for more than a quarter of a century, and had no intention of quitting the city when the going got tough, as the Conservative candidate, Jonathan Sayeed, was to recognize. When the result was declared, and Benn had lost by 1790 votes, Sayeed paid a handsome tribute to his opponent, pointing out that Benn might well have opted to contest a safe Labour seat, but preferred not to desert the city which he had served for so long.

As far as Labour's revisionists were concerned, however, Benn's defeat was no more than he deserved. That they had actively connived at creating the bogey which they now blamed for Labour's defeat was of no account. The man had finally received his come-uppance, and like wraiths they danced on socialism's grave. Having freed itself from the past, Labour could now begin building for the future, even if the auguries were not immediately propitious.

Less than forty-eight hours after the Tory victory, Michael Foot stood down as leader of the party, endorsing Neil Kinnock's nomination as his heir. Three other candidates entered the lists (Peter Shore, Roy Hattersley and Eric Heffer), but at the party conference of 1983, Kinnock received an overwhelming 71 per cent of the votes cast by the electoral college, while in the subsequent ballot for the deputy leadership, the right-winger Roy Hattersley was elected by a clear majority. While the right may have had suspicions about Kinnock's credentials, the left had no such doubts. At forty-one years of age, he had established his left-wing qualifications as a paid-up member of the Tribune group and was a fluent proponent of public ownership, unilateralism and Euro-scepticism. Indeed, at fringe meetings in 1983 he went so far as to quote Lenin and Gramsci to underline his radical credentials.

Only one thing remained unanswered as far as Peter Shore was concerned. Kinnock might have 'a complete kit of then fashionable left-wing viewpoints', but did he have a settled opinion in any of them? The answers, when they came, were to devastate his former allies. Once in office, Kinnock was to adopt Barbara Castle's axiom that to govern is to choose, and in making a virtue of pragmatism he adopted psephology as the touchstone of his mandate: the reality of a party that had 'treated realism as treachery' and of the need for it to learn from 'the harsh, electoral reality' of its recent defeat. The message was clear, yet the ambivalence remained, and in 1984 Kinnock was still insisting that Labour was 'committed to a process of renationalisation' as 'the only means to give coherence to the most efficient reorganisation of our resources'.

In the contest between principles and pragmatism, however, it was pragmatism that was to win out. With the Tories continuing to hold a commanding lead in the polls, it appeared that Labour could either ride the slipstream of free-market policies or make a political crash-landing, and with the publication of the Fabian pamphlet *The Future of Socialism* in 1985, Kinnock's conversion to revisionism finally became plain. Rejecting 'the stale vanguardism of the ultra left ... and the atavistic and timid premise of social democracy', Kinnock called for the party to adopt a 'third way' which, in recognizing the shift that had taken place in society, would allow Labour to reposition itself.

And once begun, revisionism became a self-fulfilling prophecy, whose appeal was no longer limited to the right. In 1984, Benn returned to the Commons as MP for Chesterfield, but his efforts to rally the left had diminishing impact. Five years of Thatcherism had broken the party's political will, and Benn's appeal to its historic consciousness made little difference:

> We are all taught to accept, almost without question, that our freedom and welfare depend upon centralised power struc-tures, and that we have a duty to obey the orders that are passed down to us from on high ... This oppressive political culture has now spread over the whole of our society ... There is no reason why we should accept these values, which have been consistently questioned by great numbers of people throughout our history as they challenged the established order ... and campaigned for their replacement by a set of values based on social justice, solidarity, and democracy.

For a party hell-bent on catching up with the future, or its simulacrum, Thatcherism, Benn's political reprise held few attractions. To his more generous critics it seemed that he was caught in a time trap, constantly replaying his own selective version of the past, and even his closest colleagues began to have doubts about whether his political agenda continued to have any relevance to the situation in which Labour found itself, so much so that Benn wrote in mid-summer 1986 that the majority of his advisers had deserted him. And quite possibly with good reason. Quite possibly, both he and his ideas had outlived their time. Quite possibly, the future did lie with the revisionists who, like Kinnock, had come to believe that 'the market is potentially a powerful force for good'.

In rewriting the political rule book, the Tories were dragging Labour with them, and following Labour's third consecutive electoral defeat in 1987, when the party picked up only 31 per cent of the votes, it seemed that any compromise was acceptable to avoid further political humiliation. It was a mood that the leadership was quick to exploit, and one which was to inflict a punishing defeat on Benn in the leadership contest at the party's annual conference in 1988. He had long held doubts about whether to stand, but finally resolved to declare himself following Kinnock's less than enthusiastic support for striking NHS workers earlier in the year.

Benn's candidature marked what was, in effect, the last stand of the left, and it failed calamitously. As Kinnock had forecast, Benn's campaign ended in 'a massive defeat for those who have put their self-indulgence above the interests of the party', neglectful of the fact that only recently he, too, had been self-indulgent enough to advance the policies which Benn now represented. Kinnock was right in one respect, however. When the count came, Benn picked up only 11 per cent of the votes, as opposed to an 88 per cent share for Kinnock. It was, indeed, the end of an era. On that September day in Blackpool, Labour effectively rejected the notion that there was any credible alternative to the dictates of the free market, and provided Kinnock with the sanction he sought to realign the party to the right.

The evidence of how far he succeeded was soon to become clear. In what Ivor Crewe, Professor of Government at the University of Essex, was to describe as 'the least socialist policy statement ever to be published by the party', *Meet the Challenge, Make the Change* rejected the renationalization of industries privatized by the Conservatives, accepted the restrictions imposed by the Tories on trade union rights and abandoned the party's commitment to unilateral nuclear disarmament. Indeed, there was a certain symmetry in the fact that as the Cold War was ending, and the Berlin Wall coming down – events which the American guru Francis Fukuyama described, euphorically, as marking 'the end of history' – the leadership were rewriting Labour's credo.

Apparently, there was no other option, and, as Peter Shore was to write, the party accepted the conversion with surprising ease: the commitment to what was in effect an unregulated market economy; the privatization of virtually the entire public sector; and not only continuing membership of the EC but also acceptance of the growing constraints the Single European Act imposed on state intervention in the economy. To David Marquand, a former adviser to the SDP, Kinnock was 'a better – or at any rate, a more successful – revisionist than Gaitskell ever was'. To Benn he was the man who 'gave up everything he ever believed in, so that no one believed anything he said'. But there Benn was wrong. They did.

During the post-war years between 1945 and 1979, the two major political parties had played Box and Cox in office, but Thatcherism tipped the balance heavily in the Tories' favour. A variety of factors were to account for their success, above all else the character of Thatcher herself. A product of the lower middle class, in contrast to the patriciate which, historically, had led the party, and motivated by a powerful streak of nonconformist individualism, she appealed, unashamedly, to the self-interest of Middle England, declaring famously that 'There is no such thing as society.' A heretical view as far as Benn was concerned, it challenged the fundamental text of socialism. Seemingly, however, there was no gainsaying the attractions of possessive individualism as far as the electorate was concerned, particularly when it was fuelled by the scramble for privatization.

Faced with such evidence, it appeared to Kinnock that repositioning the party was the prerequisite for its survival. To Benn, the notion was anathema. Seduced by the markets, the leadership appeared to be carrying its moderation to extremes, maintaining that There Was No Alternative (a variation on Mrs

Thatcher's dictum) to revisionism if Labour was to have any hope of ever recovering power. And the end of the Cold War accelerated the process, marking the culmination, as Benn saw it, of a contest for global hegemony that dated back to the Russian Revolution in 1917:

> I have read the correspondence between Lord Halifax, the Viceroy of India, and my Father, the Secretary of State for India in MacDonald's second administration, and it's quite clear that he was obsessed by the fear that India would go communist.

While Benn had no sympathy for Stalin or Stalinism ('a truly monstrous regime'), he firmly believed that the existence of an anti-capitalist superpower had traumatized the West, and allowed 'the right-wing or capitalist or Tory definition [of socialism] to be hung around our necks. It isn't socialism, but it has silenced us on the definition of what socialism should be.' Condemned as an apostate by the apostates of New Labour, Benn was to reaffirm his own definition of socialism in 1990:

> My belief is that of the three centres of power now existing – ownership of capital, the organisation of labour, and the ballot box – the first should be replaced by the second and the third, the ballot box and the initiative of labour ... I see this as a process rather than as an end-point, the 'socialist common-wealth' of the 1945 manifesto.

Dismissed as antediluvian, it was a formula which had no place in the strategy of Labour modernizers. Confident in their own prescriptions, the party's apparatchiks regarded Benn as a political has-been, and an embarrassing one at that. Like a ghost in the machine, he continued to rebut the myth bruited abroad by its critics that socialism had failed 'because socialism is inextricably linked with dictatorship' and to reiterate his belief that 'the main socialist message is about the democratic control of economic power.'

Since the Levellers had first challenged the compact, it had been the staple of power, and throughout the 1990s Benn continued to hammer home the message that both were inextricably linked:

'From the outset the demand for economic justice and the campaign to widen the franchise were part of the socialist movement.' And again: 'The case against capitalism is essentially the same as the case against feudalism. It is essentially about arbitrary power.' And yet again: 'Democracy is the most controversial idea in the world. Nobody minds if you make a socialist speech ... but start asking questions about the structure of power, and I tell you, you'll get into real trouble.'

And the more questions he asked, and the more insistently he asked them, the more isolated he became, a prophet whose championship of Old Testament socialism had no place in the New Testament of Labour's revisionists. Half a century had passed since the Attlee government had committed itself to building a 'socialist commonwealth', and by the 1990s Labour hierarchs (their convictions reinforced by an intake of defectors from the now defunct SDP) had no further reservations about proclaiming that 'the markets ruled, OK'. Seemingly, all that was now required to 'reinvent the party' was to jettison Clause IV, Labour's historic commitment to 'the common ownership of the means of production, distribution and exchange'.

Gaitskell was the first revisionist to propose scrapping the clause, always more of a Party icon than a policy commitment, while Neil Kinnock and Jack Straw had actively considered such a step, only to be frustrated by John Smith, who succeeded Kinnock as Labour's leader following the party's fourth consecutive election defeat in 1992. Eighteen months after taking office, Smith died, to be succeeded by Tony Blair, who was pledged to establishing 'a dynamic market economy', and whose aides, Peter Mandelson and Roger Liddle (the latter a one-time assistant to Bill Rogers, a founding member of the Gang of Four), were to put their own spin on his intentions:

Labour's current phase of reinvention was started by Neil Kinnock and continued by John Smith. But essentially they were engaged in a ground-clearing operation – first, to rid the party of the Bennite excesses that had led to the SDP split ... and then to restore its unity of purpose and to democratise its internal procedures. Tony Blair has built on that solid inheritance to lead the party in the restatement of its values and the wholesale modernisation of its policies.[6]

The words sounded well, but they disguised the intent. While the emphasis was on the need to democratize the party, the process of concentrating power in the hands of the leadership was already gathering pace, and it was the revisionist Roy Hattersley who was to voice his concern not only about the nature of the democratization process but also the direction of the New Labour project:

> Ideology is what keeps parties consistent and honest. In the long term, the party's public esteem would be protected by a robust statement of fundamental intention. Socialism – which is proclaimed in the new Clause IV – requires the bedrock of principle to be the redistribution of power and wealth.

The revised clause offered neither, but for Blair and Labour's modernizers it was central to their project of reinventing the party in their own image. Circumlocutory in style, and opaque by design, the new clause was a masterpiece of political newspeak, declaring that Labour 'believes that by the strength of our common endeavour we achieve more than we achieve alone, so as to create for each of us the means to realize our true potential', through the creation of a 'dynamic economy ... in which the enterprise of the market and the rigour of competition are joined with the forces of partnership and co-operation to produce the wealth that the nation needs'.

Unconsciously, perhaps, the echo was of Adam Smith and *The Wealth of Nations* (1776), for two centuries the handbook of free-marketeers and neo-liberals, and the reverse of all that Benn had consistently campaigned for:

> We are socialist because we believe that our rights cannot be fully realised in any society under capitalism, which, as in Britain now, has entrenched by law the power of Capital over Labour, and subordinated human values to the demand for profit, at the expense of social justice and peace.

With the party's approval of the revised Clause IV in 1995, and

6. Peter Mandelson and Roger Liddle, *The Blair Revolution: Can New Labour Deliver?* (Faber & Faber, 1996).

the leadership's confident assertion that it could make capitalism work better than the capitalists, the only problem that remained was to disabuse constituency members (Benn's longtime power base) of what residual sympathies they may have had for socialism, and 'sell in' the new corporate model of Great Britain, plc, which, in itself, posed a problem. Shortly before the new clause was accepted, David Marquand had written: 'The mission of the SDP's Gang of Four has been accomplished – by the party they left.' What he failed to explain was the precise nature of New Labour's agenda, the precise nature of its terms of reference. Twelve months later Will Hutton, then economics editor of the *Guardian*, offered what appeared to be a partial answer to the problem with the publication of *The State We're In*, in which he maintained:

> The triple requirement is to broaden the area of stake-holding in companies and institutions, so creating a greater bias to long-term commitment from owners; to extend the supply of long-term debt, and to decentralise decision taking. The financial system, in short, needs to be comprehensively republicanised.[7]

Briefly, Hutton's formula appeared to provide a solution to New Labour's need to create a new persona for capitalism, as Blair proclaimed: 'I want Britain to be a stakeholder economy where everyone has the chance to get on and succeed, where there is a clear sense of national purpose and where we leave behind the old battles between left and right.' Significantly, he delivered his message while in Singapore during a whistle-stop tour of the Far East aimed at reassuring business executives of the tiger economies of the Pacific rim that their investments would be safe in New Labour's hands.

Almost immediately, however, stakeholding was to be replaced by the more elusive vision of creating 'a radical centre', which even its exponents such as the New Labour MP, Tony Wright, a committed Blairite, had difficulty in defining ('What the radical centre means lacks precision because it reflects the uncertainties of the times'), and which Benn was to dismiss as an oxymoron on the grounds that the centre was by definition consensual rather than

7. Will Hutton, *The State We're In* (Jonathan Cape, 1995).

radical. But if the radical centre lacked clarity of meaning, so did its offspring, the Third Way, the political *via media* long championed by Jenkins and revisionists, about which Benn was as sceptical as he was suspicious ('New Labour's prime object is to destroy old Labour, but you can't wish away a movement, a history, with a sound bite'), drawing on memories of a time in his childhood when he had stood at the window of No. 10 alongside Ramsay MacDonald:

> That was in 1930. A year later [following the financial debacle of 1931] having won the support of the Tories and Liberals, MacDonald announced he was tendering his resignation to the king and would be forming a National Government ... There are some parallels with that period which we would do well to remember now ... The renaming of the Labour Party as 'New Labour', the clear indication that Clause 4 was Bolshevist and had to be dropped, the description of 'new Labour' as a new political party, and the deliberate distancing of the trade unions from that party, certainly have echoes of the past.

Roy Jenkins's subsequent assertion that the Liberal and Labour parties shared a common interest, and that it was only the century-long and unnecessary rift between them that had ensured the Tories' political predominance, tended to reinforce Benn's fears about the entire nature of the 'Blair project'. Cryptic as Blair's pronouncements were, there was no escaping the growing evidence of New Labour's determination to curb union powers (or even to sever the party's links with the unions completely, as Stephen Byers, a future Secretary of State for Industry, hinted), and, conversely, to neutralize business hostility to Labour to ensure that it became a party 'with strong and active business backing'. During his short time in office, John Smith had mounted what cynics described as a prawn cocktail offensive in the City, which was to develop into a full-frontal assault on 'the commanding heights of the economy' under his successor, with Blair going so far as to assure a meeting of Wall Street financiers that New Labour was 'the natural party of business', and to cast himself in the role of 'the entrepreneurs' champion'.

But if this was the nature of the project, the problem remained of how to market what, in effect, amounted to a new political alignment, not so much to Middle England as to Labour's traditional supporters. For almost two decades, Benn and the left had been campaigning to open up the democratic process in order to democratize the economy, a combination which New Labour was determined to reverse in order to restore the leadership's grip on policy-making and, thus, secure the acceptance of its own economic prescriptions. A leaked document prepared by Blair's pollster, Philip Gould, provided a clue to the thinking of the party's nomenklatura late in 1995. Calling for 'a unitary command structure leading straight to the leader' and a 'new culture', with the leader as 'the sole ultimate source of authority', the paper provided the groundwork for establishing a highly centralized control of all the party's activities.

Indifferent to charges that Gould's formula smacked of Leninist practices, the 'dark men', as Clare Short was to describe New Labour's apparatchiks, proceeded to impose what the Labour backbencher Richard Burden termed a new Stalinist regime on the party, which provided 'a ruthlessly effective electoral machine as the vehicle more for those who want to go into politics rather than a radical party with a definable ideological base'. And in the following half-decade the headlines told the story of the culling of dissent: 'Blair tightens grip on party: Labour to sack the disloyal and substandard' (*Observer*, June 1996); 'Labour has ways of making its MPs not talk' (*Guardian*, August 1997); 'Labour bans "old guard" MEPs' (*The Times*, October 1997); 'Labour expels rebel MPs' (*The Times*, January 1998); 'Blair unleashes party heresy hunters' (*Independent*, May 1998); 'Kinnock lays into hard left "plotters"' (*Guardian*, September 1998); 'Blair's secret purge of MEPs' (*Independent*, November 1998); 'Millbank war on dissenters' (*Guardian*, March 1999); 'Labour in new purge on left' (*Guardian*, September 1999); 'Labour's NEC to silence left troublemakers' (*The Times*, December 1999).

Marshalled by the whips, and cowed by Millbank, the silence of Labour's backbenchers was to become deafening. While Gould had declared that 'modernisation was democratising the party', the evidence mocked the assertion, particularly when reinforced by the leadership's determination to impose its diktat on the grassroots of the party. Thirty years had passed since Benn had first identified

The start of a parliamentary career: Tony Benn canvassing with his wife Caroline in Bristol, November 1950. © PA Photos.

Tony Benn being chaired by his Bristol supporters in 1963 on his return to the Commons, having renounced his peerage. From the Benn Archives Collection.

Harold Wilson, Prime Minister, and Tony Benn, the Postmaster-General, at the opening of the Post Office Tower in London, 1965.

Early days as Minister of Technology: Tony Benn in his office in 1966 with the backdrop of a trade union banner. © Ralph Gobits.

Tony Benn, Secretary of State for Energy, visiting a South Wales coal-mine, October 1975.

In defiance of a government ban, Tony Benn reads extracts from *Spycatcher* at Speakers' Corner, Hyde Park, 2 August 1987.
© *The Independent*/syndication Jeremy Nicholl.

Tony and Caroline Benn during the 1984 by-election in Chesterfield which returned him to Parliament after he had lost Bristol South-East. © PA Photos.

Tony Benn on his way to lay a wreath at a memorial to Tom Paine (whom he nominated as his Man of the Millennium), in the precincts of Lewes Castle, 14 July 2001. *Photographer Barbara E. Alcock. © Reproduced with Permission of Sussex Archaeological Society.*

Sheltering from the rain at Lewes Castle after laying the wreath. © *Brighton Argus.*

the 'democratic deficit' that infected the party, declaring: 'The power of achieving greater party democracy is now the central problem facing the movement.'

It was a challenge that had racked Labour throughout the 1980s, and one which the 'dark men' of New Labour rejected outright. In practical terms, democracy came at too high a price, and they reeled off the party's electoral defeats to justify the re-establishment of top-down control of virtually every aspect of decision-taking. And perhaps they were right. Perhaps the end did justify the means. Perhaps the means pursued to secure New Labour's return in May 1997 justified the ends by which it was achieved: the destruction of what remained of the party's democratic credentials.

For Benn, however, the cost was too high. Cautiously at first, but with increasing confidence, the apparatchiks proceeded to strip the constituencies of their powers and substitute 'the dictatorship of focus groups' for open debate; to cull potential dissenters and provide local parties with cherry-picked lists from which to select their parliamentary candidates; to convert the party conference into a rally for the leadership; and to deploy the National Policy Forum (designed to oversee policy development, and composed largely of New Labour placemen) to prevent real issues from coming to the conference.

As formulated, this was Gould's model of 'unitary command', whose central objective was to ensure that 'the leader should be the sole ultimate source of authority'; the 'new culture' in which the leadership's executive power would be augmented by control of the party machine, which, in its turn, was to be reinforced by the spinners of Millbank working to Mandelson's corporatist agenda: 'Communications means throwing your net much wider than publicity. It means deciding what we say, how we say it, and which spokesmen and women we choose to say it.'

And if the landslide of 1997 was to confirm New Labour's prescriptions, not least the abandonment of 'the antediluvian lumber of the party's principles', and the substitution of sound bites for political substance, it was to fortify the nomenklatura in pursuit of their new model agenda, provoking Mark Seddon, editor of *Tribune*, to write of living under 'the lash of New Labour's Leninists' (*Spectator*, August 1999), and reinforcing Benn's fears of the emergence of a personality cult, 'so that we now have a managed state and not a representative government and that, of course, is a huge erosion of democracy'.

It was no empty concern. In a speech delivered in Bonn in March 1998, Peter Mandelson, then Minister without Portfolio, was to reflect that 'the era of pure representative democracy' might well be coming to an end – an insupportable notion as far as Benn was concerned:

> The speech spelled out with far greater clarity than we have had before the philosophy of New Labour, which is a completely new political party that seems to have consciously repudiated trade unionism, local democracy and socialism and is trying to accommodate the party to the idea that: 'What matters for governments is that they should demonstrate that they are more popular than the alternative once every four or five years.'

This was not so much an unfinished as a virtual revolution, the apotheosis of consumer politics rooted in corporate populism, in which the chief executive has control of virtually all the levers of political power in order to market the image of Cool Britannia, plc:

> If you read the discussions of the parliamentary committee it is made quite clear that the leadership doesn't want a vote among Labour MPs. All it wants is for its decisions to be rubber stamped. And this isn't all.
>
> I'm told that no cabinet minister has put in a paper since the 1997 election. What happens is the cabinet meets for twenty minutes or so, during which the PM or the Chancellor tells ministers what their decisions are, and all pre-negotiations are done on a one-to-one basis.
>
> It is not simply that the dialogue within the Parliamentary Labour Party has gone, or even that the dialogue between the government and the party has gone, but also that the dialogue within the cabinet has gone. In effect the checks and balances of the parliamentary system have all but disappeared, to be replaced by a presidential system.

Exactly what Blair represents, however, remains obscure. Indeed, it was somewhat ironic that Roy Hattersley, a one-time committed revisionist, should find common ground with his long-standing rival, Benn, to label Blair the 'prophet of ideologically footloose politics', and to write of a man who had not only renounced his own beliefs but also derided those who continued to hold to them, insisting that apostasy was a virtue in itself: 'When bad times come, leaders hope the reservoir of affection and shared ideology has not dried up. For Blair, it has never existed.'

Bereft as Blair may be of ideology, Benn nonetheless believes that he is captivated by Jenkins's concept of achieving a political realignment and creating a new centre-ground party: the consummation of the Third Way. To Benn the notion smacks of heresy, a reprise of MacDonald's betrayal of socialism following the formation of the National Government in 1931. To Blair it represents *realpolitik*, the fulfilment of proposals drafted by Mandelson and Liddle in 1995 which recommended the formation of a coalition with the Liberal Democrats, and advanced a set of policies 'far to the right of anything previously considered by the Labour Party'. To Jenkins, it embodies the spirit of the Gang of Four: 'I think Blair is very close to an Eighties Social Democrat ... Above all I think he wants to get away from the tyrannies of party politics as they have been applied and he wants to open things up in this way.'

Once, if distantly, Benn and Jenkins had been friends. While both were committed to taking the long view of history, they disagreed fundamentally as to the direction it would take: for what Jenkins regarded as the tyranny of party politics, Benn regarded as the essence of the democratic process, the always tortuous, often fraught debate about the nature of democracy itself. While they disagreed about much else – not least, the associated question of economic policy – this central question lay at its core, the transcending issue of the location of political power.

And, if he was evasive about much else, there was no question about where Blair's preference lay. Yet, even then, he cloaked his intentions in double talk. Indeed, it was only in 1999 that a leaked document revealed how far he was willing to go in order to achieve his goal, exposing plans to include two Liberal Democrats in his first cabinet. As far back as 1996, however, Benn was becoming increasingly alarmed at the prospect of such a political *rapprochement*:

Clearly it is impossible to read Blair's mind, but it seems to me that what he'd like to do is dismantle the process of democracy in this country by creating an all-party alliance to control the political centre ground, and marginalise both the right and the left. If so, the dangers would be enormous, effectively, the creation of a one-party state, headed by an executive with almost limitless powers.

New Labour's revisionists disagreed. The predicted end of 'pure representative democracy' and the 'tyranny of party politics' not only demanded a redefinition of democracy – a redefinition which, paradoxically, led Gould to reflect that 'in periods of change a little bit of Leninism goes a long way' – but also the restructuring of the body politic. Combined with New Labour's commitment to *laissez-faire*, it appeared to Benn that this was the essence of the Blair project, and he rejected the package entirely: the assumption that there was no alternative to the free play of the markets; that representative government was nearing its sell-by date; and that the labour movement had no place on New Labour's agenda.

And as the apparatchiks of Millbank tightened their grip on the Party, Benn's own position hardened. Fifty years had passed since he had first entered the Commons. Now it appeared he was back to where he began, or before that even, back to the recrudescence of a 'dangerous estate in which centralised power is accountable only to itself'. The idea is anathema as far as Benn is concerned, all part of the Noble Lie that democracy is invulnerable:

> The whole of history gives the lie that what's been won is inviolable, and nothing's more dangerous than when democracy is eroded piecemeal so that people don't realise what they've lost.

Not that the re-emergence of the 'democratic deficit' came as any surprise to Benn, who saw it, rather, as a political response to globalization:

> You have the other process going on, that from 1976 Labour cabinets came to the conclusion that they could not move beyond the parameters set by international finance, so what we have is a managed state and not a representative government.

A historic equation, it is central to Benn's analysis: that the retreat from democracy has been coupled with the advance of globalization:

> The more governments concede to the demands of world capital, the more they have to suppress their own people ... I suspect that if a sovereign government was to challenge global finance it would be seen as a crime against the World Bank and the IMF and the WTO, and it would come to be regarded as a rogue state.

As Benn was quick to note at the turn of the millennium: 'the irony is that the new world order is, itself, vulnerable'. Only ten years had passed since 'the end of history' and yet cracks were already appearing in the carapace of power, whether in national politics or international finance. And if Ken Livingstone's election as Mayor of London reflected people's growing disillusion with being manipulated by what Benn terms 'the spinners of Millbank on behalf of the City of London', then the collapse of the World Trade Organization's meeting in late 1999 ('The siege of Seattle was a cry for freedom against dictatorship') and the run on the US stock market in the spring of 2001 revealed the fragility of the globalized economy.

Echoing the critique of Joseph Stiglitz, a former chief economist of the World Bank ('In theory, the IMF supports democratic institutions ... In practice it undermines the democratic process'), Benn regards the entire system as inherently unstable: 'When things do go wrong and the system's exposed for what it is – a 21st-century variant on the gamble for fool's gold – all we hear is that there's no alternative to the free play of the markets':

> And like some economic litany, much the same story's repeated at home. When Barclays closed 175 of their smaller branches, and Harland and Wolf lost what could have been a life-saving contract, all we heard from Blair and the government was that these were 'commercial decisions', and that there was no alternative to the free play of the markets.

The contempt is abrasive. For two decades and more Benn had argued that there was an alternative to the dictates of markets and to the Newspeak of its political agency: New Lab. Where once, however, he was demonized, an agent of Oldthink, during his last days in the Commons he was dismissed by the New Labour establishment as yesterday's man, troublesome perhaps, but passé. Yet still they listened when, like an ageing, and somewhat unkempt, lion he rose to his feet in the chamber to worry their consciences with what might have been, if only ...

But the writing of alternative history has no place on Benn's agenda when the future is out there, waiting, which perhaps partly explains the bill he drafted – The Economic Recovery (Temporary Powers) Bill – late in 2000, which he intended to table in the event of a major UK recession:

> Whereas the grave economic problems facing the peoples of the United Kingdom derive, in large measure, from the damaging effect of international market forces ... over which the country has no effective control; and

> Whereas the main responsibility for safeguarding the interests of the people of the United Kingdom necessarily, and properly, rests with the Parliament and government ...

> Now be it enacted ...

And he recited the measures like the mantra of a now heretical creed, socialism: the power to impose emergency taxation; the power to take over a company; the power to direct investment; the power to control prices; the power to control profits; the power to vet investment plans. Then he laughed: 'D'you know what, the bill is based entirely on legislation either introduced or proposed by Ted Heath's government in the 1970s. In fact, I wrote a piece on the subject for the *Sunday Times* back in 1973.' At which point he rummages through an outcrop of filing – 'It's here somewhere' – to flourish a banner headline: HEATH'S SPADEWORK FOR SOCIALISM – 'which just goes to show how far we have progressed in the meantime, but then perhaps progressed is not quite the right word.'

CHAPTER FIVE
The Enemy Within

No labour movement can ever hope to succeed in this country
without the co-operation of the trade unions.

Keir Hardie (1897)

The unions must always be an essential part of the Labour
Party. That's where it was founded, and that's where it goes.

Lord Callaghan (January 2000)

When Benn tabled Bill 147 in the Commons in July 1999, it passed largely unremarked. Only a handful of days remained until the long summer recess, and Members were in no mood to indulge Benn's radical conceits, particularly as the New Labour whips wanted no part of a measure that smacked of a past they were still trying to expunge in pursuit of a Third Way that the party was in the throes of defining. In fact Bill 147 – 'a bill to make provision for the implementation in the laws of the United Kingdom of the rights in employment which are established by certain international instruments ratified by the United Kingdom' – prompted memories that New Labour was anxious to forget at a time when the Party was preparing to celebrate the centenary of its foundation.

Not that it was altogether coincidental that Benn presented his private member's bill in the late summer of 1999. Immersed as he is in the history of the party, the proposed measure captured something of the aspirations of those trade unionists who had met almost exactly a hundred years before:

This Congress having regard to the decisions of former years, and with a view to securing a better representation of the interests of Labour in the House of Commons, hereby instructs the Parliamentary Committee of the TUC to invite the co-operation of all the Co-operative, Socialist, trade union and other working-class organisations ... to take part to devise ways and means for securing an increased number of Labour members to the next Parliament.[1]

Five months later, the Labour Representation Committee was formed, the precursor of the Labour Party. Like Banquo's ghost, the memory of the unions' initiative was to haunt the party's centenary celebrations. Neither Blair nor Margaret McDonagh, the party's General Secretary, was to make any reference to the unions' contribution to the foundation of the party in the souvenir supplement celebrating the event, omissions which prompted Roy Hattersley to reflect: 'Tony Blair has done something radically different to what the founding fathers would have wanted to see.'

What, precisely, they had wanted to see remained obscure. Beyond agreeing to establish 'a distinct Labour Group in Parliament who shall have their own whips', the political character of the 129 delegates who met in London on 27 February 1900 was as diverse as their intentions were inexact. All that was clear was that the sixty-five trade unionists present held the key to the survival of the embryo party, for as one delegate remarked: 'As capital organises, so labour must organise.' A defining statement, it was to become the touchstone of the movement. In Benn's case, however, it only began to take on any real meaning in the 1950s. Until then, the imperative had been little more than an abstraction.

Although he was brought up in a highly politicized household, the talk at Millbank during Benn's childhood was concerned more with the seemingly inexorable rise of fascism – of Mussolini's declaration that 'The century of democracy is over', and of Hitler's megalomanic ambitions – than with the humdrum business of domestic politics. Occasionally, the everyday realities would intrude, as when he saw Mosley's Blackshirts on the march:

Otherwise I can't say that events like the Jarrow march made much of an impression on me. It wasn't so much that I was

1. *The Labour Leader*, 1899.

too young to realise what was happening, just that everyone at home was more concerned with international affairs. It's hard for people to understand now, but there was this sense of impending crisis to which everything seemed to take second place.

The storm of war broke in September 1939, and another ten years were to pass before what had long been an abstraction for Benn began to be realized in concrete form. Even then, however, it proved to be of only marginal concern. In October 1950, Stafford Cripps, Attlee's Chancellor, resigned as MP for Bristol South-East. A sick man who had only months to live, he fulsomely endorsed Benn's candidature for the vacant seat:

> I want all my friends and supporters in Bristol South-East to know how heartily I support the selection of Mr Anthony Wedgwood Benn as my successor. It is splendid to see that Bristol South-East has another champion in the field – one who is as true a socialist and who is as keen a Christian as myself.[2]

For a man of Cripps's standing, it was an impressive tribute to his 25-year-old successor. Ascetic, brilliant, puritanical, Cripps had become Britain's youngest King's Counsel (KC) in 1927, winning a seat in the Commons at the 1929 election, and electrifying the party conference following the economic debacle of 1931: 'We are not here to do hospital work to the Juggernaut of Capitalism. We are here to stop that Juggernaut from his progress through the world.'[3] It was a theme that Cripps was to pursue with intensifying conviction throughout the 1930s, developing a substantive critique of 'the illusion of democracy', and advancing an ultra-left programme which, among other things, advocated the introduction of worker control in industry.

It was an issue that had long racked the party. If industries such as coal and steel were to be nationalized, as Labour proposed, then who should be responsible for managing them? The answers were as diverse as the factions who represented them, and the issue remained unresolved with the return of the Attlee government in

2. Eric Estorick, *Sir Stafford Cripps* (Heinemann, 1949).
3. *Ibid.*

1945. Indeed, when Emmanuel Shinwell, the Minister of Fuel and Power, and a one-time advocate of worker control, had to decide on who should run the National Coal Board following vesting day on 1 January 1947, he had to call on a paper translated from Welsh in an attempt to reach his decision. And Shinwell's solution proved as contentious as the problem he sought to resolve: the appointment of the nine-man board comprising eight former owners and civil servants, and one former miner.

Shinwell was not alone in performing a *volte-face*. Cripps now shared his views, having written in 1946: 'Until there has been more experience by the workers of the managerial side of industry, it would be almost impossible to have worker-controlled industry in Britain, even if it were on the whole desirable.' Critical as the issue was, it was only one among the many that concerned the electors of Bristol South-East when Benn succeeded Cripps as MP for the constituency in 1950. Its energy spent, and its spirit flagging, the Attlee government was dividing against itself, and in October 1951 the Tories were returned to power.

Labour was to remain out of office for the next thirteen years, wilderness years that would mark the opening of a divide within the party over the way ahead, particularly following its third successive electoral defeat in 1959. Campaigning on the slogan of 'You've never had it so good', the Tories were returned with an increased majority, which prompted Roy Jenkins to advocate on television that Labour should keep a wary eye on the party's link with the unions, and remain open to securing a political *rapprochement* with the Liberals: the Third Way in embryo. On his way home from the studios, Jenkins called in at Benn's house, where the two men had what Benn described as 'a flaming row'. If not the end of their friendship, the dispute marked the extent of the ideological differences between them. Whether or not Jenkins was right, and whether or not revisionism would provide an answer to Labour's time of troubles, Benn had little time for his ideas.

And neither had Wilson and the party leadership. The implication that Labour should distance itself from the unions and strike a deal with the Liberals had no place in the party's thinking, and in the run-up to the election of 1964, Labour made great play of its socialist credentials, Wilson declaring that 'the fundamental inspiration of our social life should be the age-old principle: "from each according to his means, to each according to his needs" '. The speech had been partially drafted by Benn; if Wilson's remarks did not initially allay the unions' suspicion of Labour's intentions, they were reassured by his subsequent pledge that Labour would substitute 'the planned growth of incomes' for 'a system of society where making money by whatever means is lauded as the highest service'. For left-wingers such as Frank Cousins, who was to quit his post as leader of the TGWU to join the Wilson government, it was enough to convince them that the party was bent on the root-and-branch transformation of capitalism. Cousins and Benn were soon to learn otherwise.

Forty-eight hours after Labour's election victory on 16 October 1964, Benn was appointed Postmaster-General, responsible for a rambling institution which, like Topsy, had 'just growed'. And its organizational structure was as arcane as its centuries-old history, with the Post Office's third of a million employees being managed by a freemasonry of mandarins. At thirty-nine, Benn received his first insight into the internecine mysteries of industrial relations:

> By the time I got there, there was this mixture of military-style management, the top brass were nearly all civil servants, and a union that was Guild Socialist, committed to nationalisation and industrial democracy. The result was a bit like trooping the colour, each side marching and counter-marching past each other, but never clashing.

Carefully choreographed to maintain the distinction between 'Us' and 'Them', it was an age-old ritual that Benn was determined to eradicate. Both parties to the arrangement, however, were suspicious of his intentions. As far as the hierarchs were concerned, it was all very well for Benn to lunch in the staff canteen (The Cleaners' Arms) and hold tea-and-sandwich briefings with union leaders, provided it did not compromise their own authority; while as far as the unions were concerned, he still remained one of 'Them', the bosses. For the first time in his career, Benn began to appreciate the subtleties of management, and within months of taking office what illusions he had left about establishing a new regime were put to the test when it came to negotiating a wage claim from the union of Post Office workers.

For eleven hours on 15 April 1965, Benn and his aides wrangled with a union delegation led by Ron Smith. Seven times Benn improved the management's offers, and seven times Smith rejected them, and it was only late in the evening that the deadlock was finally broken. It was a salutary experience, of which Benn was to write: 'I was expected to be very tough and they were very tough. I felt uneasy and inexperienced and got much criticism afterwards for the way I handled the issue.' Not least from George Brown, the Minister of Economic Affairs, who maintained that Benn had undermined his rudimentary prices and incomes policy by bowing to union pressure in order to reach a settlement.

The charge had significant overtones. In the decade that lay ahead, the question of how to contain price inflation while satisfying the wage demands of the unions was to dominate the political agenda, a push-me-pull-you conflict that would destroy both the Heath and Callaghan administrations. As for Wilson, he was as quick to forego his socialist principles as he was adept at selling in his new deflationary policies, albeit under mounting pressure from the capital markets. Within two years of his taking office, a sterling crisis led to the introduction of a wage freeze coupled with public spending cuts, measures which *The Economist* described as 'perhaps the biggest deflationary package that any industrial nation has imposed on itself since Keynesian economics began'. So much for the promised 'planned growth of incomes' powered by 'the white heat of technology'.

Benn's disillusionment was profound. All the high hopes of 1964 had come to nothing. While it is impossible to date Benn's shift to the left with any precision, his frustration with the old order of things, particularly the inability of the government to contain the vagaries of the capital markets, progressively fortified his radicalism. Since the turn of the century, there had been long periods when the markets had invested £2 abroad for every £1 spent at home. As he saw it, it was this that had undermined Britain's industrial capacity – that for seven decades the City had underwritten Britain's competitors at the expense of her home-based industries. And now, once again, the markets were coercing government to adopt deflationary policies, and all on the pretext that there was no alternative. Small wonder that the levels of investment were falling, and the unions growing restless.

In fact, it was Frank Cousins's resignation as Minister of

Technology in protest at the government's prices and incomes policy that led to Benn's appointment to the post in July 1966. A composite department, with responsibility for a catch-all of industries, MinTech was also the sponsoring authority for four key industrial sectors – machine tools, computers, electronics and telecommunications. It was a post that was to provide Benn with not only the authority to intervene in shaping Britain's industrial strategy but also the power to raise capital for companies that were unable to do so, and to take a stake in such companies.

Of comparable importance, MinTech was to harness Benn's enthusiasm for leading-edge technology. Like some latter-day prophet, he went on the stump to promote the new technology, challenging the capacity of government to realize the potential of the post-industrial revolution, the will of the private sector to share in the enterprise and the vision of managements and unions to exploit its economic potential:

> Every revolution begins by destroying. The constructive part of the revolution starts later. In so far as engineers and technologists are finding better ways of doing what we do now they are in effect destroying what we do now ... Our task is to harness these new energies to benefit the future.

At times, the tone was admonitory: 'It is never machines which make us slaves. It is the men who own them ... who are creating the new feudalism'; at others messianic: 'Technology serves a higher purpose than mere production. It is the light at the end of a long, dark tunnel of poverty through which most of mankind has been journeying throughout the whole of human history.' And it was exactly this – Benn's sense of history – which fused his caution: that it had taken Britain almost two centuries to come to terms with the socio-economic disruption caused by the industrial revolution. Time, however, was no longer on adaptation's side. The pace of technological change was too great for that, and it was accelerating exponentially, prompting Benn's concern that: 'As technical power increases, mankind's apparent conquest of nature may produce new tyrannical organisations to organise that conquest.'

Only four months after taking office Benn spelled out his concerns, and set out his own, self-imposed brief at an Industrial Society lunch:

Technological change has brought a new type of uncertainty into life. If the very worst happens technological change will strip people not only of their jobs but their self-respect too ... Looking a few years ahead this process could go a great deal further ... The problems of man in his working environment remain to be tackled ... This task is an urgent one. If we were to leave out of account human reactions and feelings there is no knowing how it might all end.

All of which Benn was to point and counterpoint with his concern to realize a new industrial compact:

If government-by-consent is the basic formula that makes our political system effective, it is at least as true that work-by-consent will be needed to make our industrial structure successful ... What is needed is a new dimension which recognises the need for a fuller satisfaction from work and makes it possible ... This is what we mainly mean when we talk about industrial democracy.

It was a theme that Benn was to develop, and proselytize, with growing conviction in the decade that lay ahead. Seemingly, the democratic deficit was not confined to the constitution and the Labour Party; it was equally prevalent in industry, as he learned during his time at MinTech. And the more he learned, the more radical he became.

Under the Shipbuilding Industry Act of 1967 four major yards on the Clyde were merged to form the Upper Clyde Shipbuilders. The move was an attempt to underwrite a key element in Britain's rapidly declining shipbuilding industry, and in March 1969 Benn visited the yard on the cabinet's orders to try and sell the policy of wage controls to its workforce:

I got up at four in the morning and I got there before light ... It was a foggy day and I climbed on one of the cranes and addressed the people because I always like to do it direct. I said 'Look here, we're pouring money in and yet you've got 18 per cent absenteeism', and some guy shouted at me: 'If you had to stand in an open yard working with cold metal on a foggy morning like this you'd be absent most of the time.'

The incident encapsulated Benn's dilemma: that while, on the one hand, he was committed to winning 'the new Battle of Britain' by restructuring British industry, on the other, he sympathized with the unions in their attempts to match wage increases to rising prices. For three years he had invested his hopes in the prospect of engineering an industrial renaissance. By the spring of 1969 they were stillborn, in large part as a result of an intensifying contest between the government and the unions.

As early as 1965, the left-winger Ian Mikardo had warned the government to 'watch the unions', and three years later the relationship between the two parties had deteriorated to a point where the party conference came close to passing a union-backed resolution declaring that 'the policies of this government have been and are being dictated by the monopolies and big financial institutions to the detriment of the needs and desires of the working class'. The publication of the government White Paper *In Place of Strife* only exacerbated the dispute.

Tabled by Barbara Castle, Secretary of State for Employment, the assertion that it was a charter of trade union rights – among them, the right of workers to belong to a union, and safeguards against unfair dismissal – did nothing to disguise the fact that it provided the government with the authority to interfere in the collective-bargaining process, and the power to impose penal sanctions on unofficial strikers. Described by the left-winger Eric Heffer as 'the spoonful of honey in a barrel of tar', the contents of the White Paper would split the cabinet and the party in the first half of 1969, inciting nearly a hundred Labour backbenchers to rebel against its acceptance.

By June, Wilson and Castle were virtually isolated in cabinet, and on the 18th they reached an agreement with the TUC under which the government would drop its penal sanctions in return for a 'solemn and binding undertaking' whereby the unions would review the whole contentious issue of unofficial strikes. In her diary, Castle was to note her report to cabinet on the outcome of the negotiations: 'In the end we have got complete acceptance of our formula and this is entirely due to the superb way in which the Prime Minister handled the talks.'

Benn disagreed. When *In Place of Strife* was first published, he had been in agreement with the main thrust of its argument

('Industrial life is more complex now than it has ever been and you simply cannot have a disturbance in the system anywhere without us all suffering'), but as the dispute intensified his doubts about its equity emerged. Clearly, the growing militancy of the unions was endangering his industrial strategy; and it was equally clear that something had to be done to restore a measure of peace in the workplace. In fact, only one question remained to be resolved: on what terms, and in whose interests, should such a deal be struck? If the internecine dispute that racked the cabinet concentrated his mind wonderfully, it was only after the events of June 1969 that Benn began to resolve his dilemma.

At the party conference later in the year, Eric Heffer taxed him with having betrayed the unions by supporting *In Place of Strife*. It marked a turning point in Benn's thinking: 'What I began to realise was that wages were not just a matter of economic policy, they were also about power and the workers' relationship to power.' To talk of industrial democracy was to evade the real issue. What was needed was to flesh out the idea, and make it politically meaningful. The fall of the Labour government in 1970, and Benn's subsequent appointment as shadow spokesman for industry, provided him with the opportunity to spell out his own position, and in the Fabian pamphlet *The New Politics, a Socialist Reconnaissance* he raised the difficult question of worker control for the first time:

> Here in Britain the demand for more popular power is building up most insistently in industry, and the pressure for industrial democracy has now reached such a point that a major change is now inevitable ... The campaign is very gradually crystallising into a demand for real workers' control. However revolutionary the phrase may sound, however many Trotskyite bogeys it may conjure up, that is what is being demanded and that is what we had better start thinking about.

Slowly, yet consistently, Benn's critique of the democratic deficit was evolving, for him to become the bogeyman of the establishment. Ten years had passed since he had begun questioning the arcana of the constitution in the campaign to renounce his peerage; four since he had begun to question the command structure of the

Labour Party during his time as a cabinet minister, and now:

> Certainly there is no more reason why industrial power at
> plant or office level should be exclusively linked to ownership
> of shares, than that political power should have been
> exclusively linked to the ownership of land and other
> property as it was in Britain until the 'voters control'
> movement won its battle.

By challenging the established order of things, Benn was making
powerful enemies, not least among certain elements of the trade
union leadership. While the union grandees regarded themselves
as radicals, Benn saw many of them at best as conservative, at
worst as reactionary, concerned largely with negotiating the wage
levels of their members: 'A wage claim to offset rising prices and
improve real living standards is very important ... but it doesn't
alter the relationship between the employer and the worker at all.'
As sceptical about his radical conversion as they were jealous of
their own authority, the grandees wanted nothing of his advice on
how they should manage their affairs, least of all his admonition
that they should abandon their traditional defensive attitudes
('You have allowed yourself to be presented to the public as if you
actively favoured the conservative philosophy of acquisitiveness')
and develop 'a conscious, long-term policy of negotiating [the
unions] into a position of real power in industry'.

Quick as Benn was to deny that such a policy had revolutionary
implications ('No one is suggesting that you do it by throwing
petrol bombs or starting a guerrilla war in Morecambe'), rather
that the ends could be achieved just as well 'by peaceful collective
bargaining and removing the obstacles through legislation', his
talk of worker control put the fear of God into the more
conservative trade unionists. And in this they were not alone.
Since the return of the Heath government in June 1970, with its
stated intention of taking a tough line with the unions, opinion in
the Labour Party and the unions had rapidly polarized as to how
to respond to the challenge. With memories of the fate of *In Place of
Strife* still fresh in their mind (an incident of which Healey was to
write that it had inflicted 'permanent damage' on the unions'
relation with the Labour Party), the left wing were in bullish mood,
but the right already had serious reservations about entering into a

political free-for-all with the government.

Underlying all else was the fraught question of price and wage inflation. During the first two years of Heath's administration wages had risen ahead of inflation, an imbalance that was to be compounded by the oil crisis of 1973 which, in its turn, fuelled new wage demands. As far as his critics were concerned, the situation was already sensitive enough, without Benn talking up the need for 'a great new debate within our movement' involving, among other things, the need for unions to develop 'a thread of accountability' in the management of their affairs. Always a sensitive issue, it was not something that the more conservative union leaders wished to hear. And neither did the revisionists in the party.

Roy Jenkins had long been recommending that Labour should reappraise its relationship with the unions, the problem being that it was the unions who underwrote the party. Like Siamese twins, it seemed that the two were inseparable, each dependent on the other, and as the Heath government's legislation began to bite, the left-wing unions, led by the miners, became increasingly militant. Although, privately, certain members of the shadow cabinet had some sympathy for Heath's predicament, the reality was that Labour could not afford to alienate its paymasters.

In February 1973, a joint working party published *Economic Policy and the Cost of Living*, a short but ground-breaking paper which provided an undertaking that an incoming Labour government would 'conclude with the TUC ... a wide-ranging agreement on the policies to be pursued in all these aspects of our economic life' – a commitment that promised not only a reform of industrial relations laws but also the adoption of an interventionist industrial strategy.

If the right were unhappy with the economic policy document, they were horrified by the contents of *Labour's Programme, 1973*. Drafted by Labour's Industrial Committee chaired by Benn, it reinforced the party's commitment to an interventionist strategy and advanced proposals for the takeover of twenty-five British companies, a key element in realizing Benn's goal of achieving 'a fundamental and irreversible shift in the balance of wealth and power in favour of working people'. Unpalatable as the *Programme* was to the majority of the shadow cabinet, its acceptance was

essential if the party was to retain the support of the unions, a
situation which prompted Roy Jenkins to write of the period:

> It was more that they (the shadow cabinet) regarded
> themselves as living on the lower slopes of a mountain which
> nurtured higher up a number of wild beasts, the bigger ones
> were known as union leaders, and the smaller ones as
> constituency parties.[4]

The irony was that as the unions were pushing the Labour Party
further than it wished to go in terms of economic policy, Benn was
pushing the more moderate unions further than they wished to go
over the issue of industrial relations. Not that the media
distinguished one from the other. Even before Labour's return to
office in March 1974, Benn's shadow cabinet critics had been
leaking details of his policies to the Westminster lobby, triggering
headlines about the bogey of Citizen Benn. And the more
venomous the media's attacks, the more anxious Wilson became.
Where once, and not so distantly, he had regarded Benn as the
party's next leader but one, and his own possible successor, his
one-time protégé was now the maverick who 'immatures with age'.
As for Benn, it seemed that Wilson was fast becoming 'the anti
union man', whose main concern was to secure power, whatever
the cost to his socialist principles.

And with the return of the Labour government, the demonization of Benn intensified. As Secretary of State for Industry, with a
wide-ranging, interventionist remit and his nationalization plans,
he was subjected to increasingly vitriolic headlines in the tabloids –
'Benn out to grab the lot' (the *Sun*), 'It's your money that Mr Benn
is after' (the *Daily Mail*) – and savage commentaries in the
broadsheets, with Peter Jenkins, who was later to join the SDP,
writing in the *Guardian* that 'popular worries about Mr Anthony
Wedgwood Benn appear to be that he is less a leftie than a loony'.
Even the protests of leading Tory backbenchers such as Sir
Edward du Cann ('The task is not to attack Benn alone ... There is
nothing he is proposing which has not been approved by every
Labour minister') did nothing to check the abuse, the *Daily Mail*'s
political editor, Anthony Shrimsley, writing that 'The true menace

4. Roy Jenkins, *A Life at the Centre* (Macmillan, 1991).

of citizen Benn is that he has greater ambitions than merely to take over everything that contributes to the industrial and commercial strengths of these islands. Mr Benn's aim is to obliterate democracy as we know it.'

If anything was needed to convince the left of Benn's radical credentials, it was the right-wing media's reaction to his plans. Indeed, the coverage devoted to demonizing him was a measure of how much he alarmed the City and its agents. And in that they were not alone. Within weeks of taking office, Wilson was engaged in a campaign to sabotage a proposal to extend the powers of the National Enterprise Board (NEB) by providing it with a £1 billion annual budget to be spent on the acquisition of British companies. The Confederation of British Industry protested, and Wilson concurred; the leaks continued, with the *Daily Mail* asserting that 'Wilson goes cold on Benn'.

The bitter personal disputes that racked the cabinet reflected the ideological differences that divided it. As far as Benn was concerned, Labour had won office on the strength of its radical commitments. Either it honoured them, or it betrayed the electorate. For Wilson, it was by no means so simple. In March, the party had been returned with a wafer-thin majority, and maintaining the appearance of cabinet unity was his overriding concern. Yet it seemed that Benn was hell-bent on rocking an already vulnerable ship, determined as he was to secure the powers of the NEB, and to talk up the merits of worker control.

In mid-May, Benn's Permanent Private Secretary, Anthony Part, warned him that if he continued to promote industrial democracy it would lead 'to tremendous opening of fire on us because industrialists fear you are going to establish it'. Careless of Part's advice, however, he returned to the topic in a speech at a trade union conference in early June. As Benn was to write in his diary, the speech went down 'like a pancake on a wet pavement', while at a post-conference meeting he was told in no uncertain terms what trade unionists thought of his ideas:

They think of involvement as a substitute for real power, and they know that they have power if they want to use it. I think many unions in a sense are saying: 'We want the whole thing or we'll just use our veto because we can deal with

managements any time we like as long as government keeps
out of the way.

The disillusionment with Labour governments of whatever
persuasion – left or right – was widespread and corrosive, with
Jack Jones, the left-wing leader of the TGWU, declaring that it was
a lost cause to try to convert the Labour Party to socialism. Benn,
however, was the exception to the proscription, Jones asserting that
he was 'with us if not of us' in his commitment to the redistribution
of economic power. And for those who continued to doubt his
credentials, the rescue packages he organized in support of ailing
companies allayed their suspicions that he was little better than a
counterfeit socialist.

In early June 1974, a group of Scottish MPs lobbied Benn for
support to establish a workers' co-operative in Glasgow to take
over the *Scottish Daily News*. Benn noted wryly in his diary that one
of his sternest critics, George Lawson, declared that the establishment of such a co-op reflected the best of his ideas: 'It was like
getting a hug in public from Roy Jenkins.' Three weeks later, he
was to intervene by helping the workforce to establish a co-
operative at the troubled Villiers Norton Triumph plant at
Meriden, while later in the year his department mounted a rescue
operation for the Kirby Manufacturing and Engineering combine.

Damned by the Treasury as 'Wedgie's follies', all three
companies were in serious difficulties before Benn intervened,
which prompted the *Sunday Times* to write scathingly: 'Where two
or three shop stewards are gathered together in a bankrupt firm
they only have to knock at Mr Benn's door and millions of pounds
of taxpayers' money is given away.' All three ventures eventually
failed, in part because the cabinet refused to make sufficient funds
available, but not before Benn had declared that such co-operatives
marked a new beginning in British industrial relations: 'A hundred
and fifty years ago Robert Owen's ideas were regarded as
revolutionary, and as far as some people are concerned, it seems
that they still are.'

The reference back was deliberate. The past may be another
country, but for Benn the entire socialist venture is rooted in
history, a continuum reaching back through time to its biblical
roots which provide the bedrock of his socialist beliefs: 'I was

brought up on the Old Testament, on the conflict between the kings
who exercised power and the prophets who preached righteousness. Faith must be a challenge to power.' And in challenging
power, Benn called up the history of Christian socialism, while
accepting that 'the moral force of the teachings of Jesus is not
necessarily weakened by being secularised. Indeed, it can be
argued that humanism may entrench them more strongly, for those
who cannot accept the Christian faith.'

And in the 1970s, Benn's message was strictly secular: that the
co-operative model provided an exemplar for the renewal of
British industry which would not only establish a new accord in
the workplace but also help to secure the promised 'shift in the
balance of wealth and power in favour of working people'. In June
1974, Labour published a Green Paper *The Community and the
Company*, recommending that private companies should adopt the
West German two-board system, with 50 per cent of the seats on
the supervisory board being held by union representatives.
Ironically, the German model had been developed by Ernest Bevin
and the TUC immediately after the end of the war, in direct descent
from Bevin's pre-war advocacy of the need to democratize British
industry.

The drawback to the scheme, as Benn saw it, was that it tended
to neutralize the freedom of its participants:

> Under company law it is absolutely categorical that directors
> are responsible to their shareholders, so that when you put
> trade unionists on to a board it places them in a quandary: are
> they, in fact, bound by company law to their shareholders, or
> does their first responsibility still lie with their members?

And this was not all. At the heart of Benn's reservations was the
fear that once trade unionists were absorbed into management
structures, there was a very real danger that it would compromise
their independence; as the old saw had it: 'The working class can
kiss my arse,/I've got the foreman's job at last.' A century had
passed since the craft unions, the so-called 'respectable' element of
the labour movement, had been flattered into acting as the agents
of managements, and Benn feared that much the same thing could
happen again: 'Once you get trade union representatives acting on
behalf of management in compelling their fellow trade unionists to

go along with management plans, you are really decapitating the trade union movement.'

Although the Green Paper's proposals did not go far enough for Benn, for his critics they went too far. Temporarily, however, the issue was overshadowed by the news that Benn had succeeded in driving through his proposals to nationalize the shipbuilding industry. During the Upper Clyde Shipbuilders dispute of 1969 he had promised that, given the opportunity, he would take the industry into public ownership, and in 1974 'it was a pledge I was able to discharge. It gave me a tremendous thrill.'

The media thought otherwise. On 1 August there were banner headlines in a cross-section of the dailies damning Benn's 'takeover of a great British industry', regardless of the fact that it had long been in decline, while later in the month the *Guardian* carried extracts from a paper distributed by the maverick right-winger, Colonel David Sterling, formerly of the SAS, to a shadowy group known as GB 75:

> Wedgwood Benn's two-headed purpose, elaborately planned but naively camouflaged, of steady encroachment on the public enterprise system, together with the forcing of trade union members on to the executive board of companies ... amounts between them to the realisable threat of a magnitude this country has never faced before.

The more savage the assaults on Benn, however, the more counterproductive they became as far as the left were concerned. While Jenkins might rail against the beasts on the lower slopes of socialism, the left-wing unions and the constituencies were coming to regard Benn as the champion of unreconstructed socialism, a man who was willing to challenge the entire corpus of political, economic and institutional power. It was a stand-off that was of increasing concern to Wilson: on the one hand, it seemed that the intensifying attacks on Benn were inflicting serious damage on the party's electoral prospects, and yet, on the other, Benn was the tribune of the party activists whom Wilson could not afford to alienate.

Denis Healey was to recall later that there were times when Wilson's hatred of Benn 'bordered on the hysterical', and in the mid-summer of 1974, he was actively considering downgrading

Benn – when the chance arose. Meanwhile, Wilson was more concerned with shoring up Labour's majority in the run-up to an autumn election, and campaigned tirelessly to provide Labour with a commonsensical image, in contrast to Benn's 'radical extravagances'. And for all the media hostility towards Benn and his 'loony ideas', Labour improved its working majority over the Tories by thirty-eight seats when it went to the country in October 1974, Benn winning a 17.7 per cent majority in Bristol, his share of the vote rising by more than 2 per cent. Seemingly, there was still some mileage to be won from socialism.

Rather than mollifying Wilson, however, the result intensified his antagonism towards Benn, the more so when Benn came top of the NEC election in November 1974. Six months were to pass before Wilson made his move to curb Benn's influence, and even then he was constrained by the reality that there was a formidable body of opinion opposed to sidelining his *bête noire*, Jack Jones warning that: 'Any move of Mr Benn away from the Secretaryship of Industry ... would be a grave affront to the trade union movement.' The impasse was only broken following Benn's anti-Common Market stance in the referendum of June 1975. As Wilson's biographer, Philip Ziegler, noted: 'Wilson felt no grudge against any anti-Marketeer except Benn, and only against him because he was Benn and not because he was an anti-Marketeer.'[5]

Seventy-two hours after the referendum result was announced, Benn received the call from No. 10. Wilson was abrupt: 'I'd like you to take Energy.' Benn remained silent. 'You'd enjoy it. It's a very important job.' And still Benn kept his counsel. 'Well, haven't you got any questions?' Benn had only one: 'How long are you going to give me to think about it?' Wilson's initial deadline was cursory: 'I must know soon, two hours.' The deadline came and went, however, but not before Eric Varley, a confidante of Wilson's, had revealed to Benn that Wilson 'has entered into some commitments with the City or somebody, and he has to get rid of you'.

Another twenty-four hours were to pass before Benn finally accepted what amounted to his demotion, accusing Wilson of capitulating to the CBI and the Tory press. Wilson's reply was significant: 'Well, I'm not just taking Jenkins's advice.' Whoever

5. Philip Ziegler, *Wilson* (Weidenfeld and Nicolson, 1993).

else it was who advised Wilson, it momentarily appeared that 'Commissar Wedgie' (the *Sun*) had been effectively neutralized, though as Jack Jones was to say later:

> I was relieved that he was still in the cabinet ... We wanted him in. We did regard him as a friend of the trade union movement in the cabinet, and there were people in the cabinet who weren't very friendly to us.

Jones was right. At a cabinet meeting at Chequers ten days after Benn had been reshuffled, he and Foot were the only ministers to argue for a voluntary, as opposed to a statutory, wage policy, Benn calling for an attempt to be made to win the support of the unions for such an arrangement. The Foot–Benn alliance was short-lived, however, to be replaced by what Barbara Castle termed 'the Foot–Healey axis ... round which the government revolved'. As Chancellor, Healey was faced with a dilemma as to where his loyalties should lie, to his 'trade union constituency' or to his ministerial responsibilities. In pursuit of a counter-inflationary strategy, Healey would favour the latter:

> No one in the world knows better than I the difficulties and disadvantages of trying to run an incomes policy. I spent the best part of six months each year trying to negotiate a viable policy for the next pay round, not only with the leaders of the TUC but also with the CBI.[6]

And as Healey was to say, Foot became 'an indispensable supporter in the negotiations with the TUC over pay', a point reaffirmed by Joel Barnett, Chief Secretary of the Treasury: 'Michael's position was unique. He was tremendously loyal both to Harold Wilson and later Jim Callaghan and the government would never have survived long without him.' The reason was not hard to find. Convinced of the need to retain party unity, Foot was to forego his previous radicalism, to play the role of mediator between the government and the unions in the internecine dispute over incomes policy that divided both the Wilson and Callaghan administrations. In response to what Foot termed the 'crisis of capitalism of the most formidable order', Labour progressively

6. Denis Healey, *The Time of My Life* (Michael Joseph, 1989).

abandoned Keynesianism, while seeking to woo the unions into accepting the need for wage restraint. Benn had little sympathy for either policy, and made no secret of his reservations, as Foot revealed in his recollection of one particular cabinet meeting: 'At some stage of the proceedings ... Tony Benn lost interest in the present ... and turned his brilliantly agile mind to the future.'[7]

Or more exactly, to developing an alternative to the embryo monetarist strategy favoured by Healey, the Treasury and the heavyweights in the cabinet – notably Jenkins at the Home Office and Callaghan at the Foreign Office. It was an alternative, albeit in need of amplification, that Benn was to champion in his contest for the leadership of the Labour Party in March 1976. The divide between the left and right of the party was brought into sharp focus during the campaign, and in a TV interview with Bob McKenzie on the evening of 17 March Benn staked out his claim to lead the left. Asked whether he supported the government's refusal to introduce import controls, he backed the countervailing TUC position on the issue, while on the government's refusal to reflate the economy Benn was equally forthright:

> I take the view of the TUC economic review which calls for a substantial reflation ... for government-financed investment to go into key industries, at this moment, not only to provide jobs ... but also to re-equip British industry which is otherwise bleeding to death.

The Labour Party has long made a practice of airing its differences in public – an open dialogue that has done much to account for its political vitality – and following Benn's televised interview, there was no longer any possibility of disguising the differences that rent the government and the party. Indeed, Labour's times-of-troubles-to-come could well be dated from 17 March when Benn challenged the party to decide which course it should pursue: the fiscal orthodoxy favoured by Healey and the right, or the interventionist strategy favoured by what came to be termed the hard left.

But while the campaign was to concentrate largely on economic issues, Benn widened his remit in the brief manifesto statement he

7. Michael Foot, *Loyalists and Loners* (Collins, 1986).

released on the day of the broadcast to reiterate his call for a new compact between management and labour in industry: 'We must do more than pay lip service to industrial democracy; we must provide for joint decision-making between management and workers at every level of industrial life.'

Six days later he was to expand on the point, asserting that any extension of public ownership demanded, equally, a change in the relationship between management and workers:

> All that happened [referring to previous nationalizations] was that there was a new name over the door, a new place in the headquarters, and everything else continued much as before. We said we would change it, and we will change it by going back to a very basic principle of socialism ... What we have said is not only that our greatest national asset is our people but we have said that those who invest their lives in industry are at least as strongly entitled to control it as those who invest their money.

Benn was defeated in the first ballot of the leadership contest, polling thirty-seven votes against ninety cast for Foot and eighty-four for Callaghan, and cast his vote for Foot in the second round, in which Callaghan was the eventual victor. Playing the game of alternative histories is an unproductive pastime, nonetheless it is interesting to speculate on the outcome if Benn had won the contest, particularly in view of the economic crisis of the autumn of 1976, when the IMF imposed punitive terms on the government in return for bailing out the British economy: the largest real cuts in public expenditure since the early 1930s. Would Benn have accepted the dictates of the markets, or would he have opted for a siege economy? Would Britain have weathered the subsequent financial storm engineered by the markets if he had adopted the latter policy, and if so, what would have been the consequences for Britain and the Labour Party? Who, indeed, were the realists during that 'crisis of capitalism', and was there, indeed, a credible alternative to the one adopted?

All judgements are a lottery, and by the autumn of 1976 the decision had been taken. Unbeknown to the Chancellor, Denis Healey, the Treasury had 'grossly overestimated' the Public Sector Borrowing Requirement, which increased the pressure on the pound from the capital markets. The old, old story was repeating itself, and in return for an IMF loan the government agreed to a £2 billion cut in public expenditure, prompting Benn to write in his diary on 30 September: 'The smell of 1931 is very strong in my nostrils.' And, as with 1931, his fears were compounded when, to ensure the survival of what, by 1977, had become a minority government, Callaghan entered into a pact with David Steel, leader of the Liberal Party, under which the Liberals were given consultative rights on policy matters, a development which led Callaghan to redefine the role of the collective responsibility of the cabinet: 'I certainly think that the doctrine should apply, except in cases where I announce that it does not.'

To Benn it seemed as if his concept of socialism was being dismembered piecemeal, a victim of revisionism. But if Benn was 'utterly depressed and dejected', the mood did not last for long. His standing with the constituencies and the left-wing unions, together with his post at Energy, provided him with a base to promote his ideas not only for Tripartite and Planning agreements but also for industrial democracy. All, as he saw it, were intimately related, so that by involving managements, unions and the government in developing an industrial strategy it would provide a model for wider imitation. The experiment was short-lived, but as he was to say later:

> It was an exciting experience. We sat down together – the Coal Board and the NUM, all the producers of electricity, and the ministers – and we did begin to build into it all the legitimacy of industrial democracy, but that scared the powers-that-be out of their wits. They didn't like it at all, and where once the media had treated me as if I was a Stalin – with Hitler's moustache! – they now transposed me into a Trotsky because they suddenly began to think that because I was in favour of industrial democracy it might mean that the workers would take power.

The demonization of Benn had to be set in a wider context, however. In a bid to defuse the controversy surrounding the merits, or otherwise, of industrial democracy, Callaghan appointed a committee under Lord Bullock to report on the whole fraught issue. Published in 1977, it came out in favour of an equal representation of union nominees as shareholders on the boards of private-sector companies in imitation of the German model. The employers' organizations wanted no part of the scheme, and neither did a number of the larger unions. Jealous of their authority, their leaders maintained that they should represent their members, whereas Bullock had proposed that workers should be represented on the new unitary boards.

Benn was caught between a rock and a hard place. On the one hand, he had long been an advocate of industrial democracy, but on the other, he had grave reservations not only about the nature of Bullock's proposals but also about whether the response of the union leadership cloaked their innate authoritarian leanings. Half a century had passed since Ernest Bevin had earned the title 'Boss Bevin' for the ruthless fashion in which he crushed any opposition to his authority within the TGWU. Nothing, it seemed, had changed. In all too many cases, the old authoritarianism remained, mocking the obeisance that the union bosses paid to industrial democracy.

However, there was more to the unions' objections to Bullock than the proposed composition of the new board structures. Traditionally, the unions had played a defensive role in their relationship with managements, but Bullock had exposed their unwillingness to take on more wide-ranging responsibilities for the management of company affairs. In 1978, Moss Evans, leader of the TGWU, highlighted the problem during a wage dispute at Ford of Dagenham. As Benn was to recall later:

> The pay policy had broken down and Moss came along to a meeting of the National Economic Development Council and told us bluntly 'Look, Fords are making this huge profit, but I've got no right to say "Use that profit to cut the price of your cars, or use that profit to build a new plant." All I can say is: "If you won't spend it on this or that, then I want it in wages."'

Concerned primarily with negotiating wage settlements, the unions' impotence was of their own making, yet as Benn discovered, even the more left-wing unions such as the NUM, the Praetorian Guard of the labour movement, shied away from being too closely involved in management. Since the pits had been nationalized in 1947, the issue of closures had always been a contentious one, and in 1978 Benn offered the President of the NUM, Joe Gormley, the opportunity to veto threatened closures. Gormley's reply was revealing: 'You're offering us a poisoned chalice. If we have the veto over closures we'll get the blame for every closure that occurs.'

Gormley's rejection of Benn's offer was symptomatic of the union movement's attitude towards becoming too closely involved in management affairs. Anxious to retain their own identity, and not to be charged with playing the role of Uncle Tom by their members, union leaders preferred to maintain their distance from any decisions taken at board level. Occasionally, Benn's attempts to bridge the divide were successful – as when he asked the NUM whether or not they wished to have Derek Ezra as Chairman of the National Coal Board (NCB) – but otherwise, he became increasingly sceptical about the prospects of persuading unions, let alone managements, to take even the first hesitant step towards industrial democracy. And with scepticism came disillusion.

Indeed, there was a certain irony in the fact that for all the power of the union block vote, and for all Benn's strictures on the democratic deficit within the union movement, the more left-wing unions continued to support Benn and the Campaign group in their attempts to democratize the Labour Party. While the issue continued to preoccupy the party into the early 1980s, however, what little chance remained of reshaping labour relations on a more democratic basis was effectively killed off in May 1979, when the Thatcher government came to power. Norman Tebbit, soon to be appointed Secretary of State for Employment, had already made his attitude towards the unions abundantly clear:

> Today the cloth-capped colonels of the TUC use their power for political ends ... If an evil is so powerful that the faint hearts say it must be appeased, then there is all the more reason to deal with it before it becomes stronger still.

In identifying the evil – 'the whole basis of our free society is gravely threatened by the powers arrogated by the unions' – the founding father of the new right, Friedrich von Hayek, had proposed its solution: 'to rescind every single privilege granted to the trade unions'. This is precisely what the Thatcher government set about doing with a political will that reflected its free-market ideology. Confident in their economic prescriptions, the Tories made no attempt to disguise their intentions. The 'tyranny' of labour, as Thatcher and Tebbit were fond of declaring, had to be ended, and successive Employment Acts progressively curbed the statutory power of the unions.

The challenge to the entire fabric of the labour movement was clear, and Benn made no attempt to disguise his fears when he delivered a memorial lecture for George Woodcock, formerly the General Secretary of the TUC, in March 1983. Bleak and unremitting, its contents revealed the full measure of Benn's growing despair for the future of socialism:

> We can no longer afford the luxury of liberal illusions that the bad old days are over and progress is inevitable ... The bad old days are not over. They are coming back again and progress, far from being inevitable, is now being put into reverse.

And what was true in general was particularly true of the unions:

> The trade union movement today is fighting for its survival in the most hostile economic and political environment it has faced for many decades, and none of its past achievements are free from a counterattack which could seriously harm if not actually cripple the unions in their task of representing working people.

Eighteen months had passed since Benn had been defeated in the election for the deputy leadership, and it appeared that the unions and the Labour Party were jettisoning what few socialist principles remained to them, pressurized, on the one hand, by Thatcherism, and seduced, on the other, by revisionism. The bitterness was there, along with the disillusion: 'With a revisionist party leadership and an increasingly non-political trade union leadership, the stage was set for a retreat from socialism' – a retreat that was to accelerate in the aftermath of Foot's resignation as leader of the party and the election of the 'dream ticket' of Kinnock and Hattersley after Labour's election defeat in June 1983.

It was the defeat of the miners following the year-long strike of 1984–5 that was to bring Benn's fears into sharpest focus. This was

the confrontation which the Tories had been planning since the late
1970s, when Nicholas Ridley had first detailed the party's strategy
for a showdown with 'the enemy within' – a strategy aimed at
destroying, once and for all, the van of the union movement. In the
interim, the Thatcher government had prepared its ground well.
For all of Arthur Scargill's tactical misjudgements, the forces
ranged against the miners – among them the deployment of a
police 'third force' trained in paramilitary techniques, the pre-
planned establishment of a breakaway mining union in the East
Midlands and the 'manipulation' of benefit payments to the
families of striking miners – meant that the outcome of the strike
was virtually assured from the outset.

For Benn, the defeat was a disaster of the first order which
revealed the dichotomy in his character. Cast by his critics as a
rationalist in the puritan mould – uncompromising in his pursuit of
a socialist commonwealth – those who knew him better had long
been aware that his character disguised a deep streak of
romanticism. Like so many of his middle-class predecessors, he
tended to idealize the working man and woman. Heedless of
warnings that such romanticism might well be misplaced, and that
the faith he vested in the workers might well be betrayed, he made
an icon of their struggles, not least that of the miners. During the
358-day strike, he rejected any suggestion that Scargill should
modify his strategy, declaring later: 'Arthur was one of the few
trade union leaders I have ever met in my life who wasn't looking
for a peerage – he was trying to defend his members.'

Although Scargill may have been mistaken about many things,
on the central issue that precipitated the strike – the threat of
wholesale pit closures – he was proved to be entirely correct.
Having privatized the industry, the government proceeded to
decimate it, culminating in the announcement in 1992 of a plan to
close a further thirty-one pits with the loss of some 30,000 jobs.
Political considerations aside, perhaps the rundown of the industry
was inevitable; possibly King Coal, which had powered Britain's
industrial revolution, had outlived its time. So much remains open
to debate. One thing, however, is clear: what little chance the
miners had of success in their confrontation with the Tories was
further undermined by the ambivalent attitude the Labour Party
adopted towards the strike, in particular Labour's new leader, Neil

Kinnock, who came to be dubbed 'Ramsay McKinnock' by the miners of South Wales.

As Benn saw it, the collapse of the strike in March 1985 was as much a defeat for socialism as it was a triumph for Thatcherism, a defining moment which helped break the political will of the trade unions and lay the foundations for the Labour Party's subsequent reappraisal of its relationship with them. Albeit cynically, it seemed to Benn that the Tories were doing the revisionists' work for them: 'There was a growing sense of desperation among the union leaders to ensure Labour's return at virtually any cost, careless of the damage it inflicted on the labour movement.' Where, during the 1970s, Benn had commanded a significant following among unions, that support was now imploding as their leaders came to terms with what they regarded as inevitable – the erosion of the rights which it had taken a century and more to secure.

Labour's election manifesto of 1983 had committed the party to repealing all Tory anti-union legislation and to extending the reach of industrial democracy – commitments that were to be whittled away, piecemeal, in the decade that lay ahead. Determined to distance Labour from what Kinnock and then Blair regarded as a political liability, the leadership proceeded to endorse much of Thatcher's anti-union legislation. New Labour, it seemed, wanted no part of its past, and it was left to Benn and a small group of left-wingers to mount a long rearguard action in defence of union interests. It made little difference.

In July 1986, Benn tabled the Representation of the Workpeople Bill, designed to give all company employees the right to elect board members by secret ballot, only for the party manifesto of 1987 to abandon Labour's former pledge to extend the frontiers of industrial democracy. Twelve months later, Benn tabled a bill (Re-establishment of Free Trade Unionism) aimed at repealing six Acts introduced by the Tories in the previous eight years, only for Labour's Policy Review of 1989 to recommend switching from collectivism to a 'positive framework of law', and to retain Tory legislation on strikes and union election ballots.

What, for Labour, had once been a tactical withdrawal to a new elector-friendly position had, by the early 1990s, turned into a headlong retreat from anything but the most cursory recognition of the party's long association with, and dependence upon, the union movement. In 1992 the party manifesto confirmed its commitment to the broad thrust of Tory anti-union legislation, while a review of union links with the party produced the formula of One Member One Vote for MPs' selection and cut the union's share in the leadership electoral college vote to 33 per cent. The move to eliminate the union block vote was long overdue, and reducing their influence provided Blair with the bridgehead he required to reposition the party in pursuit, variously, of a stakeholding economy, a radical centre and of a Third Way.

A barrister who specialized in trade union and industrial law, and an opposition front-bench spokesman on economic affairs, Blair gave notice of his own modernizer's agenda as early as 1989 with the announcement that Labour would not restore the legality of the closed shop. For Labour aficionados it signalled much that was to come. As a pre-emptive gesture following Blair's election to the leadership of the party in June 1994, Benn tabled a composite bill designed to provide ministers with the power to repeal restrictions on trade unions. Like those that had gone before, it failed to win parliamentary time.

Even Benn, however, had not visualized how quickly New Labour would seek to marginalize the unions, though Blair was to make his views clear soon enough, declaring in 1994 that, in pursuit of a new economic alignment, the party he led would never again 'pander to the unions'. Where once Mrs Thatcher had vowed 'to punish the trade unions', Blair was later to boast that Britain had the toughest anti-union laws in the developed world, a theme that was to be peddled, point and counterpoint, in headlines throughout the 1990s:

'Blair claims end to union armlock' (*Guardian*, July 1995); 'Blair pledges new deal for business' (*The Times*, November 1995); 'More work rights rejected by Blair' (*Daily Telegraph*, June 1996); 'Blair blows away more traces of union past' (*The Times*, September 1996); 'Blair set to sever links with unions' (*Guardian*, September 1996); 'Labour won't harm the City' (*New Statesman*, February 1997); 'Blair gets his feet under the table with business' (*Financial Times*, February 1997); 'I'll be tough with the unions says Blair' (*Guardian*, April 1997);

'Labour wins boardroom approval' (*Independent*, June 1997); 'BETTER LED THAN RED, Labour distances itself further from the unions' (*The Times*, July 1997); 'Blair seen by business as bulwark against old guard' (*Independent*, September 1997).

In the process of wooing capital, Blair was consciously distancing himself from labour, maintaining that the unions had no place in his model of a 'people's party'. Inexorably, all traces of Labour's historic commitments were being sacrificed to the dictates of the market, to the delight of right-wing commentators such as Andrew Roberts ('Tony Blair is much more an instinctive Tory than John Major was') and Roger Scruton ('Labour have accepted that Mrs Thatcher was right'). As for Benn, who had taken to asserting that he remained a member of the Labour Party, as distinct from New Labour, he regarded the right's triumphalism as the measure of New Labour's apostasy.

On coming to power in May 1997, New Labour's only significant concession to union sensibilities was to introduce a minimum wage, and this only after a bitter dispute about the level at which the minimum should be set. For the rest, the unions were treated as 'embarrassingly elderly relatives', in the sound bite of John Monks, General Secretary of the TUC, which provoked Lord Callaghan to remind the apparatchiks of Millbank that 'the unions must always be an essential part of the Labour Party. That's where it was founded and that's where it goes.'

This, in part, is what prompted Benn to table Bill 147, the Employment Rights (International Obligations) Bill, in the summer of 1999. The timing was significant, drawing, as it did, on the fiftieth anniversaries of the adoption of both the UN's Declaration of Human Rights ('Everyone has the right to form and join trade unions for the protection of their interests') and Convention 98 of the International Labour Organization: 'Workers shall enjoy adequate protection against acts of anti-union discrimination in respect of their employment.' As Benn was to say of the bill:

Globalization has conferred immense power on capital, and for socialists the answer is not nationalism, with all the economic and political dangers that would follow, but internationalism, developing trade union co-operation across frontiers to limit and control capital through the powers available to elected governments. The twenty-first century will see that conflict between world capital and world labour resolved in the only way it can be done, by a victory for the majority who create the world's wealth against the handful who happen to own it.

A century had passed since a delegate at the inaugural conference of the Labour Party had declared that labour must organize as capital was organized. For Benn, the same remains true, the marginalization of his Employment Rights Bill only serving to illustrate how far New Labour has distanced itself from its founding principles.

CHAPTER SIX
A Special Relationship: The Last Colony

They [the protestors] will say that the IMF is secretive and insulated from democratic accountability. They will say that the IMF's economic 'remedies' often make things worse ... And they'll have a point. I was chief economist at the World Bank until last November [1999] during the gravest economic crisis in half a century. I saw how the IMF in tandem with the US Treasury Department, responded. And I was appalled.
Joseph Stiglitz, *New Republic* (April 2000)

On 2 September 1998, the Commons was recalled to hear a statement by the Prime Minister on the bomb attack by a dissident faction of the IRA which had killed twenty-nine men, women and children in Omagh. Almost inevitably, the subsequent debate turned to the issue of global terrorism, the more so because, only two weeks before, the USA had launched a cruise missile attack against a Sudanese pharmaceutical plant in retaliation for a terrorist attack on their Kenya embassy. For Benn the incident had dual significance, and while quick to point out that he had no truck with terrorism, he was equally quick to remind Members of the record of Britain's imperial past: 'I finish with a historical perspective. Will the PM remember that precisely one hundred years ago today, 11,000 Sudanese were killed by the army under General Kitchener.'

Living, as so many MPs do, in the eternal present, it was not something that they wished to hear, and in the brief silence which followed, Benn resumed his seat to reflect on the happenstance that history did, indeed, repeat itself. Where, in 1898, the Prime Minister of the day, Lord Salisbury, had remarked that Kitchener's achievement was 'a humanitarian act for which the Sudanese will come to thank us', a spokesman of the Clinton administration had justified the strike on Khartoum on the grounds of 'securing the frontiers of democracy'. _Plus ça change_ ... And yet, everything was, indeed, different, for where formerly it had been Britain, it was now the USA that determined the frontiers of democracy, with Britain as a subordinate partner, prompting Benn to reflect: 'Grenada, Libya, Iraq. What we've seen in the past fifty years is a role reversal in which Britain has become little more than a colony of the US.'

The irony is inescapable, yet it is one for which Benn has little sympathy. The history of colonialism is too disquieting for that, for the truth as he sees it is that, contrary to myth, it was the subject races of imperialism who carried the white man's burden. Like so much else in Benn's make-up, his anti-colonialism is a part of his inheritance. The past, in fact, is never far below the surface of his consciousness, in particular the influence of his father who, as a twenty-year-old student, was thrown by jingoists through a window of University College, London, for his opposition to the Boer War: 'Thank God, it was a ground-floor room, otherwise the story would have ended there.'

For over thirty years in the Commons, not least during his brief spell as Secretary of State for India, and during his fifteen years in the Lords, Viscount Stansgate was a forthright champion of colonial freedom. As Chairman of the Inter-Parliamentary Union, he campaigned tirelessly during the 1950s to get China admitted to the UN, in the face of intense US opposition, and on the day of his death he was preparing to speak in the Upper House on the fraught issue of Rhodesia.

While Viscount Stansgate's influence conditioned Benn's early development ('Everything my father did in his life was about the extension of democracy'), it was to be reinforced by his own experiences as a trainee RAF pilot. Posted to Rhodesia in 1944, he saw at first hand the consequences of colonialism: the 'bug ridden and dirty huts' which housed black workers; the contrast between the overcrowded native hospital ('there were even sick people handcuffed to their beds') and its spanking new European counterpart.

If anything would convince Benn of the justice of his father's case, it was the time he spent in Rhodesia. Nonetheless, father and son had their differences, and in a debate at the Oxford Union, Benn vigorously opposed Viscount Stansgate's assertion that British foreign policy was being subverted by Washington. Although the full terms of the Potsdam conference of 1945, involving the heads of state of the USA, the Soviet Union and Britain, had yet to be revealed, as a confidante of the Labour government Stansgate may well have had his suspicions that, following the defeat of Germany and Japan, the USA's main aim was the liquidation of the British empire – a suspicion which later would be confirmed with the release of State Department documents.

At the time, however, the USA veiled its intentions in double talk, and as Benn was subsequently to confess, he was naive enough to take at face value Truman's pledge that the USA would remain 'the arsenal of democracy', and to suppose that the tacit support of the State Department for the anti-colonial movement was motivated by higher principles than US self-interest. And the ten-month airlift in response to the Soviet blockade of Berlin in 1947 tended to confirm his views. The Cold War was in its opening stages, and contrary to Viscount Stansgate's views that the USA was playing a deeper game than appeared to the casual observer, Benn regarded the Democratic administrations of Roosevelt and Truman if not as radical, then certainly as progressive, quoting in defence of their liberal credentials a speech delivered by Roosevelt in the 1930s:

> There are those who fail to read both the signs of the times and American history. They would try to refuse the worker any effective power to bargain collectively to earn a decent livelihood ... It is those short-sighted ones, not labour, who threaten this country with that class distinction which in other countries has led to dictatorship and the establishment of fear and hatred as the dominant emotions of human life.

And the residue of Roosevelt's liberalism was still evident when Benn toured the USA with a debating team from the Oxford Union in 1947:

I was always attracted by the liberal Roosevelt tradition, because when you look back to the 1930s when the world capitalist system was in crisis, every capitalist country went to the right except America. Of course, Roosevelt wasn't a socialist, but he saved American capitalism in a very imaginative way with the New Deal.

During their four-month sweep through forty-two states, the Oxford team appeared at sixty universities to wrangle the issues of the future, in particular whether or not the Soviet Union did, indeed, pose a military threat to Western democracies. At the time, Benn believed it did. He was soon to begin revising his views. Two months after the opening of the Korean War in June 1950, the Labour government announced an accelerated defence programme of £3600 million. Even then, however, there were critics in Congress who claimed that Britain was not 'fighting her weight', which led to fears that if Britain did not increase her already overstretched defence budget, the USA would reappraise its commitments to the defence of Western Europe – particularly as there was a lobby in Washington which held that it would be better for Europe to be overrun and then 'liberated' by a US atomic attack than to keep US troops in the front line of the Cold War.

Faced with intensifying US pressure, the cabinet agreed in January 1951 to raise defence expenditure to £4700 million to cover a three-year period, a concession which Washington still regarded as inadequate, but which Nye Bevan saw as going too far, particularly as the increase was at the expense of cuts in the NHS budget. As the architect of the NHS, Bevan was in no mood for compromise. ('I will never be a member of a government that makes charges on the National Health Service'), and in April he resigned from the cabinet to mount a stinging attack on what he regarded as the scaremongering of the Cold War warriors. The Soviets, he maintained, had neither the inclination nor the capacity to mount an attack on the West, and if the USA and her NATO allies pressed ahead with rearmament, it would reinforce the Cold War psychosis and lead to a witch-hunt of fellow travellers.

Bevan's line of argument made a powerful impression on Benn. Elected an MP on 30 November 1950, the day on which Truman hinted that he might give General MacArthur the authority to nuke

North Korea, he nonetheless supported the increases in the defence budget. The doubts, however, had been laid. Precisely what were the Soviet intentions? Was Russia, indeed, in expansionist mood? And what of US policy? Were Viscount Stansgate's suspicions well founded? Was the Cold War a political construct, a figment not so much of the imagination as an agent of US foreign and domestic policy? Ten years were to pass before President Eisenhower, formerly the wartime commander of the Allied Forces in Europe, provided substance for Benn's growing doubts. In his final presidential address, on 17 January 1961, Eisenhower warned:

> The conjunction of an immense military establishment and a huge arms industry is new in the American experience. The total influence – economic, political, and even spiritual – is felt in every city, every state house, and every office of the federal government. In the councils of government, we must guard against the acquisition of unwarranted influence, whether sought or unsought, by the military-industrial complex.

Eisenhower's caution was for the future – 'The potential for the disastrous rise of misplaced power exists and will persist' – and by the mid-1950s Benn already had growing reservations about the direction of US policy, while in part, at least, Bevan's fears had already been realized. As early as February 1950, an undistinguished senator from Wisconsin, Joseph McCarthy, had asserted that 205 communists had infiltrated the US State Department. When he was unable to produce evidence of a single 'card-carrying communist', the charge was quickly exposed for what it was: witch-hunting. Not that this did anything to discourage McCarthy. Over the next five years, he was to manipulate US fears to make a bogey of 'the red menace'.

The poison reached deep into the system, and with transatlantic consequences. In 1954, Benn campaigned for the right of Dr Joseph Cort to remain in Britain. A US citizen, Cort had moved to this country after being accused by the House Un-American Activities Committee (HUAC) of having been a member of the Communist Party during his time as a medical student at Yale University. The smear was enough to destroy Cort's reputation, and in 1953 he took up first a research post in Cambridge and then a lectureship in Birmingham. The committee had not done with Cort, however, and demanded his return to the USA. The Home Office rejected his appeal for asylum, provoking Benn to write:

> The Home Secretary has become the unconscious agent for the McCarthy mood ... At a time when Britain should be preserved as a haven for those who are buffeted about in this age of suspicion and intolerance, he is unwittingly co-operating with the witch-hunters.

Unwittingly or otherwise, it made little difference. The pursuit of Cort continued, and he was eventually to win asylum in Czechoslovakia. Cort's experience, later to be replicated by McCarthy's hounding of the singer Paul Robeson, whom both Lord Stansgate and Benn befriended, did more than simply prompt Benn's memories of the witch-hunts that had infected the Labour Party during the 1930s. As he saw it, they reflected a seismic shift in the US psyche. It seemed that the USA, in paranoid mood, was eschewing the liberal principles inherited from Roosevelt, to promote the ideological case against socialism by declaring: If you are critical of capitalism, then you are an agent of the Kremlin.

Apparently, his father had been right after all. Apparently, talk of a 'special relationship' disguised a different, and more subversive, agenda. Apparently, Britain was, in fact, becoming little more than an agent of Washington's designs, the 'offshore aircraft carrier' of contemporary legend. And as the build-up of US bases in Britain continued, Truman's one-time pledge that the USA would remain 'the arsenal of democracy' took on an altogether more ominous meaning.

As the USA continued its shift to the right, so Benn continued his shift to the left, particularly when it appeared that the USA was itself developing imperialist tendencies. Since 1945, it had become increasingly clear that Britain could no longer continue to play the role of a global peacekeeper, leaving a power vacuum which the USA was to fill. While meeting the conditions of the hawkish US Secretary of State, John Foster Dulles, to contain the Soviet Union with 'a ring of force', it posed a question for the anti-colonial movement: Was the USA exploiting the Cold War psychosis to extend its global reach? Committed to the emancipation of Britain's colonies, the MP Fenner Brockway had established the Congress of Peoples Against Imperialism in 1947, and strengthened by the burgeoning of home-rule movements in the colonies, there was a growing conflict between the USA's global strategy and the ambitions of the anti-colonial movement.

Benn's position was clear: 'I am anti-colonialist. I believe in national independence as the first stage towards responsible self-government', and during his early years in the Commons, he devoted much of his time and energy to colonial and common-wealth affairs, establishing a network of contacts with nationalist leaders – Hastings Banda, Kwame Nkrumah, Julius Nyerere, Kenneth Kaunda, Cheddi Jagan, Forbes Burnham – during their pilgrimages to London to plead the cause of self-government. Once begun, there could be no checking the retreat from empire, as Benn, described, half-jokingly, as one of the Honourable Members for Africa, wrote in his diary on 11 February 1954: 'At 8 p.m. a very important meeting took place – to establish one body for colonial activity – the Movement for Colonial Freedom [MCF].'

With Fenner Brockway as its Chairman and Benn as its Treasurer, the MCF helped energize the Labour Party's laggard approach to colonial affairs in much the same way as the H-Bomb National Committee helped focus the party's mind on the escalating dangers of the Cold War. Founded only two months after the establishment of the MCF, the committee gave body to Attlee's assertion that 'Time is not on the side of the survival of civilisation.' The conjunction was not coincidental. The two issues – the reach of US foreign policy and the campaign for colonial independence – were inextricably linked, each demanding an overdue reappraisal by Labour of its policies.

Without informing Parliament, the Tory government had taken the decision to develop a hydrogen bomb as early as 1952. For the next two years there were rumours, nothing more, that Britain was in the process of manufacturing an H-bomb, and at Question Time in the House on 8 April 1954, Benn taxed Churchill as to whether or not a long-standing Anglo-American agreement covered the development of thermonuclear weapons. Churchill maintained that it did, and in a significant exchange later that evening, Attlee chided Benn: 'Wouldn't it have been wiser to have consulted me before putting the question – after all *only* I know the whole truth.' As Benn was to note in his diary: 'I guess the whole truth cannot be known yet.'

The idea was anathema to Benn. Open government was his credo, a case that he had recently made in a stinging attack on McCarthyism – 'We believe that you can trust people to have good sense and good judgement if you leave people to make up their own minds and elect their own governments' – yet, seemingly, the Labour leadership was colluding with the Tories to conceal the fact that Britain itself was deeply involved in the thermonuclear arms race. In the following year, members of the H-Bomb National Committee worried away at the government front bench, demanding to know whether their suspicions were well founded, and it was only in February 1955 that the government admitted that the UK was, indeed, developing the H-bomb – with US assistance. Like some ageing relative in a Dickensian novel, terrified of impoverishment, it appeared that Britain was becoming increasingly dependent on the USA, and if anyone continued to question the fact, the Suez crisis of 1956 was to lay their doubts.

In July, President Gamal Abdel-Nasser nationalized the Suez Canal and all its assets, an act that divided the Labour Party against itself. On 2 August Gaitskell mounted a savage attack on Nasser, prompting Benn to write in his diary: 'I felt so sick as I listened. I wanted to shout "Shame".' Throughout the late summer, tensions continued to mount, and on 16 September Benn addressed a rally in Trafalgar Square, deploring the government's sabre-rattling and demanding an international initiative to resolve the dispute. It made no difference. Anthony Eden, who had replaced Churchill as the Tory leader in April 1955, was bent on confrontation, and with Anglo-French complicity, Israel launched an attack on Egypt on 29 October. The following day, Britain and France announced their intention to intervene in support of Israel, leading Gaitskell to reverse his former position, and move a censure motion on the government.

The subsequent debate degenerated into uproar, particularly when Benn asserted that 'to put troops in any illegal war of aggression is a crime against those troops'. It was as nothing, however, compared with the reception Benn was given forty-eight hours later at the Cambridge Union:

The UN flag had been stolen and there were wildly noisy scenes and shouts. Great posters hung from the gallery reading 'Support Eden, not Nasser' and 'We are now committed and must support our troops'. The crowd of students laughing and screaming for war gave me an icy hatred of them.

The incident crystallized all that Benn detested most, a recrudescence of that jingoism to which his father had been subjected more than half a century before.

On 5 November, Britain and France invaded Egypt, and within forty-eight hours the war was over, in large part due to the intervention of the USA, which, having tabled a cease-fire resolution at the UN, made it plain that it was willing to employ economic sanctions against two of its principal allies. If anything was to confirm Benn's suspicions, not so much about Britain's impotence as a world power as of the extent of US influence, with all that implied, it was the outcome of the Suez debacle of 1956. Indeed, the paradox was that in exposing Britain's pretensions, the USA revealed the reach of its own power, not least in the Middle East, formerly within the Anglo-French sphere of influence. The old order may have changed, but the burlesque of imperialism remained.

Nevertheless, the Tory government continued to harbour its pretensions, and only six months after the Suez fiasco, Britain intervened militarily in Muscat and Oman, provoking Benn to call for an emergency debate on the issue. The Speaker refused, but not to be outdone, Benn tabled a motion of censure on the Speaker, asserting the right of individual MPs to be heard:

> It is not the vote at the end of the day that limits our rights. It is the right of free speech and thought unfettered by the party system. If an individual backbencher cannot raise a point without the support of his party ... then you give to the party a power over the members which I believe would be an imposition on the rights of this House ... I am not forming an anti-party faction at all ... I am one of the thousand flowers asking permission to be allowed to bloom.

The episode did something to account for Benn's resignation as Labour's second spokesman on the RAF after little more than a year in office. Appointed to the post by Gaitskell in March 1957, there was always a conflict of interests implicit between the role he had played in founding the H-Bomb National Committee and his role as a spokesman for Labour's multilateral defence policy, a conflict compounded by the restrictions that the appointment placed on his own freedom of expression.

Committed as he was to the party he had joined at eighteen years of age, Benn nonetheless remained a loner. It was a trait that was to be a feature of his fifty-year career in the House, a restless individualism which questioned the mores of the political establishment, whether of party or government, to the despair of a succession of colleagues. There could be no question about either his originality or his talents. All too often, however, they damned him. Indeed, he began as he was to continue, proud to call himself a House of Commons man.

In March 1958, Benn returned to the back benches, to reflect on the growing need for Britain to adjust to a new world order without becoming bitter or defeatist:

> This problem of power contraction does threaten our political system. Someone said the Angry Young Men were a symptom of the shrinking pains of the British Empire. The answer probably lies in two things – a widening of Britain's horizons so that we can get satisfaction from the achievements of others, and a domestic revolution to modernise ourselves.

In setting an agenda for the future, Benn had growing confidence in his own prescriptions. By the close of the 1950s, he had helped persuade the Labour leadership to include a commitment to decolonization in the party manifesto. As for the 'domestic revolution', that remained to be tackled, and in November 1960, it appeared that Benn would have a diminishing role to play in the pursuit of modernization. On 17 November Viscount Stansgate died, leading to Benn's expulsion from the Commons. While he was to remain in political exile for the next thirty months, he was far from politically inactive, and not only in the punishing constitutional contest to recover his parliamentary seat.

On 25 March 1957, the six founding members of the European Economic Community had signed the Treaty of Rome. A new player had entered the power game, in part to act as a counter-weight to burgeoning US influence. It was a development that was to condition political debate in Britain for the next four decades, and shape the cast of Benn's future career. Ultimately, as he saw it, the question was simple: with the end of empire, should Britain go into Europe or remain a free agent? As leader of the party in the late 1950s, Gaitskell had no doubts – Britain should retain her independence in order 'to continue playing her historic role in world affairs'. His confrère, Roy Jenkins, disagreed, and in 1959 published a short book setting out his unreserved commitment to the European project, prompting Gaitskell to confide to Benn: 'Roy's an extremist, you know, when it comes to the question of Europe.'

The ground was laid for the bitter disputes that were to come, and in a brief article published in the magazine *Encounter* in January 1963, Benn catechized himself as to the alternatives:

> The idea of Britain joining the Common Market is emotionally very attractive. To throw open our windows to new influences, to help shape the destiny of a new community, even to merge our sovereignty in a wider unit – these offer an exciting prospect. By contrast the xenophobic, parochial delusions of grandeur fostered by the Beaverbrook press appear petty, old-fashioned and reactionary.

Nonetheless, the reservations remained: that the Treaty of Rome entrenched *laissez-faire* and preferred bureaucracy as its administrative tool; that the political inspiration of the EEC amounted to the institutionalizing of NATO and the reinforcement of the East–West divide in Europe; and that the trading policy of the Market would damage underdeveloped countries and widen the gap between the first and third worlds.

On balance, Benn's conclusion was that Britain would have more rather than less influence in world affairs if she remained a free agent. Clearly, the pursuit of such a course of action would demand radical changes in Britain's economic, social and foreign policies: 'But we should be free to make them in the light of the wider needs of the world as we see them', for 'the Market as it now exists is inspired by narrow regionalism'.

Appointed Postmaster-General by Wilson in the incoming Labour administration of 1964, Benn was provided with a platform for the modernization he championed – and an insight into the seemingly insatiable appetite of US commercial interests. Less than two years had passed since he had debated the question of whether Britain should enter Europe or remain a free agent. Now the question had changed, prompting Benn to ponder in a diary entry of 14 January 1965:

> Defence, colour television, Concorde, rocket development – these are all issues raising economic considerations that reveal this country's basic inability to stay in the top league ... in reality the choice lies between Britain as an island and a US protectorate, or Britain as a full member of the Six, followed by a wider European federation. I was always against the Common Market but the reality of our isolation is being borne in on me all the time. This country is so decrepit and hidebound that only activities in a wider sphere can help us to escape the myths which surround our politics.

And the wider sphere was to be Europe, which appeared to be the only political instrument capable of containing the growing power of multinational companies, a high percentage of which were US-controlled: 'As British economic policy had failed, I thought that Europe might provide the basis for securing some democratic control of these new mega-creations.' Benn's views keyed in closely with those of Harold Wilson who, in championing the potential of 'the white heat of technology', advanced the argument for the creation of a European Technological Community, an argument which was later to play a significant role in leading the government to the historic decision to apply for full membership of the EEC.

For all Benn's previous reservations, it appeared that this was the only viable alternative to Britain becoming what he termed 'an American satellite: the last colony' – a view reinforced following his appointment as Minister of Technology in 1966:

> My department is becoming increasingly involved in the development of a closer relationship with our fellow European countries ... The full benefits of integrated European technology can only be achieved when Britain is a member of the EEC ... We must co-operate now and prepare for the day when the Community can be enlarged.

Seemingly, all the old doubts about the nature of an institution which 'preferred bureaucracy as its administrative tool' had been laid. Seemingly, the innate conflict between the *laissez-faire* policies favoured by Brussels and the interventionist strategy advanced by Benn had been resolved. Seemingly, the *volte-face* was complete and Benn had become a convert to the European project in pursuit of a technological renaissance that would empower his modernizing vision. Roy Jenkins was delighted and welcomed him to 'the club'. Benn's membership proved short-lived. Temporarily, his reservations about the democratic accountability of the Market had been suspended, but they remained nonetheless. In the best of all possible worlds, a case could be made out for Britain's entry into the Community, provided ...

The longer Benn considered the provisos, the more compelling they became. Less than a decade had passed since he had challenged the whole arcane system of representation in order to renounce his peerage, to learn how easy it was to dupe the electorate with a semblance of democracy: the Noble Lie, indeed. Yet now it appeared that what had been achieved was in danger of being sacrificed to some new and equally arcane construct. Benn, however, remained ambivalent, and on balance continued to favour Market entry, with the caveat that if Britain was to take such a step, then it was only right that the public should decide the issue in a referendum. In October 1969, he floated the idea in cabinet. It received no support. Another twelve months were to pass, twelve months which marked the return of a Tory government committed to Europe, before he went public with his proposal in a letter to his Bristol constituents:

> The whole history of British democracy has been about how *you* take decisions, and this has always been seen to be more important than what the decisions were. All political parties in Britain are willing to accept electoral defeat because they believe that the machinery represented by the ballot box is more important than the result it produces. If the Common Market question is decided without consulting the people, it will split the country and both parties.

Few people appreciated Benn's percipience, least of all Labour's shadow cabinet, who rejected his call for a referendum for a second time in November 1970, but not before Jim Callaghan had mused: 'Tony may be launching a little rubber life raft which we will all be glad of in a year's time.' Concerned above all else with retaining the appearance of unity, the shadow cabinet's decision disguised the reality that Labour was bitterly divided on the issue, the pro-Marketeers led by Roy Jenkins being ranged against such fellow front-benchers as Peter Shore, who regarded the Market's blandishments as largely illusory. As for Benn, he continued to debate the issue with himself – 'I don't think that economics are everything, but if we are to have some sort of organisation to control international companies, the Common Market is probably the right one' – while continuing to press the case for a referendum, arguing in the Commons on 22 July 1971:

> It would be the end of democratic politics as we know it in Britain if the Labour Party embraced an aristocratic view of its function, believed itself to be cleverer, wiser, more knowledgeable than those it is here to serve ... Indeed I believe that this is the whole heart of the argument now going on inside the Labour Party.

His plea made little difference. At the party conference that year, a resolution calling for a referendum was heavily defeated, and following a five-day debate in October, the government won a 112-vote majority in favour of Britain's entering the Community, thanks to the support of sixty-nine Labour MPs who defied a three-line whip and voted with the government, an event that was to provoke Benn to write in his diary: 'This is the moment when the right wing decides that Europe is more important than the Labour Party, and, more importantly, that they are not interested in a party they don't control.'

As the internecine wrangling within the party intensified, however, Wilson came to recognize the benefits to be gained from adopting Benn's strategy. It was de Gaulle's decision to hold a referendum in France in 1972 to establish whether or not Britain should be permitted to enter the Market that finally persuaded the shadow cabinet that Benn's proposal did, indeed, provide Labour with the 'little rubber life raft' that Callaghan had envisaged, and on 29 March the shadow cabinet reversed its former decision, voting six to eight in favour of a referendum.

Ironically, in light of subsequent assertions, during the early 1970s Benn's proposal provided Labour with a formula, if not for unity, then with the means by which, in calling for a referendum, it could claim that it would respect the electorate's views when Labour was re-elected. The decision established a constitutional precedent – until 1972 the notion of referenda had been anathema to both major parties – and led to Jenkins's resignation as Deputy Leader of the party on 10 April 1972. A patrician by inclination, Jenkins was opposed to the idea of what he called 'direct democracy', which he compared with Hitler's plebiscites. He made it quite clear that if such a referendum was ever held, and if the result went against Britain's entry into the Market, he would quit British politics.

Not that Jenkins was alone, rather the first among equals in a group of dedicated pro-Marketeers, for as early as 30 May 1971, Benn had noted in his diary: 'This group working with conservative pro-Europeans really represents a new political party in Britain ... It is inconceivable that such a group, consistently voting with the [Conservative] government, could do this without severing their links with the Labour Party.' Another ten years were to pass before his prediction was realized, years of growing hostility among the Labour leadership, not least over Europe.

In March 1974, the Heath government fell, and Benn's appointment as Secretary of State for Industry provided him with his first personal insight into the workings of the Market. What he discovered shocked him, more especially when the Foreign Office submitted his Industry Bill to Brussels to have it cleared by the Commission before it had been published in the UK. Apparently, the mandarins were replicating themselves, as bureaucratic clones contemptuous of democratic accountability, provided, always, that the correct procedures were followed, that the correct formalities were observed. And all this with the constitutional sanction of the Treaty of Rome:

> When I got there I met people who hadn't been elected who were simply telling me what I could and couldn't do ... I felt that whatever notion I had of democracy was being over-ridden by people who had no interest in democracy at all ... What they really wanted was to build capitalism, and

gradually I came to realise that while the Commission might harbour ambitions of becoming a super-power, they certainly didn't want it to be a democratic one, but one that they controlled themselves.

Benn had long suspected as much, and now his suspicions were confirmed: that *laissez-faire* was the driving force behind the Market, regardless of the democratic deficit which that entailed. Eleven years had passed since he had first wrangled with the issue, but this was the moment of truth: either he subscribed to the Treaty of Rome or he stood by his democratic ideals. The choice was as clear-cut as that, and at a cabinet meeting in July 1974, he announced his intention of campaigning against Britain's continuing membership of the Community.

Six months were to pass before the cabinet fixed 5 June 1975 as the date when the electorate would decide on the future of Britain's role in Europe, and the launch of the Britain in Europe campaign – fronted by Jenkins, flanked by two Tory grandees, Willie Whitelaw and Reggie Maudling, and the former Liberal leader, Jo Grimond – provided substance for Benn's long-standing fears. This, indeed, was breaking the political mould, and as the campaign intensified, it became increasingly acerbic. Once begun, in fact, there could be no further compromises, and in the run-up to the referendum, Benn became the favourite hate figure of the political establishment and the right-wing media, Mrs Thatcher's guru, Sir Keith Joseph, describing him as Dracula, and Edward Heath warning that 'before you could say Lord Stansgate, he would be leading us into his vision of the promised land, not flowing with milk and honey but swamped by ration books and state directives'.

And to the media's delight, the pro-Marketeers in the Labour Party were equally vituperative at Benn's expense, particularly when he focused much of his campaign on what he regarded as the deleterious economic consequences of Britain's continuing membership of the Market: 'We have lost half a million jobs as a result of our trade deficit with the Six. Three years of EEC membership has been an industrial disaster for Britain.' Harold Wilson was dismissive, describing Benn as 'an Old Testament prophet, without a beard, who dreams about the New Jerusalem he looks forward to at some future time'; Denis Healey contemptuous, accusing Benn of 'escaping from real life and retreating into cocoons of myth and fantasy'; and Roy Jenkins abusive: 'I find it increasingly difficult to take Mr Benn seriously as an economic minister.'

Ranged against the combined forces of the establishment, the media and much of the government front bench, the National Referendum Campaign (NRC) had little chance of success, particularly when it was operating on a budget of only £133,000 compared with the £1,410,000 war chest of the Britain in Europe movement. For all the mass audiences attending the NRC meetings – in Cardiff more than 2000 people attended a Britain Out rally that a young Welsh MP, Neil Kinnock, had helped to stage – the outcome of the referendum was virtually preordained, though the magnitude of the pro-European majority took even Benn by surprise. More than twenty-five million electors cast their vote, eighteen million of them in favour of Britain remaining in the Market. At half-past midnight on 5 June, Benn drafted the statement that he was to issue the following day:

> By an overwhelming majority the British people have voted to stay in, and I am sure everyone would want to accept that ... I am very proud that the people had the right to vote ... and will enter the community as free men and women and not as serfs taken in by their masters.

Four days later, Wilson stripped Benn of his post as Secretary of State for Industry, and downgraded him to the Department of Energy, thus fulfilling the media's predictions: 'Time to say goodbye to Wedgie'; 'The debunking of Tony Benn'. While the epitaphs were premature, they set the tone for the character assassinations that had yet to come. At fifty years of age, and having already served almost a quarter of a century in the Commons, Benn had no intention of quitting politics. Quite the reverse. On 9 June he asked his Private Secretary, Roy Williams, to clear out his office at the Department of Industry – 'take everything out as if I had never been here' – and moved to his new department. Committed to Labour's interventionist economic strategy and, not least, to the party's programme of public control of North Sea oil, he faced powerful opposition from the multi-national oil companies, which, in the words of the Chairman of the British National Oil Corporation, Lord Kearton, were 'treating

Britain like an offshore Arab state'.

During his three-year tenure at Energy, Benn was to lay the foundations for an agreement under which Britain would secure a quarter share of the North Sea holdings; it was a period that would confirm Benn's suspicions about the influence of the multi-nationals, and of their seemingly incestuous relationship with the nomenklatura of Brussels:

> Far from the European Commission being a source of strength against the multinationals, when the multinationals made no progress with me they would go to Brussels and use the Community's laws to break our control over them. In short, they used Brussels as the last court of appeal over national governments.

Ironically, in light of their later differences, David Owen, appointed Foreign Secretary by Callaghan in February 1977, shared certain of Benn's reservations. Concerned, like Benn, at what he regarded as Britain's relative economic decline, and the country's penchant for selling itself short, he tabled a paper on the Common Market at a cabinet meeting in July. Benn accepted much of Owen's critique, which sparked a major confrontation between the pro and anti factions, and prompted Benn to declare:

> I am quite happy to go along with David Owen's general approach ... You hear all this about parliamentary democracy being undermined by Marxists or by extending the public sector, but the plain truth is that it has been undermined by Brussels.

For Benn, the problem was that he was equally sceptical of Britain's 'special relationship' with the USA. Since the McCarthy era he had had serious reservations about the direction of US policy – reservations that had been reinforced by the USA's intervention in the war in Vietnam. In 1960, President Kennedy had been the first to deploy significant numbers of US troops – euphemistically termed 'military advisers' – in the conflict. Four years later President Johnson escalated the commitment, having received congressional authority for full-scale US intervention, a decision that was to reveal the full potency of the military-industrial complex. In the twelve years that followed, the USA lost

47,000 men in the killing fields of Vietnam, only to admit eventual defeat, but not before Benn had concluded that the war had revealed the USA's intention of becoming 'a regular imperial power'.

What few lingering doubts Benn still harboured about the role of the 'special relationship' within US designs were quickly dispelled during his time at the Department of Energy. As the minister responsible for Britain's nuclear industry, he was soon to learn that the USA had only lent Britain nuclear know-how, including the Polaris and Trident systems, in return for their control of Britain's intelligence network, most notably GCHQ, and to discover that if Britain was to develop certain items of hardware essential for the development of its nuclear energy programme, permission had first to be obtained from the US Atomic Energy Commission. And the more he learned, the more convinced he became that the relationship was little more than a charade that disguised Britain's subordination to the USA: 'They lend us the bomb and let us pretend that it is an independent deterrent, but it isn't. This is really the fraud that lies at the pretence of Britain being a great power.'

While the illusion may have heartened the xenophobes, it was unsustainable in reality, though the return of a Conservative government in May 1979 did something to revive the pretension. Twelve months before, Benn noted in his diary Callaghan's warning that Thatcher was moving further and further to the right, to which Peter Shore had added the rider: 'Mrs Thatcher is beginning to reflect a genuine English nationalist feeling.' Benn agreed entirely, suspecting that, if elected, Mrs Thatcher would abandon One Nation conservatism and, wrapped in the Union Jack, appeal unashamedly to the public's chauvinistic instincts. It was a strategy that was to underlie her later hostility to the Common Market and, conversely, to invest her faith in the US connection, particularly when it appeared that she had, indeed, established a special relationship with Ronald Reagan.

Although a critic of the Common Market, Benn was as sceptical of Thatcher's anti-European posturings, remarking to the former German Chancellor, Willy Brandt, that the Labour Party wanted 'nothing of her nationalism', as he was of her friendship with President Reagan. Shortly before Christmas 1980, he visited

Washington for a conference arranged by the Democratic Socialist
Organizing Committee and attended by, among others, François
Mitterrand, Olaf Palme and Willy Brandt.

Their object was to examine the possibility of developing a Third
Way between capitalism and communism, a concept that already
had a respectable history. In the 1930s a young Tory backbencher,
Harold Macmillan, had been explicit in calling for a planned
economy in *The Middle Way* ('such a wise governance of the
economic system as will eliminate or control our trade cycle'),
while post-1945, the so-called Third Force movement opposed both
the virulent anti-Soviet policy pursued by Ernest Bevin and the
Attlee government and its equally noxious alternative, Stalinism.
Instead, it had sought to develop a more independent policy which
would allow Britain to work more closely with the UN and those
colonial territories seeking independence.

The Washington conference was to fortify Benn's belief that there
was, indeed, an alternative to the diktat of the Market:

> At the time the Common Market did have a more progressive,
> socialist-democratic-internationalist element in it, which
> people such as Palme and Brandt and Mitterrand believed
> could have a significant influence on the Community. In a
> funny way, it was the real Third Way, of democracy
> intervening in the economy to safeguard the interests of the
> workers.

What optimism Benn felt may well have been dampened when,
on the morning of 6 December, he woke early and turned on the
TV. For an hour he was transfixed by the rantings of the right-
wing, born-again Christian evangelist Pat Robertson, who talked
up Reagan's achievements as the political Superman who, single-
handedly, had defeated the liberals – a utility phrase which,
seemingly, embraced all forms of leftists:

> I couldn't switch it off. It was so frightening, the feeling that
> we are now entering a holy war between that type of
> reactionary Christianity and communism. It is a thoroughly
> wicked and evil interpretation of Christianity.

A quarter of a century had passed since McCarthy had finally
been ostracized for his extremism and yet here, once again, was the

virus, which this time was laying claim to the political sympathies of a man who, within the month, would become President of the USA.

Symbolically, Mrs Thatcher was the first head of state to visit Reagan after his inauguration. Since their first meeting in 1975, they had shared common cause in their ardent embrace of the free market, and their detestation of anything to the left of their own right-wing persuasions. Only eighteen months had separated Thatcher's election and Reagan's inauguration, but as Hugo Young was to write in *One of Us*, his incisive biography of Thatcher's first decade in power: 'to a certain extent Mrs Thatcher was a kind of Baptist to Reagan's Messiah'. But if this was the apotheosis of pan-Atlantic conservatism, there could be no mistaking where the source of that power lay. On the lawn of the White House, with the Iron Lady beside him, Reagan may have pledged that Britain and the USA would 'stand side by side' in defending freedom – just so long as it was on US terms.

And as Benn saw them, the terms were becoming increasingly onerous. In 1981, he again reappraised his position to ask, once again, whether Britain had, indeed, become a colony, and if so: 'to which empire do we belong?' His answer, spelled out in *Arguments for Democracy*, was as bleak as it was uncompromising:

> My personal experience ... from the mid-1960s as Minister of Technology to the late 1970s as Secretary of State for Energy, convinced me of the colonial status which the multinationals have succeeded in imposing upon Britain.

Not that they operated in isolation:

> Parallel with the colonisation of post-war Britain by the multinationals and bankers came the much more specifically political supervision of another area of our policy – defence – by the United States ... As Britain's commercial rival, America has been quite ready to exploit British weakness in Iran, the Middle East and elsewhere for its own advantage. But these factors are of little account compared to the 'special relationship' between the UK and the US, whereby the situation before 1776 [the date of the Declaration of

Independence] has been reversed, so that Britain is now to a large extent a colony in an American empire.

Benn's critics were derisive. There could be no questioning the nature of Britain's continuing role as a great power, and for all of Benn's eleven years in government, his appraisal was widely dismissed as the work of a conspiracy theorist, not least by the Tory right. They were soon to learn, if not the full extent of their illusion, then something of the nature of the special relationship.

The British sovereignty of the Falkland Islands had long been disputed by Argentina, and on 1 April 1982, an Argentinian task force invaded the islands and occupied Port Stanley. At an emergency sitting of the Commons forty-eight hours later, the Tories were in bullish mood, Julian Amery declaring that the government must 'wipe the stain from British honour', as was much of the Labour front bench, Michael Foot asserting that such acts of 'foul and brutal aggression' should not be allowed to succeed. Only a handful of backbenchers questioned the government's proposal to despatch a task force to the South Atlantic, and it was left to a former Minister of State at the Foreign Office, Ted Rowlands, to point out that 'the United States is very close to the Argentine regime'.

Since the formulation of the Monroe Doctrine in 1823, the USA had regarded Latin America as falling within its sphere of influence, and in 1973 a coup backed by President Nixon and bankrolled by the CIA had overthrown President Allende's left-wing government, to install General Pinochet in power. The coup revealed how far Washington was willing to go to secure its interests in the Americas, whether in Guatemala or El Salvador, in Nicaragua or, most notably, in Cuba. In each case, Washington had intervened, directly or indirectly, in attempts to destabilize or overthrow left-wing regimes and replace them with puppets of its own choosing.

And as Rowlands had made clear, the USA was 'very close' to Galtieri and the right-wing junta that governed Argentina, a point that Benn was to note briefly in his diary on the evening of 3 April ('The last thing they want is a big British fleet in the South Atlantic overturning the Argentinian dictatorship'), and was later to flesh out:

The Americans did not want Mrs Thatcher stirring up trouble with one of their favourite dictators, and they only went along with us because Reagan favoured Mrs Thatcher politically, though it was significant how slow he was to provide her with any backing.

A month was to pass between the Argentinian invasion and Reagan declaring his support for Britain. With the notable exception of Chile, the majority of South American states sided with Argentina, which led Reagan to despatch his Secretary of State, Alexander Haig, on a mission of shuttle diplomacy in an attempt to avert the crisis escalating and, thus, jeopardizing Washington's influence in the region. Seemingly, all talk of fighting 'side by side' in defence of freedom had temporarily been put on hold, and it was only on 30 April that Haig's mission was finally terminated, and Reagan announced his intention of imposing economic sanctions on Argentina, and providing logistical back-up for Britain's task force.

Four days later, on Tuesday, 4 May, the Commons again debated the Falklands crisis, with Benn recommending that the sovereignty of the islands should be transferred to the UN pending a settlement under UN auspices. The proposal was in line with a previous UN resolution, and reflected the stress that Benn placed on the role of the UN as a broker in international affairs. The House wanted nothing of his proposal. In bellicose mood it would settle for nothing less than total victory, a mood personified by Mrs Thatcher, which prompted one cabinet member to reflect that her public appearances reminded him of the Nuremberg rallies, and for Benn to declare: 'The purpose of the battle fleet is to recover Mrs Thatcher's reputation.'

With the news that the first British troops had landed in the Falklands on 21 May, the war fever mounted, reaching a climax with news of the Argentinian surrender. Benn was disconsolate. This was the antithesis of all that he represented: 'I went to the House to hear the Prime Minister's statement announcing the surrender. Michael Foot congratulated her and her forces, somehow it was odious and excessive.' Neither the Commons nor the public agreed. All too soon, however, his prediction proved to have been correct, for it was largely on the strength of the Falklands factor that the Iron Lady reversed her negative standing in the opinion polls to lead the Conservatives to a landslide victory in the election of June 1983.

The Tories' triumphalism was soon to be tempered by *realpolitik*, however. While Mrs Thatcher was fulsome in her appreciation of Reagan's support during the Falklands campaign and what, subsequently, it had done for her re-election prospects, she was compelled to reappraise what it meant to stand 'side by side' with the USA only four months after the election. Since 1979 the tiny Caribbean island of Grenada, a member of the Commonwealth, had been ruled by a Marxist regime which Washington regarded as posing a threat to the security of the region. In the third week of October, a US invasion force was assembled in the Caribbean, without informing either the Queen, Grenada's head of state, or the British government of Washington's intentions to invest the island. In fact, when questioned in the Commons about rumours of a possible landing, the Foreign Secretary replied: 'I know of no such intention.'

When the deception was exposed, Mrs Thatcher was incensed at what she regarded as US treachery. Benn, however, was not altogether surprised, for the action revealed the exact nature of the 'special relationship'. Rhetoric aside, the phrase disguised the reality not only of Britain's subordinate role in the partnership but also of the contempt with which Washington regarded her 'closest ally'. Benn's suspicions were subsequently reaffirmed when, shortly after Clinton's election to the presidency, he received John Major in the White House. Before Major's arrival, Clinton and his aides sat joking in the Oval Office: 'Don't forget to say "special relationship" when the press comes in', one of them joked. 'Oh yes, the special relationship', said Clinton. 'How could I forget?' Then he threw back his head and laughed uproariously.

The story, told by Raymond Seitz, formerly a US ambassador to London, summed up the extent of Britain's decline. As Benn was to point out, however, the cost to Britain of playing the puppet's role was high and escalating, with military expenditure in the late 1980s accounting for well over 5 per cent of gross domestic product: 'which in real terms is 20 per cent above what it was when Mrs Thatcher became Prime Minister' – the highest percentage of any country in NATO with the exception of the USA.

Seemingly, Britain was, indeed, little better than an offshore aircraft carrier – a suspicion reaffirmed in April 1986, when Reagan informed rather than consulted Thatcher about his intention to mount a strike against Libya by US F-111 bombers based in the UK. And all for what? Benn had no doubts as to the answer:

> The NATO alliance was intended to act as a *cordon sanitaire* to prevent the spread of socialism. But meanwhile this system also provided a cover for the growth of a formidable American empire, sustaining, with the help of 3,000 American bases across the world, the huge economic, industrial, and political interests of the USA.

Whether or not the Cold War was an agent of US foreign policy, the consequent arms race succeeded in crippling the Soviet economy, and yet, as Benn was to note at a 1987 conference on non-alignment, the contest continued unabated:

> With only 11 per cent of the world's population, the superpowers account for 60 per cent of all military expenditure, 80 per cent of all weapons research and 97 per cent of all nuclear weapons ... At constant prices the world total spent on defence is now two and a quarter times greater than it was in 1960.

In the case of the USA, the expansion of the military-industrial complex had achieved its twofold objective, namely securing the dynamism of the US economy via a mutant form of Keynesianism, whilst crippling that of the Soviet Union. By the mid-1980s, it was a Cold War game that Russia could no longer afford to continue playing, and as her domestic problems intensified, her East European satellites grew increasingly restless. For all of Gorbachev's attempt to shore up the system, not least by launching a programme of economic and political reforms (*perestroika*), Reagan's 'evil empire' was on the point of collapse, an event vividly symbolized by the fall of the Berlin Wall in 1989.

Coincidentally, a US academic, Francis Fukuyama, was to argue in the journal *The National Interest* that a consensus concerning the legitimacy of liberal democracy as a system of government had emerged throughout the world, which had conquered rival ideologies such as fascism and communism: 'I [Fukuyama] argued that "liberal democracy" may constitute "the end point of man's ideological evolution" and the "final form of human government", and as such constituted "the end of history".[1] The phrase encapsulated the mood of the times. Apparently, there was no further place for ideological debate. All that remained to be done was to fine-tune the US model of liberal democracy and its economic adjunct, capitalism.

If Fukuyama regarded the collapse of the Soviet empire as the end of history, Benn regarded it as the apotheosis of US imperialism, deriding Mrs Thatcher's declaration that the opening of a McDonald's hamburger outlet in Moscow was 'a giant leap forward for democracy'. The notion mocked his sense of history:

> The more I've thought about East–West relations, and how they have developed over the years, the more I've come to realise that the whole period from 1917 to the present time has been a long-drawn-out war to eliminate socialism in every shape and form ... In Russia's case, all the talk of democratisation was so much eye-wash. The long game was not concerned with the democratisation of the Soviet Union, rather its colonisation by capital.

Colonization! In Benn's vocabulary the word has powerful connotations, a prompt to the memory of his own and his father's experiences in combating imperialism, and yet ...

In August 1991, Benn was in New York when Boris Yeltsin faced down an attempted coup by communist hard-liners in Moscow. Gorbachev had already lost control of the quiet revolution he had initiated, and as far as Benn was concerned, Yeltsin was little better than 'an agent for the final subversion of the Soviet Union', the man who, on becoming President, was to oversee the wholesale sell-off of Russia's industrial and commercial assets.

The collapse of the Soviet Union appeared to have fortified, rather than diminished, Washington's resolve to eliminate all vestiges of socialism and those 'rogue states' who continued to challenge US hegemony. For eight years, the USA and its NATO partners had sided with Iraq in its bloody war with Iran, which had replaced the Soviet

---

1. *The National Interest*, summer 1989.

Union as Washington's favourite bogey, but with Iraq's annexation of Kuwait in August 1990, the situation changed radically.

On 2 August, a UN resolution condemned the invasion, which the Iraqi President, Saddam Hussein, was quick to dismiss as gesture politics. In fact, the indications were that he was playing for higher stakes, particularly following the deployment of Iraqi forces on the border with Saudi Arabia, a move which threatened the fragile stability of the region. Determined to defend US interests in the Gulf and, coincidentally, Israeli security, the State Department began to flex its muscle in a reprise of gunboat diplomacy of the colonial era. Regardless both of the build-up of US forces in the Gulf and of a subsequent Security Council ruling imposing economic sanctions on Iraq, Hussein continued to pursue his confrontational strategy.

As far as Benn was concerned, it was only a matter of time before this post-Cold War turned hot, and throughout the autumn he campaigned energetically in favour of the UN sanctions. Initially, it was a policy shared by the Labour leader, Neil Kinnock, with the crucial additive that such measures should be backed up by the use of force if, and when, necessary – the hard-line policy already favoured by Margaret Thatcher and the US President, George Bush. Aimed at maintaining unity, Kinnock's twin-track approach did nothing to disguise the differences within the party, and the Chair, Jo Richardson's, petty-minded gesture in deliberately ignoring Benn's request to speak at the party conference in October merely reinforced his standing with those dissidents who shared his fears that it was the USA rather than the UN that was dictating the political agenda.

Indeed, in part it may have been as a result of Richardson's snub that the Iraqi government invited Benn to visit Baghdad in early November in an attempt to break the diplomatic impasse, and negotiate for the release of thirty-three western hostages taken by the Iraqis. Before flying out, Benn articulated his fears:

> The possibility that President Bush, supported by Mrs Thatcher, may launch an all-out attack on Iraq, and their refusal to seek a settlement by negotiation, represents a threat to world peace ... I believe that this position is criminal folly.

He made his own position clear: 'If war is to be avoided we must seek an overall settlement of the many interconnected problems of the area, under the auspices of the United Nations, in line with its Charter.' It was a view which received widespread support from the world leaders Benn canvassed before leaving for Baghdad, among them Nelson Mandela, Julius Nyerere, Rajiv Gandhi, Pierre Trudeau, Kenneth Kaunda and Willy Brandt.

On 28 November, the day on which the *Spectator* named him Backbencher of the Year, Benn had a meeting with Saddam Hussein in a small villa which, as he recalled later, 'might well have come out of a set for Brookside'. On being invited to speak his mind, Benn warned Hussein that if he did not quit Kuwait the Americans intended to destroy him, to which Hussein replied: 'The Americans are going to destroy me even if I do get out of Kuwait.' The meeting lasted for three hours, but Benn's plea that Hussein should consider the long-term perspective for peace – 'Today is the crisis, tomorrow is war, but there is a day after' – appeared to make little impression on the Iraqi leader. As for the fate of the hostages, Benn became so excited during the meeting that it was only as he was leaving the villa that he recalled: 'Oh God, I've forgotten the main purpose of my mission.'

Despite Benn's oversight, the hostages were released within a week of his return. Meanwhile, the countdown to war continued with a steady build-up of forces in the Gulf, now sanctioned by a UN resolution that force could be used failing Iraq's withdrawal from Kuwait. On 12 January 1991, Congress approved the use of US troops for an offensive operation against Iraq, and on 17 January Operation Desert Storm began with a series of massive air strikes against Iraqi targets. In the following forty days as many as 150,000 Iraqis, troops and civilians, died, and a further 300,000 were wounded, and when a cease-fire was announced on 28 February, President Bush declared, euphorically, that it marked the beginning of a New World Order. In Benn's vocabulary, the phrase had ominous undertones. He had heard it too often before:

It wasn't simply that Bush's declaration reminded me of Hitler's vain boasting, more that it was evident that imperialism was coming back again as an acceptable thing ... Despite all the hopes raised when the Cold War ended,

Desert Storm provided a clear indication that nationalism, militarism and imperialism were all re-emerging.

Pax Americana may have substituted for Pax Britannica, but Benn had no sympathies for either. Seemingly, the old order had changed, only to be replicated by the new. Indeed, the only difference was that whereas colonialism had formerly secured the interests of capitalism, globalization was now the name of the game, with the World Bank and the IMF acting as the agents of US neo-colonialism in a drive to impose free-market conditions on rogue states by threatening to withdraw investment funds: 'The so-called cancellation of the world debt is actually privatisation under economic threat.' The combination of the reach of US strategic power, allied to the reach of US economic interests, may have done something to account for the shift in Benn's attitude to the European Community in the 1990s. The reservations remained but tempered now by a more malleable approach.

As early as 1988, when Benn tabled his European Communities (Amendment) Bill calling for the 'return of full and unfettered powers to the United Kingdom over all legislation enacted by the European Communities', he was quick to add the qualification that all members of the Community should continue to co-operate closely with one another. Three years later he was to reaffirm his position ('I'm a great believer in close co-operation in Europe') with the threefold caveat that the Community only represented a part of Europe; that the Treaty of Rome 'is the only one in the world committed to capitalism'; and that the Community was totally undemocratic: 'It is run by Commissioners who are not elected and cannot be removed.'

Desirable as the idea of closer collaboration with Europe was, the existing Community was damned by a structure which, since its establishment, had subordinated political to economic objectives, resulting in the democratic deficit that had degraded the concept itself. Given that this situation could be reversed, and democratic accountability established, it appeared to Benn that the ideal of a European commonwealth might, indeed, be realized. For five years he worked on his Commonwealth of Europe Bill, before tabling it in the summer of 1996. The preamble to the bill was straight-forward – 'Whereas it would be in the interests of the people of the

United Kingdom to co-operate closely with the people in all the other countries in the continent of Europe for the welfare of all' – and its qualifications equally specific: that the existing structure of the Community overrode the domestic laws of member states, and that proposed economic and monetary union 'would necessarily undermine still further the democratic accountability of those with power to those over whom that power would be exercised'.

Benn's solution lay in restructuring the entire institution to establish the primacy of political decision-taking, reversing the existing polarities of power by vesting policy-making in an elected Assembly to secure democratic accountability, and to provide member states with a high degree of autonomy in the management of their own domestic affairs. Consisting of five hundred members, the Assembly would be empowered to determine 'the policy of the Commonwealth as a whole', while a restructured Council of Ministers would 'actively seek to harmonise the policies of all nations of the Commonwealth'. Then, and only then, would the Secretariat be authorized to act. A qualified form of Lionel Jospin's 'federation of nation states', Benn's Commonwealth Bill did, indeed, threaten to turn the world upside down, not least that of the Eurocrats who, for forty years, had determined the Community's policies, while paying scant attention to the democratic deficit on which their authority was based.

While the Eurocrats would reject Benn's proposals, Mrs Thatcher was to misread his intentions. At a dinner in the Speaker's House to celebrate Ted Heath's fifty years as an MP, she aired her hostility to the EU and claimed that as 'a true-born Englishman' Benn could not but agree with her. Benn's reply was instructive:

> My wife is an American of French, Irish and Scottish descent. Our son is married to a woman who is half Jewish and half Indian, and another is about to marry a Muslim, so I suppose we are breeding a UN peacekeeping force.

There was a momentary pause before Mrs Thatcher replied: 'Ah yes, but they all *speak* English, don't they?' Her chauvinism was as evident as Benn's internationalism, for as he has asserted so often, 'I've always been a world government man myself'.

Like so much else, it was part of his inheritance, his father and mother having spent their honeymoon at the League of Nations in

Geneva. And as with the fate of the League, it seemed to Benn that even before the end of the Cold War, the UN was being marginalized as the forum of international government. Deliberately sited in New York in an attempt to avert the danger of the USA developing such isolationist tendencies as had been the case after the First World War, when it refused to join the League, in its early days the fifty founding member states of the organization reflected its Western origins and its consequent mind-set.

Ironically, it was the drive for decolonization, in which Benn had played a significant role, that was to change both the composition and the character of the organization, and lead to its deteriorating relationship with the USA. By the early 1980s, the UN's original membership had almost tripled, and as Western influence diminished, so Washington's disillusion with its role intensified. As the largest contributor to the organization's budget, this was not what the State Department had envisaged, and in an attempt to retain its authority, Washington progressively tightened its squeeze on the organization's finances, whilst seeking to develop an alternative power base.

And the means, as Benn saw it, were already to hand. As the IMF, the World Bank and the World Trade Organization served US economic interests, so the North Atlantic Treaty Organization could be reoriented to serve its strategic ends. Established in the early days of the Cold War to provide a military counterweight to the Soviet presence in Eastern Europe, NATO was later to be described by Gore Vidal as 'the *cosa nostra* which we [the United States] used to control Western Europe'. With the ending of the Cold War, NATO's *raison d'être* effectively came to an end. As Benn was to note, however: 'Rather than disbanding NATO, the United States extended its remit, as became quite apparent during the Kosovan crisis, when it deliberately set out to destroy the last remnants of socialism in the Balkans.'

Always a political flashpoint, the break-up of the Yugoslav republic following the withdrawal of Croatia in the early 1990s had led to growing tensions in the region, a situation exacerbated by the influx of Albanians into the Serbian province of Kosovo, to the point where, by the late 1990s, the Muslim immigrants outnumbered the native, largely Christian population. Since the Middle Ages, the two faiths had waged sporadic holy wars in the name of their beliefs. Now they were to become super-numeraries in a wider power game, for as the situation deteriorated, the Americans and Germans covertly armed the self-appointed 'freedom fighters', the Kosovan Liberation Army, while the Serbian leader, Slobodan Milošević, intensified his brutal campaign of ethnic cleansing against the incomers.

In a TV debate with Benn during the early days of the crisis, a British general admitted that the USA was already gearing up to intervene militarily in the region, an admission confirmed by the findings of a US Senate committee in August 1998 that: 'Planning for a US-led NATO intervention in Kosovo is now largely in place.' Before that, however, the charade of 'negotiating for peace' remained to be played out, and at Rambouillet on 24 February 1999, the US Secretary of State, Madeleine Albright, supported by the British Foreign Secretary, Robin Cook, presented the Serbians with a coercive ultimatum – surrender or be occupied – though the majority of Washington's NATO partners knew nothing of the details of the US terms.

Ignorant as he, too, was of the terms of the Rambouillet ultimatum, Benn was nonetheless scathing in his critique of NATO, and more especially of Britain's involvement in the escalating crisis. Blair had declared that NATO was involved in a 'crusade for civilization', whereas Benn was adamant that the government was talking up peace while arming for war:

> Ministers say that it will be a war for humanitarian purposes. Can anyone name any war in history fought for humanitarian purposes? ... War is about power, for the control of countries and resources ... We are told that Kosovo is to be a protectorate. Has international law advanced to the point where, if we do not like a country, we can take one of its provinces and call it a protectorate? That reminds me of Victorian England, which was a bit before my time.

Benn's intervention made little difference. On 24 March, NATO launched its first air strike against Serbia, and for the next ten weeks the assault continued, the RAF alone dropping 78,000 cluster bomblets, a high proportion of which failed to hit their military targets, thus belying the claims of Clare Short, Secretary of State for International Development, that 'NATO is not killing civilians. The very carefulness of our operations is to ensure that there is minimum damage to civilians.' On 10 June, a cease-fire was called, prompting Benn to reflect: 'Not only has NATO been guilty of a crime against humanity, but even more seriously, it is now itself a direct threat to peace and security', and for Britain's second most senior defence minister during the conflict, Lord Gilbert, subsequently to confirm much that Benn had suspected. In his evidence to a select committee of the Commons, Gilbert maintained that NATO had forced Milošević into a war: 'I think certain people were spoiling for a fight in NATO at that time. I think that the terms put to Milošević at Rambouillet were absolutely intolerable. How could he possibly accept them? It was absolutely deliberate.'

If the terms of Rambouillet were intolerable, precisely what was it that motivated the USA and its military satellites to adopt such a bellicose policy? For public consumption, the answer was to check the ethnic cleansing that was taking place in Kosovo. A simplistic message, assiduously peddled throughout the war, it disguised what Benn regarded as a self-serving rather than a humanitarian agenda which signalled that, having sidelined the UN, the USA could unilaterally dictate the shape of things to come in the interests of the free markets which, in their turn, were dominated by the USA. Rather than resolving the problem, however, the Kosovan venture compounded it, and by the early spring of 2001 the region was again at flash point, as Benn noted:

'The damage that's been done to Balkan stability is enormous. There's no doubt that the so-called Kosovan 'peacekeeping operation' has triggered a whole series of consequential conflicts to the point where the Kosovan Liberation Army, which in 1999 was an arm of NATO in its confrontation with Serbia, is now being demonised because it is digging into Serbia and Macedonia, and consequently destabilising the entire region. I don't think that it will be long before the whole Kosovan war will be looked back upon by responsible opinion as being as great a disaster as Suez or Vietnam.

It was not only the Balkan crisis that exposed the limitations of US designs, however. Five months after the ending of the Kosovo conflict, the Commons debated what Benn was derisively to refer to as 'another triumph for free trade ... the celebration of the success of the World Trade Organization conference in Seattle'. His sarcasm was well founded, for rather than celebrating the accomplishments of *laissez-faire*, the Seattle conference, which had been designed, among other things, to provide a showcase for President Clinton, had degenerated into a running battle between upwards of 50,000 protesters and a screen of riot police guarding the conference delegates. What, for so long, had gone virtually unquestioned – the gospel of the globalizers and free-marketeers – had been challenged, full frontally, by a coalition of churchmen and women, environmentalists and voluntary agencies. In the Commons on 9 December, Benn articulated the concerns that had been heard on the streets of Seattle the previous week.

In an indictment of what he regarded if not as a conspiracy, then as a combination of power – a piecemeal alliance of transnational corporations, financial speculators and the media – legitimized by US transcendence, and grounded on Fukuyama's model of 'a liberal democracy', Benn mocked the notion of the trickle-down of wealth: 'The world's 447 billionaires ... have a combined wealth equivalent to the annual income of half the world's population'; derided the myth of both the efficacy and the benevolence of the free markets: 'One-fifth of the world's 5.6 billion live in extreme poverty ... 12 million children under five years of age die ... '; exposed the ambitions of multinationals by quoting, as one instance, a comment by the right-wing Institute of Economic Affairs: 'Africa should be privatised and leases to run individual countries auctioned off'; outlined his own agenda for the twenty-first century:

> In the next century, people will want co-operation and not competition in self-sustaining economies, working with other nations ...   They will want to plan for peace as we have always planned for war ... They will want democratic control over their own destiny. That is the real lesson that this century must teach the next one.

During his first quarter-century in the Commons, Benn had campaigned tirelessly for decolonization. In the second quarter-century of his time in the House, he had seen the re-emergence of neo-colonialism, though, seemingly, Seattle had already done something to expose the vulnerability of this New World Order ...

CHAPTER SEVEN

Interview

The socialist who is a Christian is more to be dreaded than a socialist who is an atheist.

> Fyodor Dostoevsky, *The Brothers Karamazov* (1880)

The future is the only kind of property that the masters willingly concede to the slaves.

> Albert Camus, *The Rebel* (1953)

The office in the basement of the house on the hill is large and seemingly chaotic, a warren of files, folders, books and papers: Benn's retreat, though not from reality. For almost half a century this has been that 'other place', well distanced from Westminster and Whitehall, that has been the nerve centre of Benn's political life. He smiles and gestures vaguely at the four quarters of his sanctum – 'Sorry about the mess' – then takes up the mug of tea, a ubiquitous sacrament, and wonders: 'Now, where were we?'

DAVID POWELL: *Before taking office in 1997, New Labour made much of the need to eliminate what you call 'the democratic deficit' by reforming the constitution. How far do you think they have succeeded?*

TONY BENN: The Scottish Parliament is an achievement. The Welsh Assembly is an achievement. The restoration of government to London is an achievement. The attempt to establish a constitutional settlement in Northern Ireland is wholly admirable, while the move towards a federal Europe is a constitutional change of even greater importance and one which I regard as a shift towards bureaucracy and bankers' control.

In practice, however, power is becoming more centralized. Local government is being stripped of its educational and housing roles, and local authorities are being rate-capped and given grants that are tied to particular purposes so that they have no discretion over their use. The NHS and education are suffering from the Private Finance Initiative, which is transferring power from the electors to the business community and leading to the creeping privatization of services. I remember Harold Wilson once saying to me that the engine of economic growth is the public sector. It was a very profound thing to say, and I've thought about it a lot since. Of course, defence has always been a classic example of what he was talking about, but now the other engines of growth – health and education – are being handed over to private companies. Today there are at least seven companies operating in the health and educational fields, one of which has shown a profit increase of 50 per cent this year, because they have their eyes on what they regard as a privatized gold mine.

But this isn't all. When private companies take over health and education, profit becomes dominant over need, and in no time at all you'll have a two-tier health and education service. We hear a great deal from New Labour about inclusivity, but in reality what they are about is exclusivity, especially in education, where they are concerned with creating an elite who will run the world, and shunting everyone else onto the labour market. They don't want the working class to be trained to question, simply to obey – and they call that raising standards! In effect, I think that if this isn't prevented, it will mean the total dismantling of the welfare state, and modernizing backwards to Victorian times. In fact, every one of the so-called 'Blair projects' is backward-looking.

DP: *And the Prime Minister?*

TB: As for the Prime Minister, his powers are greater than they ever were through his control of the party. Conference has been gravely weakened as the voice of the movement and become a huge trade fair which does little more than provide ministers with a platform to air their policies, while the party machine has used the National Executive Committee to influence which candidates are selected for the House of Commons.

On balance, I think there has been a formal change which has covered a substantial increase of presidential powers. The House of Commons and the cabinet have been completely sidelined. Parliament is now regarded as virtually unimportant, and with the move towards privatization, power is moving from the ballot box to the bank balance and that, I think, is a very serious erosion of Parliament's role.

DP: *Surely everything's not as bleak as you suggest. Recent opinion polls have shown that a growing number of people are questioning the unreformed role of the monarchy. Do you detect any evidence that New Labour have any intention of reforming the monarchy's role, and curbing the powers vested in the royal prerogative?*

TB: Buckingham Palace and No. 10 are locked in an embrace of mutual convenience. The prime minister depends on royal powers, and the Queen has no power but depends on the support of the prime minister to prop up the monarchy. That will not change until you have a democratic constitution, and as I see it the likelihood of that being seriously discussed is minimal.

DP: *Surely the reform of the Lords has been a step in the right direction?*

TB: Not at all. It has simply increased the prime minister's power of patronage by reverting to the medieval practice of Edward I. Hereditary peers only came in in the fourteenth century. To begin with, all peers were life peers, and to be made a peer didn't guarantee that you would be in the next Parliament. New Labour's reforms take us right back to the days when the king appointed his Parliament. It is totally undemocratic. The idea of election and accountability has been completely sidetracked, so what we've got is a sort of constitutional conjuring trick – now you see it, now you don't – to fool people that the government is committed to democratic reform.

Every civilized country has two chambers, both of which are elected, but there is an absolute hostility to democracy at the heart of the British establishment. They do not believe in it. They do not want it, and if they could get rid of what little we have of it, I believe that they would, and I think that the European Union would actually remove what exists of our parliamentary democracy, because power would be sited elsewhere.

DP: *What you are saying is that, contrary to its former pledges, New Labour is concentrating rather than devolving power. How long do you think that this can continue?*

TB: As long as New Labour can get away with it. Put crudely, while electors have the power to sack governments, which is the bottom line of democracy, you will find pressures building up. In fact, I think that is noticeable already. Although the party pulled out all the stops over the pensions issue at Brighton in 2000, they couldn't persuade the unions to go along with a means test instead of providing a decent basic pension. Don't forget that the National Executive Committee went along with MacDonald in '31, but the TUC wouldn't, and Bevin saved the party. It may be that John Edmonds and Rodney Bickerstaffe have done it again, but that remains to be seen.

And something else is happening. The hostilities between different ministers, of which the Mandelson affair was a symptom, are nothing like the real arguments that took place in the governments in which I served. Then we were arguing about principles – about Vietnam or the alternative economic strategy, Europe or trade union rights – but now there are struggles between jealous and ambitious courtiers fighting each other for privilege and power. In fact, I think that all this talk of the Third Way is just a sort of theatre for personal conflicts that have little substance, and it damages the government enormously. At least the arguments that took place in Old Labour were arguments about the substance of policies. There are no arguments going on now, just squabbles between Blair's courtiers.

DP: *The cult of personality?*

TB: Well, you've got to remember that a lot of ex-communists joined New Labour because they recognized democratic centralism was alive and well and therefore they felt at home there. Other people joined just to be on the winning side. As they used to say about Mussolini, 'He rushed to the aid of the victors', and there are a lot of New Labour politicians who rushed to the aid of the victor.

If you look at the individual role played by some of the leading New Labour people, they were Trotskyites, they were left-wing, they were CND, they were for democratic reforms of the party, they were for the alternative economic policy, but when they realized that their political bread was buttered on the other side they shifted. I don't want to mix metaphors, or appear too cynical, but my Dad used to talk about loose ballast, and there is a lot of loose ballast in New Labour.

DP: *Are you saying that New Labour has no ideological substance?*

TB: You have to remember that New Labour is the smallest political party in the history of British politics – so small that they are almost all in the cabinet! – but it has few roots in the labour movement, or any ideological roots. And because there is no ideology – just a kind of political pick 'n' mix: people are told, 'Watch us. We're so brilliant. Here's our latest scheme' – there is little role for members in New Labour, except as spectators and admirers and fans.

Of course, the condition isn't peculiar to Labour. In terms of right and left, the ideology of political leaders has lost its meaning. There is little real ideological debate between the major parties any more. When the Labour Party was formed at the end of the nineteenth century there was growing discontent among the working class that the old order – which provided a kind of political Buggins turn for Liberals and Tories – did not represent a satisfactory realization of their aspirations, and so the new movement was formed and for a very long time the Labour Party was proud of its socialism. What's happened, however, is that capital is now so powerful that party leaders have come to terms with it, and that the most powerful advocates of capitalism of an allegedly humane kind are now New Labour.

DP: *But, surely, capitalism itself is an ideology?*

TB: Certainly, and I suppose in a sense you could say that New Labour is the most ideological government we have had. It is utterly committed to market forces, utterly committed to monetarism, utterly committed to global capital, utterly committed to NATO. It is an ideological government posing as a pragmatic one, which does much to account for its appeal to much of the political establishment.

DP: *Do you think that this situation could lead to a coalition emerging?*

TB: There has always been a desire at the top, from Labour and Liberals, to get into coalition, as the Blair–Ashdown talks revealed.

DP: *Blair's reported remark on the subject following the 1997 election was revealing: 'Who knows what the ultimate destination down the track might be. It could be a merger ... or maybe not. We don't have to discuss that now.'*

TB: Before the 2001 election I had the feeling that New Labour wouldn't have minded if they suffered a lot of losses, because that would open up the way for the coalition they clearly want. Indeed, I suspected that what they really feared was being returned with a large majority, because that would make it more difficult to bring a coalition about.

DP: *If, as you say, New Labour lacks ideological substance, what of its longer-term prospects?*

TB: That depends on how it continues to perform but if, at some stage, it finds that its core vote has disappeared, one of two things could happen: either you would have a right-wing government, which is a possibility, or, and I think this more likely, New Labour will decide to go into a coalition with the Liberals and progressive Tories like Ken Clarke, and have a National Government, so they can say: 'We're the ones who stand up against the extreme right and left, as we stand up for Europe.'

Once that happened, whether a right-wing Tory government or a coalition was elected or, a third possibility, that New Labour went even further to the right – which is already happening – then I think that the labour movement, which, after all, is an independent organization made up of the trade unions and lots of other active people, would realize that its historic function would have to be revived. New Labour could command the loyalty of the party after it had been out of office for eighteen years, but if Kennedy and Clarke were in the cabinet, they wouldn't support it. I am not really a pessimist, but I think that in the cycle of political development we haven't reached the nadir yet.

DP: *Again, that's a pretty bleak prospect.*

TB: Possibly, but I think that what's happening represents a huddling together of the professional leaders of all parties who, lacking any clear ideology, don't really know what to do. All that they do know is that if they are seen to be fighting one another they are likely to be picked off by the voters, whereas if they all huddle together they are able to talk about 'the national purpose, the national interest'.

DP: *The election of 2001 certainly didn't engage the electorate, with a 60 per cent turnout, the lowest since 1918. In fact, it seems that a growing number of people, frustrated by their apparent powerlessness, are taking to the streets, as in Seattle and Davos and Gothenburg, to protest at their disenfranchisement.*

TB: We hear a great deal about the corruption of power, but little about the corruption of powerlessness. Powerlessness is a very powerful political force. In the end, the ballot paper and the polling station are the buckle that links feelings to action, and when governments or parties break that link and say 'We're not listening', and people outside begin to think that the link has got no value, then you do create, I don't say a revolutionary situation, but a breakdown in the social contact, and I certainly think that the social contract has been broken.

When I look back on it, that's really why I left Parliament. If you are a back-bench MP today, you have a very small role, but if you are linked to what is going on outside, and can teach people to see that there is a link between Maastricht, globalization, corporate power and privatization, then you are laying the foundations for a political organization which is capable of doing something.

DP: *That's all very fine, but what of such deep-rooted, countervailing* *factors as nationalism? The devolution issue seems to have opened up the whole question of what it means to be British, which provoked an outburst from Jack Straw, who castigated the left for its lack of 'Britishness'. Do you think that there is any real danger that New Labour will coat-tail the Tories and play the nationalist card?*

TB: I think that that is a very real danger. You see it happening everywhere. Zuganov, the Russian communist leader, became a nationalist. Saddam is a nationalist. The SNP is nationalist. The Basques are nationalist. The Israelis and Palestinians are nationalist. Nationalism is certainly back on the agenda due to a combination of factors, one of which is that there is no clear international philosophy.

Religion is international, and while it's very divisive in some places, at least there is one God: monotheism. Socialism is international, but destroy socialism, and the idea that people share a common purpose, and people will turn on foreigners and asylum seekers and Jews and blacks. I think that is a great danger, and add to that despair and cynicism, as with the Germans before the war when they elected Hitler – and they did elect him – and you have the ingredients of a most dangerous situation.

DP: *The more so if there should be a downturn in the economy?*

TB: If the world economy does go down, if there's war in the Middle East and oil prices rise, if the whole dot.com, South Sea bubble should burst, then it seems to me that there's a very real danger that someone will come along and say, 'Leave it to me. I'll clean up the mess.' That's how you end up with Haider in Austria, or with this right-wing racist in Belgium, or with Umberto Bossi and the Northern League in Italy. One way or another, they all say, 'Leave it to us. We'll sort things out,' and that's the death knell for democracy.

I don't want to sound alarmist, but the answer to it is a dose of explanation so that people understand why they are being told to turn on asylum seekers, or why the Germans were told to turn on the Jews, plus support for movements that are in favour of justice and the recognition that democracy is not just a game played out in Parliament, but about something you do yourself. Until then, until people become engaged in the democratic process, there will be no messages to the government from underneath, and the only messages they'll be getting are from Bernie Ecclestone, from Esso and Shell and BP, from IBM and Ford and the like. That is the problem. Governments are now the agents of international corporate finance, and until people start saying, 'We won't have it', then prime ministers will be unable to say, 'Sorry, I'd like to help you, but I can't get away with it. I won't be re-elected.'

DP: *As with the pensions issue, do you think that single-issue groups and the unions will begin to exert more pressure on the government?*

TB: It's certainly true that pressures are building up that no one dares to neglect. Even the Conservative Party have had to come to terms with the fact that you can't be prejudiced against gays, and the same goes for drugs ...

DP: *But the prejudices remain. Over the law and order issue, for instance, it seems that in contrast to the party's humanist traditions, New Labour is pursuing a populist strategy to compete with the Conservatives as to who can advance the toughest, most punitive policies.*

TB: I think that is broadly true. If you look very carefully at the Home Office, it seems that it's in a push-me-pull-you contest with the Tories to establish its hard-line credentials, and appeal to the populist vote. One day they are talking about fining so-called yobs on the streets without conviction, punishment without trial, and the next about taking away the right to trial by jury, which means that people who feel that local magistrates are prejudiced will lose their historic rights.

Add to that the extension of the anti-terrorism measures, the culture of secrecy implicit in the Freedom of Information Bill, the bugging of people's phones, the use of riot police, even the appointment of Chris Woodhead, who went around destroying teachers' morale, and a very sinister picture begins to emerge.

DP: *One way or another, that is a pretty serious indictment of the so-called New Labour project. If things continue as they are – if Blair continues to play up the enterprise culture in imitation of Margaret*

Thatcher; if Blunkett continues to pursue the hard-line policies followed by Straw; if New Labour continues to prefer sound bites to substance; if there is no effective check on the erosion of democracy – do you see a breakaway party emerging on the left?

TB: I doubt it. Sectarianism is the curse of the left, as it is of religion, but my opinion, based on my own experiences of the 1970s and 1980s, is that a sectarian approach is a switch-off for a number of reasons. First of all, people don't like sectarian squabbling. Secondly, sectarian politics are always very frightening, and what people want now is reassurance. Thirdly, people are suspicious of all parties, and if they don't believe Labour or Tory, are they really going to believe that sectarians can do any better?

What's got to be done is to build alliances around issues – support the pensioners, support the unemployed, support the women's movement, support the environmentalists, support the multiethnic movement, and so on. I don't say that when you do campaign on specific issues you won't attract the sects, they'll come along, but what it's all about is improving the quality of life for people in their daily lives, and developing movements to protect them. That is the essence of politics, and always has been. The Levellers, the Tolpuddle Martyrs, the early trade unionists didn't have a fully worked-out alternative strategy, they were just saying, 'We won't put up with this'.

DP: *How long do you think that the unions will 'put up with this', when New Labour has made it clear that it is anxious to distance itself from the movement?*

TB: Well, if you take the Marxist analysis that there is a difference between those who create wealth and those who own it, there is a natural majority for social equality. However many advertising agencies they may employ, big business does not have any votes. They have power and money, and own the media, and can bring pressure to bear via the IMF and the banks, but they don't have any votes, so in the end, and unless I am wholly wrong, we won't go back to some kind of medieval serfdom, because it's not something they could get away with.

In fact, that's one of the reasons that they have cleverly redefined class. We are all middle-class now, except for a handful of people who are so brilliant that they are entitled to millions in share options – the entrepreneurs – and another group who, so we're told, prefer to sleep rough on the streets. As for the rest of us, we are all middle-class. When you analyse it, however, and look at the insecurity of the so-called middle class – of the man or the woman on the short-term contract who is always wondering 'What next?'; of the consultant faced with the sack under a PFI scheme; of the workforce in a company that's going to be downsized – you realize that insecurity is the characteristic of this new class system.

I find that a socialist analysis helps me to understand what is going on. Without some hope for a better future, fear and insecurity will continue to predominate. As with nationalism, in fact, there are always those who are ready to exploit our fears and insecurity, and say: 'If you are insecure, vote for a strong man who will clean it up.'

DP: *I'm sorry to press the question, but if your analysis about the complicity between business, the banks, the media and New Labour is correct, do you think it is possible that a time will come when the unions will say, 'Enough is enough?'*

TB: If I was a trade unionist, I would continue to pay my subs to the Labour Party, but would consider putting all my extra money into campaigns on behalf of my members. I don't see why they should fund Labour policies that they don't like. I am not in favour of the trade unions disaffiliating as some people say they should. The worst-case scenario is '31 when MacDonald came along, did an alliance with the Tories and Liberals, and in the subsequent election there were only fifty Labour MPs elected. If that did happen, we would be in a situation where the unions would have to create a political instrument again, as they did, then, when they saved the party.

DP: *So the left would be back to the beginning again?*

TB: What we need now, and I have been saying this for nearly twenty years, is a new Labour Representation Committee. When the original LRC was set up in the 1890s, Keir Hardie said that this was labour's answer to the federation of masters and trusts. If things continue as they are, I think that something similar to the LRC could emerge. Of course, it won't be a carbon copy of the original, it will be a much broader movement. My Dad said that when he joined the party what really impressed him was the annual conference, which was so widely representative. Now we need to extend that representation even further.

DP: *In the wider context, how do you view New Labour's attitude towards Europe and the Euro, more especially Tony Blair's ambivalent approach to the issue?*

TB: I don't think that there can be any doubt that Tony Blair and Stephen Byers are passionately committed to a European super state, and this for political reasons. I used to think that they were prepared to sacrifice democracy in Britain, which is the price you have to pay for what they call 'greater influence in Europe'. I now conclude somewhat differently that one of the real advantages to them of the European super state is that it does destroy British democracy, and that it is part of the counter-revolution against the democratic advances made in Britain by the labour movement.

As for the Euro, it is an integral part of the transfer of power over our economy from the Chancellor, who is answerable to the Commons, to the governor of the Bank of England. If the Euro project is realized, it will lead to a subsequent transfer of power to the European Central Bank in Frankfurt. Under the Maastricht Treaty, it is illegal for any government to try to influence Central Bank policy, in a deliberate attempt to concentrate economic power in a body that has no democratic legitimacy and is accountable to no one but itself. Having said that, New Labour do recognize that for other reasons, some of them nationalistic, the Euro option is not going down well with the general public. Even on the European issue, the supposed clash of ideologies between the Little Englanders and the Europhiles is dissolving, with the Tories saying that there won't be a referendum on the single currency in this Parliament, and New Labour's spin doctors and focus groups saying: 'Hold on, you'll never get away with it if you try.'

As I see it, it is all part of a double process, of a return to nationalism and the destruction of democracy. The two go together. The destruction of democracy is what the European idea is about, and nationalism is a response to it. The trouble is that when democracy goes, and you respond to it nationalistically, you are in deep trouble, and this is at the heart of the dilemma we are facing.

DP: *You have talked a great deal about the dangers of nationalism, but isn't there a danger that your critics will say that you, too, are a Little Englander?*

TB: They'll try it, they always do – Thatcher and Benn, Benn and Thatcher – but at no stage have I ever appeared on a platform with the right, because I am fundamentally in disagreement with them. Some Labour people, even one or two Labour MPs, joined the Bruges Group, but I can't work with them.

We had the Danish socialists over recently, and they decided to run absolutely separate campaigns during the Danish referendum on the Euro, and to have no dealings with the right. I think that is the correct thing to do. In effect, it is difficult to argue that there is any common interest between the Tory Eurosceptics and the Campaign Group of Labour MPs. Of course, they will try to make the connection to disguise the fact that the real cross-party link is between New Labour, the Lib Dems and Tories such as Clarke. That is the real coalition. I recognize that if we don't go into the Euro we will still have huge problems to face, whereas from the Tory Eurosceptics' point of view, if we keep the Queen's head on our pound notes that will be a victory. It certainly won't be a victory for me.

DP: *Given your reservations about the nature of the EU, how do you see our relationship with Europe developing? Is there a way ahead?*

TB: The argument against the EU as it is presently constructed is basically a democratic argument. If you transformed the EU into the United States of Europe, with a President, a Senate, a House of Representatives and a system by which the laws were made not by the Council of Ministers but by the European Parliament, you could not argue that it was not democratic. The problem is that it would be totally unworkable, first because it would be much too big, and secondly because member states are at different stages of development, the more so if the enlargement process continues.

Put crudely, if it turned out that the laws of the EU were made in a hung European Parliament, and the balance of power lay with the Albanian Greens, would people accept it? I doubt it. After all, it is difficult enough to get people to accept government as it is. More than this, the European lobby would be passionately opposed to such a move towards democratization. If the Commission and the Council of Ministers were abolished, they wouldn't look at it for two minutes.

DP: *For all its failings, not least during the farrago that surrounded the US presidential election, isn't it possible that the USA provides a working model for federalism?*

TB: Even in America there are poor states and rich states, but they are all, broadly, at the same level of development, and they all share a common language, while if you look carefully at the United States there are none of the rigid rules laid down from Washington as there are from Brussels. Texas can't introduce import controls on goods from California, but it can subsidize goods from Texas if the Texan voters decide that's what they want to do, because government in the States is far more devolved.

DP: *On Europe it seems that we are a bit like that character in* Through the Looking Glass: *'If it was so, it might be; and if it were so, it would be; but as it isn't, it ain't.' I know that it is a compromised expression, but do you see a Third Way out of the dilemma?*

TB: I was trying to find a Third Way forward in my Commonwealth of Europe Bill modelled on a mini-United Nations with a General Assembly and a Council of Ministers, both acting with the consent of national parliaments. There is no reason why you could not have a Continental Commonwealth, including Russia, which could work together, but would be much more democratic because decisions would be taken by consent. I published the bill not only because I didn't want anyone to think I was anti-European but also to try and see a way through the current impasse, and prevent

Europe becoming so centralized under the EU that eventually it breaks up like Yugoslavia.

DP: *A gloomy scenario.*

TB: The EU is not durable, and I don't rule out the possibility that by fanning nationalism it could actually bust up, which would precipitate the very danger that the best pro-Europeans are trying to avoid, namely the re-emergence of the right and the recurrence of the old wars and trade wars, which I certainly don't want to see.

DP: *You once said that Britain had to make a choice between joining the EU or becoming a colony of the USA. Do you think that that still remains true?*

TB: I remember it very well. That was when I thought that the EU would be a bigger and more democratic answer to the global corporations. I now realize that the EU is an instrument of globalization and that the Commission in Brussels is trying to work for global corporations.

DP: *The point is, is it realistic to think that Britain could go it alone?*

TB: I don't think that we should go it alone. I think that a foreign policy based on the United Nations would be very formidable. At their best, some of the semi-neutral countries like Canada and Ireland and India have been very influential, and in its day the non-aligned movement was extremely important. In fact, I suspect that there is a growing demand for the re-creation of a non-aligned movement, but this time it would be non-aligned against globalization rather than non-aligned in the old East–West, Cold War context.

DP: *And what of the so-called 'special relationship' which has been the touchstone of our foreign policy since 1945?*

TB: It is an illusion that has been fostered to disguise the nature of our semi-colonial relationship with the US. With two exceptions, Suez and Vietnam, British foreign policy has largely been dictated by Washington since the end of the war, but the reality is that the Americans are no longer interested in us. They are more interested in the Germans now, which provides us with the opportunity to develop an independent role, for I believe that as a non-aligned state we would have far more influence in the world. After all, we are members of the Commonwealth and the EU, and have a seat on the Security Council, all of which exercise considerable influence, but all too often we remain an instrument of Washington.

DP: *As a mediator between the USA and the EU? If Britain has cast itself in the role, do you think that it now has any credibility?*

TB: I remember Dick Crossman saying, 'Let's join the Common Market and wreck it from the inside', whereas Ted Heath took the view that a strong Europe would act as the counterweight to American domination. I am not sure that either of these views is right. I think that our co-operation with Europe should be durable and genuine, but I doubt whether our perception of acting as a mediator has any relevance now, because the American attitude towards the EU is somewhat confused. During the Cold War they were all for it, because they thought that it would act as a bulwark to communism, but now they are beginning to wonder whether a strong Europe would provide what Ted envisaged: a counterweight to their own influence. Add to this that there is an isolationist element in Bush's thinking, which is gaining ground in the States, and it becomes increasingly difficult to read Washington's mind.

DP: *And add to this the pressures brought to bear by lobbyists and Washington's agenda becomes even more opaque. Indeed, it seems that Eisenhower's warning of the dangers of a military-industrial complex emerging has now been reinforced by economic imperialism determined by corporate interests.*

TB: Big business spent more than $300 million on the last presidential campaign, and there can be no escaping the fact that it will be corporate America that will be calling the shots in the years ahead. This makes their talk of being 'the arsenal of democracy' increasingly implausible. In fact, Bush is little more than the mouthpiece for American multinationals, and if he were to tackle such isues as global warming and the environment, it would jeopardize the profits of his corporate sponsors.

DP: *Which, presumably, influences his global strategy?*

TB: Bush is a sort of militarist-imperialist, and I think that with the American economy turning down, he won't have failed to notice that a big boost in defence expenditure, as exemplified by his commitment to a National Missile Defence System, with all that implies as far as arms control treaties are concerned, could, in Keynesian terms, be counter-cyclical. Of course, it has happened before. You've got to remember that full employment in America in 1940 was not just the result of the New Deal; the rearmament programme played its part. Similarly, full employment during the Cold War years resulted from a huge investment in the military-industry complex.

DP: *But surely, if the Bush administration attempts to reflate the economy via increased defence expenditure, it will have to find a new enemy?*

TB: Everyone needs an enemy, don't they, some real and some fake? If you look back at the Cold War, the idea that Russia, which lost twenty-five million people during the Second World War, was planning to invade Western Europe and take on the United States is revealed for what it was: ludicrous. But the pass was sold that if you were critical of capitalism, you worked for the Kremlin. And now the Bush administration have identified China as America's new Public Enemy No.1. I think it's a big mistake, but it's all part and parcel of Bush's plan, for no one really believes that North Korea or Libya or Cuba or any of the other so-called 'rogue states' poses a threat to the United States, or has the capacity to undermine world stability.

DP: *And what of Britain in this scheme of things?*

TB: As far as corporate power is concerned, we seem to be following the American model. People are now spending enormous sums to buy political favours, and then bringing pressure to bear on whichever party wins office. That is one of the reasons why Parliament is being sidelined. It is not so much that it has failed, more that it has been overtaken by new centres of power that have no democratic legitimacy, which is why I wonder whether the politics of advanced global capitalism is not a new form of feudalism. Once it was the landlords who were sent up to the Lords to do the king's business. Now it is big business that is running the world, and when people say that I'm an idealist in favour of world government, they seem to forget that we've got a world government already. The World Trade Organization, the International Monetary Fund, the World Bank are the world government, and political leaders such as Blair are no longer the representatives of the people, simply the regional managers of the global authorities.

DP: *What of the United Nations?*

TB: It's been sidelined like parliament. The Americans always thought they could dictate to the UN by controlling their contributions to its funds, which was a form of economic blackmail. Now I don't think that the US wants the UN any more than kings wanted parliaments, because however primitive parliaments were, they had the potentiality for bringing democratic pressure to bear.

DP: *You have protested several times that you are not a pessimist . . .*

TB: . . . I can't afford to be . . .

DP: *. . . yet you continue to paint a pretty bleak picture. Surely, there is some encouragement to be gleaned from the protests in Seattle and Prague and Gothenburg? In fact, it seems there is growing popular resistance to the US model of corporate globalization, and that while traditional political forms are in decline, new political forms are emerging, and people are beginning to find a new political voice?*

TB: Certainly people are beginning to connect corporate power with global poverty, with environmental disaster, with the outbreak of war and so on. It is a strange thing that we were told for years and years that socialism was a worldwide conspiracy, but now that communism of the Stalinist pattern has died, people are seeing for the first time what capitalism is really like. Without an enemy, capitalism can no longer make excuses for its failures by saying, 'Well, we're defending the free world', and people are now beginning to see capitalism for what it always was: red in tooth and claw – yet Blair talks of 'an anarchist circus'. I ask you, for him to dismiss church leaders and trade unionists and environmentalists as a bunch of anarchists was a bit like Thatcher calling Mandela a terrorist. Indeed, there's a certain irony in the fact that the establishment were lionizing protest in Eastern Europe (and let's not forget Tiananmen Square) only a handful of years ago, yet now protesters against the globalizers' New World Order are being demonized as anarchists.

The truth is that the protesters in Seattle and Prague and Gothenburg represented an upbeat response to globalization and revealed that there is a huge vacuum in our political spectrum, and a huge audience that is waiting to find its voice. I don't believe in a world of imminent socialist revolution, but people are beginning to see through the double-talk of capitalism, and anyone who comes forward with a rational explanation of how things have come to the present pass is going to win a significant following.

DP: *The trouble is that all too often single-issue groups are easy to isolate and pick off. Do you believe that such disparate groups are really capable of achieving unity and political coherence?*

TB: If you look at the history of the early Labour Party, which represented a diversity of political interests – the Fabians, the Marxists, the trade unions, the co-operative movement – they came together, and they had a programme, and Clause IV was a simple aspiration of what they wished to achieve. Whether the Labour Party can be saved, I can't say, but if you were to refound the party, which I would like to see happen, then you would extend it to a whole range of other organizations – the women's movement, the environmental movement, and so on – and then work with similar organizations in other countries that are beginning to move in the same direction.

DP: *A pipe dream, surely?*

TB: Not so. After all, when the Chartists demanded the vote, it seemed that there was no possibility of the franchise being extended, and when the suffragettes campaigned for the vote, it was regarded as an absurd demand, yet now ... The refounding of a progressive movement is certainly a legitimate aspiration, but no question, it would mean that we would have to be very bold.

DP: *New Labour certainly wouldn't take kindly to such a project, and the party has never been averse to witch-hunting in the past – Laski, Cripps, Bevan, to name but a few.*

TB: All the best people have been expelled, but you can't crush an idea when its time has come.

A Note on Sources

Bibliographies are notoriously misleading, apparently providing equal weight to all the sources involved in a publication. Clearly, this is not so, especially as far as *Tony Benn: A Political Life* is concerned. Certainly, it was important to read around the subject, and in this connection the biographies and autobiographies of the other major players during Benn's fifty years in the House were required reading – John Campbell's *Nye Bevan*, George Brown's *In My Way*, James Callaghan's *Time and Chance*, Barbara Castle's *The Castle Diaries*, Richard Crossman's *The Crossman Diaries*, Michael Foot's *Loyalists and Loners*, Denis Healey's *The Time of My Life*, Roy Jenkins's *A Life at the Centre*, Brian Brivati's *Hugh Gaitskell*, George Drower's *Kinnock* and Philip Ziegler's *Wilson*. Of comparable importance were the three existing biographies of Benn, those by Robert Jenkins, Russell Lewes and more especially J. A. D. Adams's perceptive study, first published in 1992. Ultimately, however, it is Benn's own works – not least, the five volumes of his *Diaries* – that have provided the core material for the present work. Since the publication of his first Fabian Society pamphlet (*The Privy Council as a Second Chamber*) in January 1957, Benn has either written or co-authored a range of political studies in hardback, paperback or pamphlet form, among them *Arguments for Socialism*, *Arguments for Democracy* (both of which were edited by Chris Mullin), *Parliament, People and Power*, *Fighting Back* and *Common Sense*. In addition, of course, there are Benn's speeches, for which Hansard provided the primary source, reinforced by the 1974 publication of his earlier speeches: *Speeches by Tony Benn*.

One final point, while I hope that *A Political Life* will be of interest to students of politics, the work is equally directed at a wider audience, and thus, rather than overburdening readers with copious references, I have preferred to include the above note on the major sources that have formed the staple for my own research.

Bibliography

J. A. D. Adams, *Tony Benn*. Macmillan, 1992.

Paul Anderson and Nyta Mann, *Safety First: The Making of New Labour*. Granta Books, 1997.

C. R. Attlee, *The Labour Party in Perspective*. Victor Gollancz, 1937.

M. Beer, *History of British Socialism*. G. Bell and Sons, 1929.

Tony Benn, *Speeches by Tony Benn*. Spokesman Books, 1974.

Tony Benn, *Arguments for Socialism*, edited by Chris Mullin. Jonathan Cape, 1979.

Tony Benn, *Arguments for Democracy*, edited by Chris Mullin. Jonathan Cape, 1981.

Tony Benn, *Parliament, People and Power*. Verso, 1982.

Tony Benn (ed.), *Writings on the Wall*. Faber and Faber, 1984.

Tony Benn, *Fighting Back*. Hutchinson, 1988.

Tony Benn, *A Future for Socialism*. HarperCollins, 1991.

Tony Benn, *The Benn Diaries*. Hutchinson, 1995.

Tony Benn, *Talking about Socialism*. Unity Books, 1996.

Tony Benn, *The Speaker, the Commons – and Democracy*. Spokesman Books, 2000.

Tony Benn and Andrew Hood, *Common Sense*. Hutchinson, 1993.

Aneurin Bevan, *In Place of Fear*. Heinemann, 1952.

Tony Blair, *New Britain*. Fourth Estate, 1996.

Tony Blair, *The Third Way*. Fabian Society, 1998.

Brian Brivati, *Hugh Gaitskell*. Richard Cohen Books, 1996.

Brian Brivati and Richard Heffernan (eds), *The Labour Party*. Macmillan, 2000.

Michael Barratt Brown and Ken Coates, *The Blair Revelation*. Spokesman Books, 1996.

George Brown, *In My Way*. Victor Gollancz, 1970.

James Callaghan, *Time and Chance*. Collins, 1987.

John Campbell, *Nye Bevan*. Weidenfeld and Nicolson, 1987.

Barbara Castle, *The Castle Diaries*. Weidenfeld and Nicolson, 1980 and 1984.

Barbara Castle, *Fighting All the Way*. Macmillan, 1993.

Noam Chomsky, *Deterring Democracy*. Vintage, 1992.

Peter Clarke, *A Question of Leadership: From Gladstone to Thatcher*. Penguin, 1992.

Ken Coates, *The Crisis of British Socialism*. Spokesman Books, 1971.

G. D. H. Cole, *A History of the Labour Party from 1914*. Routledge and Kegan Paul, 1948.

John Cole, *As It Seemed to Me*. Weidenfeld and Nicolson, 1995.

Ivor Crewe and Anthony King, *SDP: The Birth, Life, and Death of the Social Democratic Party*. Oxford University Press, 1995.

Michael Crick, *The March of the Militant*. Faber and Faber, 1986.

C. A. R. Crosland, *The Future of Socialism*. Jonathan Cape, 1956.

Richard Crossman, *The Crossman Diaries*. Vols. 1–3, edited by Anthony Howard. Hamish Hamilton and Jonathan Cape, 1975, 1976, 1977.

Ralf Dahrendorf, *The New Liberty*. Routledge and Kegan Paul, 1975.

Ralf Dahrendorf, *On Britain*. BBC Books, 1982.

A. J. Davies, *To Build a New Jerusalem*. Michael Joseph, 1992.

George Drower, *Kinnock*. The Publishing Corporation, 1994.

Gregory Elliott, *Labourism and the English Genius*. Verso, 1993.

Eric Estorick, *Sir Stafford Cripps*, Heinemann, 1949.

Michael Foot, *Loyalists and Loners*, Collins, 1986.

Alan Freeman, *The Benn Heresy*. Pluto Press, 1982.

J. K. Galbraith, *The Culture of Contentment*. Sinclair-Stevenson, 1992.

Ernest Gellner, *Conditions of Liberty*. Hamish Hamilton, 1994.

Anthony Giddens, *The Third Way*. Polity Press, 1998.

Ian Gilmour, *Dancing with Dogma*. Simon and Schuster, 1992.

Philip Gould, *The Unfinished Revolution*. Little, Brown and Company, 1998.

John Gray, *False Dawn*. Granta Books, 1998.

Peter Hain, *Ayes to the Left*. Lawrence and Wishart, 1995.

Stuart Hall and Martin Jacques (eds), *The Politics of Thatcherism*. Lawrence and Wishart, 1983.

Brian Harrison, *The Transformation of British Politics*. Oxford University Press, 1996.

Denis Healey, *The Time of My Life*. Michael Joseph, 1989.

Peter Hennessey, *The Hidden Wiring*. Victor Gollancz, 1985.

Eric Hobsbawm, *The Forward March of Labour Halted*, edited by Martin Jacques and Francis Mulhern. Verso, 1981.

Mark Hollingsworth, *The Press and Political Dissent*. Pluto Press, 1986.

Alan Hutt, *British Trade Unionism*. Lawrence and Wishart, 1975.

Will Hutton, *The State We're In*. Jonathan Cape, 1995.

Robert Jenkins, *Tony Benn*. Writers' and Readers' Publishing Co-operative, 1980.

Roy Jenkins, *A Life at the Centre*. Macmillan, 1991.

Simon Jenkins, *Accountable to None*. Hamish Hamilton, 1995.

Eileen Jones, *Neil Kinnock*. Robert Hale, 1994.

Tudor Jones, *The Remaking of the Labour Party: From Gaitskell to Blair.* Routledge, 1996.

Dennis Kavanagh (ed.), *The Politics of the Labour Party.* University of Nottingham, 1982.

David Kogan and Maurice Kogan, *The Battle for the Labour Party.* Fontana, 1982.

Dick Leonard (ed.), *Crosland and New Labour.* Macmillan, 1999.

Russell Lewes, *Tony Benn.* Associated Business Press, 1978.

Andy McSmith, *John Smith.* Verso, 1993.

David Marquand, *The Progressive Dilemma.* Heinemann, 1991.

David Marquand and Anthony Seldon, *The Ideas That Shaped Post-War Britain.* Fontana Press, 1996.

Kenneth Morgan, *Labour People: Hardie to Kinnock.* Oxford University Press, 1992.

George Orwell, *Nineteen Eighty-four.* Secker and Warburg, 1949.

David Owen, *Time to Declare.* Michael Joseph, 1991.

Leo Panitch and Colin Leys, *The End of Parliamentary Socialism.* Verso, 1997.

Henry Pelling, *A History of British Trade Unionism.* Penguin, 1987.

Ben Pimlott, *Harold Wilson.* HarperCollins, 1992.

David Powell, *What's Left.* Peter Owen, 1998.

A. J. P. Taylor, *Essays in English History.* Hamish Hamilton, 1977.

Willie Thompson, *The Long Death of British Labourism.* Pluto Press, 1993.

David Selborne, *One Year On.* Centre for Policy Studies, 1998.

Patrick Seyd, *The Rise and Fall of the Labour Left.* Macmillan, 1987.

Eric Shaw, *Discipline and Discord in the Labour Party.* Manchester University Press, 1988.

Peter Shore, *Leading the Left.* Weidenfeld and Nicolson, 1993.

Keith Sutherland (ed.), *The Rape of the Constitution.* Imprint Academic, 2000.

Hilary Wainwright, *Labour: A Tale of Two Parties.* Hogarth Press, 1987.

David Widgery, *The Left in Britain.* Penguin, 1976.

Tony Wright, *Socialism Old and New.* Routledge, 1996.

Hugo Young, *One of Us.* Macmillan, 1989.

Philip Ziegler, *Wilson.* Weidenfeld and Nicolson, 1993.

Index

Adeane, Sir Michael   26
Asquith, H. H.   13
Attlee, Clement   43, 145

Barnett, Joel   127
Benn, Caroline   38
Benn, Margaret, Lady
    Stansgate   12–13
Benn, Michael   14
Benn, William, Viscount
    Stansgate   4, 12, 13–14, 18, 49,
    140–1, 143, 148
Bevan, Aneurin   10, 44, 47, 142
Bevin, Ernest   124, 131, 176
Bickerstaffe, Rodney   176
Blair, Tony   11, 41, 98, 99, 100–1,
    104–5, 110, 135, 136–7, 170, 174,
    181, 184, 190
Boothroyd, Betty   11, 36–7
Brockway, Fenner   144–5
Brown, George   114
Bullock, Lord   130–1
Burke, Edmund   3, 21, 34, 58
Bush, George, Snr   166–7
Bush, George, Jnr   188–9
Butler, R. A.   20
Byers, Stephen   184

Callaghan, James   29, 31, 65, 70,
    73–9, 85–6, 114, 128, 129, 137,
    152
Castle, Barbara   28, 52, 53, 59, 66,
    69, 117, 127
Chamberlin, Neville   14
Churchill, Sir Winston   14, 145

Clarke, Kenneth   178
Clinton, Bill   162
Cook, Robin   170
Cousins, Frank   113–15
Cripps, Sir Stafford   43, 84, 111
Cromwell, Oliver   5, 15
Crosland, Anthony   5, 45, 51, 70
Crossman, Richard   23, 44, 49, 51,
    54, 188

Dahrendorf, Ralf   2
Dalyell, Tam   37
Davidson, Randall   13
Douglas-Home, Sir Alec   26
Dulles, John Foster   144

Eden, Sir Anthony   46
Edmonds, John   176
Eisenhower, Dwight D.   143

Foot, Michael   56, 62, 65–70, 86–9,
    92–3, 127–8, 129, 133, 160, 161
Fukuyama, Francis   96, 163–4

Gaitskell, Hugh   19, 22, 24, 44, 46,
    48, 50, 96, 98, 146, 147
Gilbert, Lord   171
Gilmour, Ian   7, 79
Gormley, Joe   132
Gould, Philip   7, 102–3, 106

Hailsham, Lord   10
Hardie, Keir   42, 183
Hattersley, Roy   93, 99, 104–5, 110,
    133

Hayek, Friedrick von   132–3
Healey, Denis   6, 50, 65, 65–71, 83,
    88, 89, 91–2, 125, 127, 128, 129,
    130, 154
Heath, Edward   28, 108, 119, 120,
    154, 188
Heffer, Eric   117, 118
Hobsbawm, Eric   78
Hussein, Saddam   165–6
Hutton, Will   100

Jay, Baroness   36
Jenkins, Clive   53, 89
Jenkins, Roy   53, 55, 60–1, 66, 70,
    85, 88, 105, 112, 120, 123, 125,
    149, 151, 152, 153
Jones, Jack   53, 69, 123, 126, 127

Kaufman, Gerald   92
Kearton, Lord   155–6
Kennedy, John F.   156
Kinnock, Neil   7, 90–1, 93–6, 98,
    133, 135

Laski, Harold   10, 43
Livingstone, Ken   40, 107
Lloyd George, David   13, 17, 18

McCarthy, Joseph   143
MacDonald, Ramsay   13, 18, 43,
    101, 105
McKenzie, Bob   128
MacLeod, Ian   24
Macmillan, Harold   78
Major, John   38, 162
Mandelson, Peter   98, 103–4
Marquand, David   100
Maurice, Denison   17
Maxton, Jimmy   1, 10, 43
Meacher, Michael   87, 90
Mikardo, Ian   67, 117
Monks, John   137
Morris, William   10, 42–4

Nasser, Gamal Abdel   146

Orwell, George   2, 10
Owen, David   85, 87, 156

Paine, Tom   1, 10, 16, 25, 33, 81
Prentice, Reg   60, 66, 75

Radice, Giles   6, 91
Rainborough, Thomas   5–6, 14
Reagan, Ronald   157, 159, 161, 162
Ridley, Nicholas   134
Rogers, Bill   88
Roosevelt, Franklin D.   141–2
Russell, Bertrand   3–4

Sayeed, Jonathan   93
Scargill, Arthur   40, 134
Scruton, Roger   8, 34
Shaw, George Bernard   3, 42, 44
Shinwell, Emmanuel   111–12
Shore, Peter   6, 87, 93, 152
Short, Claire   102, 170–1
Smith, John   98, 101
Steel, David   130
Stiglitz, Joseph   107, 139
Straw, Jack   98, 180, 182

Taverne, Dick   60, 61, 63
Tawney, R. H.   4
Tebbit, Norman   132–3
Thatcher, Margaret   6, 7, 8, 30, 79,
    84, 88, 96–9, 133, 136, 157, 159,
    161, 162, 168, 181–2
Thorpe, Jeremy   20
Truman, Harry S.   141, 142, 143

Varley, Eric   126

Wilkes, John   15, 16, 20
Williams, Shirley   66, 88
Wilson, Harold   20, 26, 27, 30, 32,
    48, 52, 64–5, 70–1, 92, 112–13,
    114, 117, 121–2, 126–7, 150, 154,
    155, 174
Winstanley, Gerrard   1, 10, 15, 41